BASIC TEXTS IN COUNSELLING AND PSYCHOTHERAPY

Series editors: Arlene Vetere and Rudi Dallos

This series introduces readers to the theory and practice of counselling and psychotherapy across a wide range of topic areas. The books appeal to anyone wishing to use counselling and psychotherapeutic skills and are particularly relevant to workers in health, education, social work and related settings. The books are unusual in being rooted in psychodynamic and systemic ideas, yet being written at an accessible, readable and introductory level. Each text offers theoretical background and guidance for practice, with creative use of clinical examples.

Published

Jenny Altschuler
COUNSELLING AND PSYCHOTHERAPY FOR FAMILIES IN TIMES OF ILLNESS AND DEATH, 2nd edition

Bill Barnes, Sheila Ernst and Keith Hyde
AN INTRODUCTION TO GROUPWORK

Stephen Briggs
WORKING WITH ADOLESCENTS AND YOUNG ADULTS, 2nd edition

Alex Coren
SHORT-TERM PSYCHOTHERAPY

Jim Crawley and Jan Grant
COUPLE THERAPY: THE SELF IN THE RELATIONSHIP

Emilia Dowling and Gill Gorell Barnes
WORKING WITH CHILDREN AND PARENTS THROUGH SEPARATION AND DIVORCE

Loretta Franklin
AN INTRODUCTION TO WORKPLACE COUNSELLING: A PRACTITIONER'S GUIDE

Gill Gorell Barnes
FAMILY THERAPY IN CHANGING TIMES, 2nd edition

Fran Hedges
AN INTRODUCTION TO SYSTEMIC THERAPY WITH INDIVIDUALS

Fran Hedges
REFLEXIVITY IN THERAPEUTIC PRACTICE

John Hills
INTRODUCTION TO SYSTEMIC AND FAMILY THERAPY

Margaret Henning
POSITIVE DYNAMICS: A SYSTEMIC NARRATIVE APPROACH TO FACILITATING GROUPS

Sally Hodges
COUNSELLING ADULTS WITH LEARNING DISABILITIES

Linda Hopper
COUNSELLING AND PSYCHOTHERAPY WITH CHILDREN AND ADOLESCENTS: AN INTRODUCTION

Sue Kegerreis
PSYCHODYNAMIC COUNSELLING WITH CHILDREN AND YOUNG PEOPLE: AN INTRODUCTION

continued overleaf...

Invitation to authors
The Series Editors welcome proposals for new books with the Basic Texts in Counselling and Psychotherapy series. They should be sent to Arlene Vetere at the University of Surrey (email a.vetere@surrey.ac.uk) or Rudi Dallos at Plymouth University (email R.Dallos@plymouth.ac.uk).

FAMILY CONFLICT AFTER SEPARATION AND DIVORCE

MENTAL HEALTH PROFESSIONAL INTERVENTIONS IN CHANGING SOCIETIES

JIM SHEEHAN

First published 2018 by
PALGRAVE

Palgrave in the UK is an imprint of Macmillan Publishers Limited, registered in England, company number 785998, of 4 Crinan Street, London, N1 9XW.

Palgrave® and Macmillan® are registered trademarks in the United States, the United Kingdom, Europe and other countries.

ISBN 978–1–137–60657–0 paperback

This book is printed on paper suitable for recycling and made from fully managed and sustained forest sources. Logging, pulping and manufacturing processes are expected to conform to the environmental regulations of the country of origin.

A catalogue record for this book is available from the British Library.

A catalog record for this book is available from the Library of Congress.

CONTENTS

CONTENTS

PART I

CHANGING CONTEXTS OF FAMILY CONFLICT AFTER SEPARATION AND DIVORCE

INTRODUCING THE TERRITORY OF FAMILY CONFLICT AFTER SEPARATION AND DIVORCE

The theme of family conflict after separation and divorce presents itself to mental health and social care professionals in many different ways and contexts. A young mother may arrive at a statutory income mainte- nance service because of repeated and unexplained delays in the receipt of child support from her ex-partner. A school counsellor may be asked by a teacher to see a nine-year-old boy who confides in her that he is unable to play football for his local team because his separated parents cannot agree about who will pay his club membership fee. An eight-year- old girl may be seen by a psychotherapist attached to a medical practice after her father brought her to the doctor because of bouts of vomiting for the 24-hour period prior to her weekend contact with her mother and new partner. A 13-year-old girl may report incidents of self-harm to an adolescent mental health professional in the context of her refusal to accompany her younger siblings on court-ordered contact weekends with her father, following an episode of loud and angry exchanges between her parents at handovers. A mother may present to a child protection social worker the day after her ex-partner has hit her in the face with a school bag in front of their ten-year-old daughter as her father returns the child after a period of midweek contact. A 36-year-old father may attend his local doctor with symptoms of depression following a three-month period in which his 11-year-old son has refused to get in the car to accompany him for his weekly contact period, as his mother insists that the boy must not be forced to do anything he does not want to do. A 55-year-old father may be referred to a psychiatrist with depressive symptoms following a dictate from his 25-year-old daughter that he should not attend her wedding ceremony. A 45-year-old mother of 15-year-old twin boys may be referred to her workplace counsellor as a result of a deteriorating work performance in the context of her twins' refusal to either meet with her or speak with her. Behind each of these snapshots of professional encounters with people in distress lies a story of family conflict following separation and divorce.

Professionals to Whom This Book is Addressed

The above examples give some idea of the broad range of mental health, health and social care professionals for whom this book will be relevant. Child protection social workers, community-based child, adolescent and adult psychologists and psychiatrists, school counsellors and general medical practitioners all frequently encounter the arena of post-separation family conflict. Such professionals are regularly challenged to broaden their focus away from the immediacy of the presenting symptom or complaint and towards processes of post-separation conflict as the key contextual background to a complaint's presentation. Residential care and fostering social workers also meet the phenomenon where parental conflict in the process of separation has led to neglectful or abusive parenting which requires the placement of children in either foster or residential care. Likewise, addiction counsellors in either in-patient or out-patient settings meet the territory when crises in alcohol or drug consumption following separation leads to separations of indeterminate length between substance-misusing parents and their dependent children. Domestic violence refuge workers are immersed in such conflict every time a parent tries to find out from them the whereabouts of their children following their partner's fleeing to safety in the context of intimate partner violence. Prison officers meet the territory when they manage and respond to an unusually troubled, angry and distressed prisoner whose separating spouse has withdrawn both herself and their children from prison visits. Police officers all too frequently meet the issue when anxious and fearful resident parents appear at police stations to report that their children have not arrived home from either regular or holiday contact with a nonresident parent and are neither geographically traceable nor contactable by phone. A later chapter in this book examines a small sample of typical contexts in which children become the victims of child abduction.

Professional Contexts in Which Post-separation Conflict Appears

The reader will notice that many of the above-mentioned professionals meet the phenomenon of post-separation conflict in the context of a *crisis* of some kind. In facing such crises professionals must find a way of responding to the immediate needs of a symptomatic child, a poorly functioning employee or an anguished and anxious imprisoned parent. In other words, the primary function of many professionals encountering the phenomenon has nothing to do with the management of post-separation conflict as such, but focuses upon meeting the crisis-related needs of individuals in front of them for such services as a safe shelter, financial aid, a child-tracing or child-placement service, anger containment or anxiety-managing medication. These professionals, depending upon the scope of their role, may also try to find a way to address the broader relational dimensions of the issues presenting. This second level of their response can be accomplished either by way of a referral of the persons engaged in and affected by the conflict to an appropriate service or by attempting to directly engage those involved in efforts to better manage their conflict should they have the required skills and should their service boundaries permit them to undertake this task. It is hoped that this text will enhance the *understanding* of such professionals of the very complex phenomenon that post-separation family conflict can be while assisting them to recognise the *skills* that they either already have or require to be able to help the family and its members in the context of their conflict.

The theme of assistance through referral to an appropriate service has just been mentioned. It is not too early in this text to note the importance for families and their members of their earliest possible engagement with relevant assistance. While those specialist professionals working in this area have varying perspectives on many of the complex challenges facing them there is widespread agreement on the need for *early intervention* if some of the most negative outcomes for child and parent mental health, and family relational well-being, are to be prevented. The skill of referral is very often the pathway through which early intervention can become a reality and an adequate understanding of the phenomenon of post-separation conflict is a prerequisite for the exercise of such skill.

This book, however, is also addressed to that group of professionals whose meetings with the family and its members occur in more *formal* settings. Within this group I include family therapists, family mediators, family psychologists, family lawyers and judges presiding over family law proceedings, as well as those mental health professionals who assist the family courts by undertaking evaluations with respect to child residence and contact arrangements and/or related therapeutic tasks of different kinds with parents and children. By the time that families and individuals meet these services and their professionals it does not mean that their crisis is over. What it does mean, however, is that this crisis is now in the process of building a structure of potential containment around it. And it is this *structure of potential containment* that carries the hope for the family and the separating couple within it of being able to manage, if not resolve, their conflict. The reader will note the use of the word *potential* in the preceding sentence, which alerts us to the fact that these structures (therapy, mediation, legal assistance, the family court) don't always succeed in containing conflict and sometimes, retrospectively, seem like further contexts through which conflict deepens and spreads. The word *containment*, however, signals what, perhaps, is the most important intention and skill that mental health and other professionals bring to the task of addressing post-separation conflict at whatever stage of its evolution. In all that is done the mental health professional uses whatever personal and professional resources she has at a moment in time to provide for the troubled family a safe, containing space in which their problem-solving capacities can be mobilised. Many of the professional skills mentioned in this book are precisely related to, and often dependent upon, this primary task of containment and many of the personal/professional exercises at the end of each chapter are designed to further the capacities of professionals to provide such containment as they attempt to deliver core aspects of their service to the family as a whole or to some of its members. And what is it we are trying to contain in the troubled family in conflict? We are trying to contain their fears and anxieties about the present and the future, out-of-control thoughts and behaviours in children and parents, and a variety of fantasies about themselves and one another as they move about their worlds, which have begun to feel uncertain and unsafe to varying degrees.

The Conflict Continuum in Post-separation Family Relationships

All the scenes mentioned in the opening paragraph of this chapter can be expressions at a moment in time of conflict processes, and responses to these processes, impacting upon family members during or following separation and divorce. The shape and dynamics of these processes can and do change over time with respect to each family, and indeed, the length of time over which conflict dynamics organise the character of post-separation/ divorce family relationships varies enormously. Although this book is about family conflict after separation and divorce we must not forget that there is a whole group of separating families in our communities who transition through the experience, bringing new family structures into existence, through negotiation processes which exhibit consensus-seeking rather than conflict. The term *amicable separation* belongs to our ordinary language for a reason. It attests to the reality that some separating couples and families seem to be able to bring about such transformations while maintaining relatively friendly relations among all members of the group. It is not the case that these families experience zero conflict, but they do seem to be able to resolve their conflicts in a relatively amicable way. Readers of this book will find themselves engaged in repeated reflection concerning why some families, and not others, appear to be able to make these transitions in this way even in the context of the painful experiences of sadness and loss that appear to strike everyone engaged in family separation processes. As we make the journey through this text we will see how some of the theoretical perspectives deployed throw some light upon this important puzzle without resolving all the dilemmas to which the puzzle gives rise.

We can think about this 'amicable' group as representing one end of a continuum of separating/divorcing families. The other end of the continuum is represented by a group of families where conflict appears to find no end. In these families the conflict between the separating couple members can maintain itself right up to the death of one member of the couple. Indeed, their conflict often continues beyond that point when the conflict 'drama' appears to conscript new members to fill conflict performance positions vacated by those now deceased. We will see how this end of the continuum can teach us something about the way some patterns of post-separation/divorce family conflict gather their own power and momentum over time such that they appear to observers to have a life of their own. The participants in these conflicts sometimes seem to observers like puppets in a drama whose plot origins have long disappeared from view. Such powerful patterns are often implicit in familial conflicts that get passed on from one generation to the next. Family therapists who conduct genogram exercises (McGoldrick and Gerson, 1985) where clients are helped to map the character of family relationships over time both within and across several generations, and often discover that previously unexplained disconnections between some members of an extended family group have their origins in the post-separation conflict of a couple who have long since passed on. In other words, conflict can be a legacy passed on from one generation to the next and part of the professional task in such situations is to recognise and interrupt these intergenerational transmission processes.

Mental health and social care professionals will probably have relatively little to do with those on the 'amicable' end of the continuum, but quite a lot to do with those on the other end of the continuum; however, there is a very large group in the middle space of this continuum where professionals can be engaged or required to assist and intervene for different lengths of time. Many families successfully use family mediation services to work out negotiated settlements which pave the way for orderly transitions into new structures of post-separation family life, and require a limited amount of legal assistance as they make their way through to a divorce decree. The structure of mediation aims to enable them to manage their conflicts and negotiate a settlement concerning the key parameters at stake in the separation process, which principally include housing and residence, income and financial support, and residence arrangements for children as well as plans for their contact with the nonresident parent.

Other families are less successful in their efforts to mediate their way through this challenging passage and it may be that the speed and intensity with which their conflict has developed leaves one or both participants ill-disposed to do business with their ex-partner in the context of mediation. The adults in many such separating families often require a significant amount of legal assistance and family court involvement to bring their conflict to a resting point.

Another group of families requires even greater amounts of legal and court involvement. These are families where mental health professionals are often required to work closely with the court in the management of the details of family conflict and to foster compliance in family members with respect to the implementation of court orders. Later chapters in this book consider the evidence emerging from some different jurisdictions regarding the relative size of each of these groups.

The Grounds and Processes Underpinning Contemporary Post-separation Conflict

In advance of the journey through many faces of the territory of post-separation conflict a distinction will be made between two ever-present facets of this conflict – namely, the *grounds* on which the conflict takes place and the relational *processes* through which the same conflict is brought into being and maintained. By the *grounds* of conflict is meant the things, themes and issues that people fight about, such as the amount of child support that should be paid; whether children should be introduced to the new partner of a parent; whether a parent can take children out of their country of residence for a holiday; who should reside in the home where the separating couple have habitually resided; whether one parent should have 'the lion's share' of the children's care or whether it should be shared more equally between the two parents; and if and how grandparent involvement with children should be facilitated. In the fourth chapter of this work, the word *goods* is also given to these many different grounds around which post-separation conflict takes place. This additional term is used to underline the fact that these themes or issues have relative *value* for each of the key conflict participants. The list mentioned above is just a small initial sample of the 'mainstream' grounds on which post-separation conflict can find expression.

Relational processes refer to the ways that the main parties of the conflict actually interact with each other as they each go about trying to achieve the results they wish to achieve on a particular matter or issue. And it is at this level that the mental health professional will find that addressing post-separation conflict can become particularly complex. This is because the interactional cycles through which the conflict happens are not always confined to the behaviours and actions of the principal parties, namely the separating adult couple who are often parents as well. Indeed, as mental health professionals know well, children are regularly brought in as additional players into the conflict 'drama' and become part of a complex triangular web of interactions in which they generally seem to have more to lose than gain. Grandparents, friends and childminders can often be added to the list of conflict participants as the interactional web increases laterally at the same time as the intensity with which the conflict is addressed by key participants increases. Where serious disputes exist about parent–child contact after separation and divorce, these others are sometimes referred to as 'negative advocates' (Eddy, 2010) when the performance of their roles acquires alienating characteristics with respect to a child's relationship with one parent.

The Changing Context of Contemporary Post-separation Conflict

Most of the family conflict themes mentioned in the paragraph above might belong to any decade over the last 50 years, or even longer. However, the shape and appearance of family conflict over that period has evolved in response to both new configurations of family life and new conditions in which that life is being lived. Although some of what is pointed to about *contemporary* post-separation family conflict in these paragraphs relates mostly to urban and town living in the Western part of our world, much of it also relates to post-separation family life in both rural and thinly populated towns and villages. This is because there are some facets of our newly emerging ways of living that make the conditions of life across these seemingly different kinds of localities increasingly similar.

Contemporary twenty-first-century family life is characterised by the global exchange of information through the Internet; easy and immediate contact to communication via the mobile telephone; a labour market that expects rapid mobility of its workers; vastly increased participation of women in the workplace; and family incomes, for some at least, that don't carry the risk of a life in poverty should separation and divorce be the choice or felt necessity for one or both partners in a couple. Long working hours for parents, along with increased dependence on extra-familial sources of childcare in the context of the ever-busier lives of pre-adolescent and adolescent children, all make for a hugely changing experience of family life and living. They also make for a vastly changing context in which post-separation family conflict is performed. Parents can now have a series of rapidly escalating text or email exchanges about any of the themes or issues mentioned in earlier paragraphs without having to meet each other face to face (with all the accompanying risk of more direct aggression) as would have been necessary in pre-mobile telephone days. Such messages can be rapidly sent on to others as they are invited to become either witnesses to the conflict performance or participants within it. The posting of 'information' on social media allows for an enormous number of potential witnesses to be speedily annexed in to post-separation conflict dramas. All of this communication speed has profound implications for the commencement of mediation, for example, if ex-partners can get themselves to the mediation table before their own conflict performances or those of their 'allies' blow their low level of trust completely out of the water. It means that the mediator is required to direct his or her containment strategies towards the range of communication moves being deployed by the principal parties to the conflict before they begin to look at any of the more concrete issues in themselves. This and other related themes find further elaboration in the second chapter of this book.

The above remarks are not intended to suggest that contemporary modes of information contact and communication only have a negative impact on post-separation conflict scenarios. Such an implication would be far from the truth. Skype now allows parents separated from their children by long distances to have 'face-to-face' contact with their children, and the availability of email allows ex-partners to risk some level of direct communication and negotiation with each other without the fear that such exchanges will erupt into immediate verbal or physical violence. Texting or making contact via 'apps' permits some parents to communicate messages of love and concern to children who are refusing to have any direct contact with them and permits those same children to receive such messages without the burden of having to acknowledge them in a response. Readers will be able to supplement this list with many other advantageous consequences of twenty-first-century media and communications for families caught in cycles of post-separation conflict.

The increased demand for the mobility of workers and the increased reliance of families on extra-familial sources of childcare both have significant consequences for the contemporary post-separation family in conflict. Only a few of these consequences are mentioned here. Separated fathers who work long distances away from their children and ex-partners often have no base from which to have contact with their children as they have already moved far away from their own familial resources. Their lack of resources often reduces their opportunities for contact with their children to infrequent weekend daytime contact in the context where their children are already leading very busy social and recreational lives. A mixture of factors not really in the family's control make increased conflict a more than likely outcome.

A major consequence for post-separation family conflict arises out of the necessary reliance on extra-familial sources of childcare. One key figure in this picture is the 'nanny' or childminder who either lives in or comes in to the house where the children reside with one of the separating parents. Not enough research has been done to elucidate the role that these family-near professionals play in post-separation conflict scenarios and to what degree the more formal vehicles of conflict response such as family therapists, family mediators or the family courts include these persons in planned interventions. But it is certain that these individuals, who have a greater or lesser degree of professionalisation, become conscripted into the conflict patterns in some ways, and the assisting mental health professional must always consider the part she might play either as a potential resource towards conflict resolution around some matters, as an additional victim of parental conflict or as a significant ally of one parent in the performance of conflict strategies.

Eight Theoretical Perspectives at Work in This Text

No phenomenon can be explored and examined without some set of guiding theories or perspectives. These perspectives are like a set of assumptions or lenses through which we look at what we are interested in. In this text eight central theories are at work:

1. Family Systems Theory (Bateson, 1979; Hoffman, 1981; Campbell and Draper, 1985; Carr, 2000; Minuchin, 1984; Napier and Whitaker 1978; Von Bertalanffy, 1968).
2. Attachment Theory (Bowlby, 1969, 1973; Ainsworth, 1967; Belesky and Cassidy, 1994; Birnbaum, Orr, Mikulincer and Florian, 1997; Crittenden, 2008; Dallos, 2006; Dallos and Vetere, 2009; Hazan and Shaver, 1987; Howe, 2011; Schore, 2014).
3. Poststructuralist Theory (Bourdieu, 2004; Derrida, 1981; Foucault, 1980; Dickerson, 2014).
4. Narrative Theory (Parry and Doan, 1996; Ricoeur, 1984, 1992; Sheehan, 1995, 2004; White and Epston, 1990; Freedman and Combs, 1996; White, 2007).
5. Family Conflict Theory (Wilmot and Hocker, 2014; Jones, 2015; Mayer, 2015).
6. Family Conflict Resolution Theory (Deutsch, 1973; Irving and Benjamin, 2002; Barky, 2015).
7. Trauma Theory (Herman, 1998; Van Der Kolk, 2014; Rothschild, 2017; Akhtar, 2017).
8. Reflexivity Theory (Hildebrand, 1995; Jensen, 2008; Schon, 1991).

Although these are eight separate perspectives, the chapters ahead show how their application to an understanding of post-separation family conflict reveals a considerable amount of connection between them. Additional perspectives are used as well at different moments on the journey through this multifaceted phenomenon, and readers will, of course, also bring other theories to bear on their own understanding of what appears before them in the text. Although the richness of these different perspectives for our task will unfold across the different chapters ahead, this opening chapter is confined to a brief 'snapshot' of the key concepts attaching to each theory as well as an indication of how we might expect these theories to assist in the understanding of the text's key focus.

Family Systems Theory, as a development of general systems theory (Von Bertalanffy, 1968), grew out of the efforts of a group of researchers in California in the 1950s to better understand the behaviour and experiences of young adult males with a schizophrenic condition. As they first observed these young men in the company of their mothers, and later took the reality of their fathers into account, as well as the reality of marital strife, they noticed a predictability with respect to the timing of psychotic crises, as these related to increases in the intensity levels of parents' marital unhappiness. Following a rich and detailed observation of these young men and their parents, the researchers felt they were encountering something new with respect to the way they perceived the family. Napier and Whitaker (1978, p. 47) explain: 'Rather than look at it as a collection of individuals, they began to view the family as having almost the same kind of organised integrity that the biological organism does'. The researchers were beginning to understand that the 'family functioned as an entity, as a "whole", with its own structure, rules and goals'. It was a short step from the recognition of the family as this kind of patterned wholeness to viewing it as a *system*.

This first identification of the family as a system meant that all the different parts of the system (each of the adults/parents and each of the children) were understood to be in an ongoing relationship of mutual influence with one another. The family was also seen as an *open system* (Von Bertalanffy, 1968) in that it exchanged information not just internally between its own members but also between itself and the environment in which it was located. The family as a system was seen as going through changes and variations, but this changing was seen as occurring within limits, thus giving the family organisation a kind of stability over time.

A central concept addressing the character of the family as an openly evolving, changing structure was that of the *family life cycle* (Carter and McGoldrick, 1980; Duvall, 1977). This concept pointed to the predictable transitions family members had to make in their mode of organisation as they absorbed such events as the arrival of new children, their eventual emergence into adolescence and young adulthood, their departure from home and the death of parents. Parental separation can be seen as a transition point within a family's ongoing evolving life cycle, and the persistence of family conflict after separation and divorce can be seen as an indicator of the difficulty some of their members are experiencing in addressing the tasks associated with this transition.

A further contribution of systemic theory to the understanding of what happens in families concerns its view of problems experienced by people as *interpersonal* in nature, rather than individual. It perceives individually experienced problems as emerging out of the daily interactions the person has with all others with whom he interacts, both inside and outside the family. It is a theory that constantly foregrounds *relationships, communication* and *interaction* as the key parameters through which personal identity is both developed and experienced. In its continuing emphasis on this triangle of concepts, systemic theory has relied heavily on the work of Bateson (1972).

A further idea encapsulated in the system notion as it related to the family was the principle of *non-summativity*. This implied that, as a whole entity, the family was more than the sum of its parts. This 'moreness' helped to account somewhat for the power of the family interactional cycles, operating at a level 'above' the individual, within which individuals often felt caught, trapped or relatively powerless. The family was also seen to be organised *hierarchically*. Minuchin (1974) referred to the family as a system comprised of *subsystems*. As we look 'down' from the level of the family as a whole system, we can think of the parent(s) as forming one subsystem, and the children or siblings another. If we were to look 'up' to the level of the local community as a system, we might think of each of the families within it as subsystems of that community system. In order for family systems to function well their internal *boundaries* are required to be sufficiently robust to enable them to protect the integrity of each of the subsystems (the individual, the sibling subsystem, the parental subsystem, the couple) at the same time as being sufficiently permeable to allow information to pass between the subsystems.

The reader will note from the above brief review of some systemic concepts that systemic theory is a very broad level of theory. Despite this breadth, it has some important implications for our task of understanding and assisting families in post-separation conflict. For example, it might alert us to ask who are the key participants in this conflict and how the family has now organised itself in the process of the conflict performance. What is the new formation of subsystems within the post-separation family, and how is this formation meeting, or not, the needs of different family members? Systemic theory informs us that if mental health professionals are to have a constructive role in assisting the family to resolve its conflict, they not only need to understand the grounds and themes around which the family is engaged in its conflict but must also have an appreciation of the interactional processes through which the struggle persists, as well as an understanding of the costs to the family, its individual members and its different subsystems arising from the particular system formation that has come in to being around the conflict. It is a major assumption of this book that the mental health practitioner working in this area needs *a systemic understanding* of the family in conflict.

If systems theory could be considered a very broad theory, **attachment theory**, originating in the work of Bowlby (1969) and others (Ainsworth, Blehar, Walters and Wall, 1978; Crittenden, 1995), was to become a much more specific theory addressing the significance for the ongoing

14

development of human lives of the early bond that the infant makes with his caretaker, who is usually, but not always, his mother. Dallos (2006, p. 13) explains that central to attachment theory is 'the proposition that we share with other species an evolutionary-based instinct to seek protection from a parent (or carer) when we experience danger'. Attachment behaviours are responses that develop in children between the ages of six months and three years when they encounter danger or threat as they explore the world around them. In the face of danger, the infant/child will seek proximity with the parent and, once comforted, will return to showing interest in and exploring the world immediately around him. Over the course of multiple repetitions of this cycle, in which the child returns to the parent for comfort and safety following the experience of danger in the external world, the child develops an *internal working model* informing him of what he can expect in the context of his relationship to attachment figures. Carr (2000, p. 166) describes how these models are 'cognitive relationship maps, based on early attachment experiences, which serve as a template for later intimate relationships'. Hazan and Shaver (1987) also propose that these initial attachment patterns can be seen in later romantic relationships in which each member of a couple seems to function as an attachment figure for the other person.

Bowlby (1969) had become aware, from his study of infants and children in residential care, that once they had been removed from maternal care and opened up to a range of uncertain and varying responses from other caretakers, they appeared to have a greater likelihood of becoming unhappy outsiders in society, distrustful of others, given to deceitfulness and appearing unwilling or unable to empathise with the situation of others. Bowlby was most struck by the differences he found in children who had parents from whom they were temporarily separated as opposed to children who had either been fully separated from their parents or who had lost their parents. He noticed three distinct attachment patterns across all the children he observed. One pattern was a *secure attachment pattern*, wherein children would protest and be distressed at being separated from their parents but could be reassured quite speedily and showed signs of being able to get on with their play with a degree of autonomy. The other two patterns were examples of *insecure attachment patterns*, and they are referred to either as 'avoidant', where the child avoids the parents after a separation; or 'ambivalent/anxious', where, following separation, the child shows contradictory behaviour which moves between being dependant, clingy and crying to displaying anger, resistance and tantrums. Empirical research has confirmed the presence of each of these three attachment patterns as well as a fourth, referred to as a *disorganised attachment pattern*, which shows aspects of both the 'avoidant' and 'ambivalent/anxious', types and is commonly associated with significant child abuse and neglect and/or early parental absence or death. The significant piece of information from the point of view of our topic is that these four attachment patterns seem to show continuity over the individual's life cycle, and the type of adult attachments that individuals make in later romantic relationships can be classified into four equivalent categories (Carr, 2000). Such adult attachment patterns may go some way towards helping us to understand the kind of pre-separation struggles that some relational pairs endure, as well as throwing some light on the styles of post-separation conflict engagement exhibited by these same pairs.

Poststructuralist theory emerged in the latter decades of the twentieth century as a response to, and critique of, structuralism. As a critique, Hoffman (1992, p. 7) tells us that poststructuralism 'challenges any kind of framework that posits some kind of structure internal to the entity in question, whether we are talking about a text, a family or a play'. A poststructuralist perspective invites us to surrender the search for the 'essence' of something – whether this 'something' is a person, a problem or a family in conflict – in favour of understanding the way the character of a phenomenon is constructed through particular ways of speaking and thinking about it. Although it shares with narrative theory, described below, a focus on the pivotal role played by language in the construction of the meaning attaching to events, the central thrust of poststructuralism within the field of human practices derives from the work of Foucault (1980), who directed attention to the intimate connection between power and knowledge. For Foucault, power and knowledge are two sides of the same coin. The dominant way a phenomenon is 'known' in any culture or society becomes the vehicle through which a set of power relations is established in which different individuals and groups are assigned different places. In the field with which we are particularly concerned in this text, family conflict after separation and divorce, poststructuralist theory invites us to consider the operation of power and power relationships in those social fields where such conflicts are negotiated and managed. For example, poststructuralist theory can assist the mental health practitioner to consider the way power operates within certain discursive practices deployed in the court setting to produce 'knowledges' of different kinds about the identities of parents and children at the heart of legal proceedings. In its focus on power and power relations, poststructuralist theory maintains a close bond with feminist theory (Hare-Mustin, 1987), which casts light on the way power relations implicit in discursive practices produce particular kinds of gendered subjectivities. As we carry out many different kinds of work within this field of practice, we need to remind ourselves that we are gendered subjects, gendered mental health practitioners and that we meet gendered parents and gendered children. Poststructural theory provides the impetus for continuous and ongoing critical reflection concerning the way our different ways of thinking and speaking about women, men, boys, girls and their post-separation family conflicts either reproduces or challenges certain kinds of power relations that are productive of certain 'knowledges' of each of us as gendered subjects.

Narrative theory rests upon the idea that meaning is made through the vehicle of language and that narrative is the linguistic form towards which our linguistic exchanges evolve as we try to make sense of experience both within ourselves and with others. Narrative can be seen as the specifically human way of *making meaning* out of our experiences. Aristotle (1895) was the first to draw our attention to the centrality of the concept of the *plot* to the idea of narrative. There is no narrative without a plot. A plot is that act of the imagination, individual or collective, by which we select a variety of heterogeneous elements from our experience – events, goals, chance, actions – and draw a circle around these elements while saying to ourselves and others that this group of elements, if organised in terms of a proposed set of relationships between them, constitute a meaningful whole.

Narratives, Ricoeur (1984) tells us, are the way we have of making our existence in time a *human existence*. Unfathomable time, which appears to us without beginning or end, is made human and manageable in so far as it can be told in the form of a story, which is a structure with a beginning, a middle and an end. In the act of plot-making, narratives turn a sequence or succession (one thing after another after another) of things/events into a configuration.

Narratives are also the way we compose a picture of the self, or an *identity*. Arendt (1958) suggests to us that when someone asks us who we are, we always respond with a story, and Ricoeur (1992) affirms that self-identity is always a narrative identity. Our sense of who we are does not, of course, come solely out of that inner act of imagination, a composition made by the self about itself in isolation. Others also make stories about us, and for the most part the self-identities we live with and by emerge from the exchanges between our own picture of ourselves and the range of stories others make about us. The metaphor of *entanglement*, used by the German historian Schapp (1976), nicely captures that sense each of us has of being caught in a web of such stories. Legal affidavits in family law are wonderful examples of plot-making around key family events that confer differential identities on the parties to the proceedings. Such affidavits and responding affidavits regularly tell of many events and episodes in a family's life over time, and the telling is moulded into stories of different kinds – for example a story of betrayal which confers a narrative identity of 'deceiving betrayer' on the *other* party to the proceedings while also conferring a narrative identity of 'innocent victim' on the *self*. Some legal affidavits draw attention to a certain set of events while forgetting a range of other events. Every act of narrative memory, Ricoeur (2004) tells us, is at the same time an act of forgetting. Narrative theory helps us understand something of the extreme stories that family members often make about themselves and others during and after separation while pointing to the place that modified or alternative stories (White and Epston, 1990) can play in facilitating conflict containment or resolution.

Most theories of **family conflict** (Wilmot and Hocker, 2014; Jones, 2015; Mayer, 2015) and **family conflict resolution** (Deutsch, 1973; Irving and Benjamin, 2002; Folberg, Milne and Salem, 2004; Deutsch, Coleman and Marcus, 2006; Barky, 2015; Murphy and Rubinson, 2015) emphasise the normality and ubiquitous character of conflict in human lives and relationships. Pre-separation couple scenarios often reveal individuals who have been in conflict within themselves ('Should I stay or should I go?') for different lengths of time. Nor do these theories perceive conflict just in negative terms. Indeed, theories concerning family conflict suggest that when conflict performance is exercised within limits with respect to both duration and grounds, it can operate as an avenue towards transformation and growth for both the family as a whole as well as for its individual members. Parent–adolescent conflict can be seen, often in retrospect rather than contemporaneously, as a transitional vehicle of this kind where a developing adolescent autonomy is accompanied by a corresponding reduction in dependence. Conflict, however, can also be seen to be destructive and system-dissolving when it escalates in an out-of-control kind of way. Family therapy (Carr, 2000) is often sought or recommended when a family is unable to bring its own regulatory resources to bear on an internal, escalating conflict and seeks to generate this regulation within the context of the therapy and the relationship with the family therapist. Such assistance is often required both before and after separation.

Theories of conflict management and conflict resolution point to the importance of both utilising and developing *negotiation* skills. The activity of negotiation is directed towards reaching an agreement between people with respect to something that is important to each of them, and it is done through a mechanism of dialogue or discussion of different kinds. This concept of negotiation appears many times within this text and will be seen to underpin a host of different activities that mental health professionals engage in with families in post-separation conflict. Negotiation and its associated skills come into play in family therapy, family mediation, family court exchanges and assistance, family court order implementation, parent co-ordination, parent coaching and other activities. And negotiation skills are required, of course, by both family members *and* the mental health professional.

Trauma theory (Herman, 1998; Rothschild, 2017) provides an important framework for addressing a number of different contexts met by the mental health professional working with post-separation conflict. Parent and child victims of domestic violence and abuse, separated adults catapulted into separation by the unforeseen betrayal of an ex-partner, as well as abducted children and their left-behind parents, are some of the participants in these conflicts who suffer trauma responses of different kinds. The word *trauma* comes into our language from the Greek word for 'wound'. Its earlier medical meaning, pointing to physical injury, is joined here, for our purposes, by a psychological meaning which refers to 'highly distressing events that have the power to overwhelm' (Akhtar, 2017, p. 23). Herman (1998) refers to a dialectic at the heart of trauma which is made up of both the natural desire to deny the awfulness of certain horrific events as well as the impetus within the horrible to be brought into the light of day and to be recognised for what it was. In victims, this dialectic gives rise to what mental health specialists refer to as 'dissociation'. Witnesses to the horrible, as well as its victims, are subject to the dialectic of trauma. The mind, brain and body all participate in both the expression of trauma and its transformation (Van Der Kolk, 2014).

Reflexivity theory finds its relevance for the mental health professional in its recognition that in each moment of professional engagement with a client or clients, we are part of many contexts which have a bearing, often outside of our consciousness, on the way we feel, think, behave and decide. Hawes (1998, pp. 97–98) tells us that reflexivity is essentially about 'turning one's critical gaze back on oneself as well as the professional, historical and cultural discourses that empower and constrain one's capabilities to think and act in the context of a relationship'. The practice of reflexivity is about trying to bring a deep level of self-questioning into our consciousness about the way our membership in different groups such as our gender, class, culture, race, sexual orientation, professional discipline or age can both throw light upon as well as occlude certain themes pertinent to the professional task we are engaged in, or certain aspects of the professional–client relationship through which these tasks are being accomplished. Reflexivity is certainly about the exercise of power within professional–client relationships and making a critical examination of the way the performance of such power relations either facilitates or inhibits the helpful completion of contracted tasks. *Self-reflexivity* refers to that part of this process that professionals do either on their own or in the company of a professional supervisor, whereas *relational reflexivity* (Burnham, 1993) refers to the process of critical questioning that is done by the professional and client together, often at the invitation of the professional, about the inner workings of the interpersonal professional context they find themselves in.

Although self-reflexivity and relational reflexivity are important in all aspects of work with families after separation and divorce, they seem to take on an added significance during evaluation processes that the mental health professional may be asked to undertake by the court with respect to the residence and parent contact arrangements for the children of a separating couple. There is so much at stake for both parents and children that the onus falls on professionals to bring as much reflexivity into the context as possible as they exercise their role of deciding what to recommend to the court. This performance of reflexivity extends not just to the act of deciding what to recommend in such contexts but to the process through which the assessment is accomplished. Among the many questions that the professional must ask are the following: has each person in the family been afforded the time and the comfort to enable them to communicate his different feelings and desires? Has each person's perspective been seen and heard in a manner that is fitting for his developmental stage? What are the different discourses (gender, culture, class etc.) which I and this particular client inhabit that may be having a bearing upon the decision-making processes I am engaged in? How might the unique way I am positioned within these discourses be contributing to some blinkered vision on my part? The lack of agreement between separating parents about matters of residence and contact automatically renders them relatively powerless as the decision-making is handed over to the court and assessment agents acting on its behalf. It is critical that the manner in which assessment/evaluation processes are carried out do not add to this diminishment of parental power that is already written into the context. The reflexivity practice of the assessing professional is one central pathway to the protection of parental and child power.

The Design and Scope of This Book

This book is divided into three parts. The three chapters following this introductory chapter will form the first part of the book which sets the scene for the different stages of conflict escalation and management which are the subject of the second part of the work. The second chapter will look at the way the changing conditions of contemporary life in Western societies alter the shape of family conflict following separation. An expanding variety of family forms, the mobile telephone and social media, the busyness of daily life, the world of cybersex, and changing patterns in the daytime care of dependent children all give rise to new conflict-related themes as well as new avenues for the performance of post-separation conflict. The third chapter examines the way that patterns of conflict engagement and management in both the in-house phase of separation as well as in the period immediately following residential separation can, without timely mental health professional intervention, have a detrimental effect on family relationships in the years ahead. The fourth chapter takes a step back to examine the nature of the different 'goods' that are being struggled about in the context of post-separation conflict as well as considering the implications for conflict management arising from the different kinds of post-separation parenting relationships that take shape over time.

The sequence of the following five chapters, which form the second part of the book, reflects the movement in post-separation family conflict from milder forms of conflict involving temporary disruption to parent–child contact to the more serious forms of conflict which include domestic violence, the cessation of parent–child contact, parental alienating behaviours and, allegations of child abuse. The final two chapters make up the third part of the text. The penultimate chapter considers the challenges posed for the management of post-separation family conflict by the phenomena of child relocation and child abduction. Themes relating to parent and child mental health and illness, as well as to parental substance abuse, will be explored in the final chapter of the book. The mental health and well-being of mental health professionals engaged in this area of practice also receives consideration in this final chapter. In each of the chapters, consideration is given to the range of skills and interventions needed by the mental health practitioner to contain and address evolving patterns of post-separation conflict.

The Case Vignettes in This Book

The reader will quickly realise that a host of different case vignettes are being used in this book to illustrate different facets of post-separation family conflict and its management. A text such as this would be extremely dry and dense without them. These vignettes are based upon the writer's experiences of hundreds of families seen over a 40-year practice period in which the phenomenon of post-separation conflict has been encountered in a variety of professional roles such as child protection social worker, family therapist, family mediator, court-appointed assessor in parental disputes over residence and contact arrangements for children, post-separation parenting plan advisor, order implementation assistant, parenting co-ordinator and other therapeutic roles with children and parents proposed by parents themselves or by the family courts. Although the vignettes represent a faithful rendering of the variety of relational processes encountered in family conflict after separation and divorce, none of the vignettes refer to any particular family the writer has been engaged with. Hence, these vignettes are a mixture of *fiction* and *fidelity*. They are fictional with respect to the personal profiles of the family members, their locations and movements, yet faithful to the relational processes to be found in real families during the performance and resolution of different kinds of conflict. If you, as either a professional or lay reader, have been a participant in this phenomenon, it is hoped that you will recognise yourself and other family members in some of the relationship processes described, but you will not recognise yourself in any of the purely fictional descriptive detail.

Language and Terminology

Multiple kinds of language and terminology are used to describe post-separation parenting roles and responsibilities in different jurisdictions. The language used in current and past legislation, as well the everyday language used by parents themselves, all give some shape to the terminology used in our daily dialogues about families after separation. Terms such as *custody, joint custody, sole custody, primary care* and *contact* have all been used in many jurisdictions for a very long time and continue to be used in everyday dialogue. Despite this tradition, the current text moves away from this tradition and uses terms such as *residence, resident parent, nonresident parent* in place of the language of *custody* and uses the term *contact* instead of *access*.

The reader should also note that the text is written with the purpose of reaching the greatest possible number of professional audiences from a wide range of jurisdictions. This means that the language used to refer to specific services and agencies does not follow the language used in any one jurisdiction, but is as general as possible, with this wider reach in mind.

Personal Reflexive Exercises at the End of Each Chapter

The whole of this book is an invitation to readers to consider the phenomenon we are exploring from different angles. For those experienced professional readers who are intimately involved with the area on a day-to-day basis, some of the content may feel so familiar as to border on the banal. Yet it is hoped that even these readers will find that some aspects of the text which encourage them to reflect again on things they already 'know'. For other professionals who may be at an earlier stage of their engagement with the area, the first message of this book is that this field of professional practice, while bringing its own satisfaction and rewards, is very difficult. The second message is that it remains very difficult even for those experienced professionals who have mastered many of the skills relevant to practice in the area. One of the things that makes the practice difficult is that coming face-to-face with family conflict, its casualties and consequences, often evokes in us quite intense feelings and memories from earlier parts of our lives. It can also trigger a range of feelings about events that are happening currently in our personal lives. Reflexivity theory, which we just introduced some paragraphs ago, alerts us to the fact that it is much more likely that our behaviour and decision-making in practice contexts will be driven by these intense emotions and past experiences rather than by the immediate needs of the family in focus if our memories and experiences and their attaching emotions are not brought as fully as possible out into the open space of our present awareness, where they can be acknowledged and processed by ourselves and with others such as supervisors and colleagues. In fact, a reflexive practice requires of the practitioner a constant vigilance with respect to the relationship between our own life and experiences and the particular piece of practice we are engaged with at a moment in time (Jensen, 2012). Reflexivity implies an effort on the part of the mental health practitioner to consider the mutual influences that may be at work between these two elements of the professional's context (Jensen, 2008).

With the above in mind, this text includes a series of personal, reflexive exercises at the end of each chapter. The reader can complete these exercises alone, or they can be done as part of a class group or professional development group in learning settings of different kinds. Although it is certainly fine to do these exercises just within the confines of the reader's own private thinking and remembering, it is strongly advised to use a personal journal and to do these exercises in written form. In this way, the reader can return to past exercises and add to what was originally written from time to time. The exercises relate to the themes of the chapter and invite you to develop a three-cornered reflection and dialogue between these themes, where you have encountered them in your practice, and your own life experiences. Here are the first set of exercises.

Personal and Reflective Exercises

Write some notes for yourself in response to the following three questions:

1. What experiences do you have now, or have you had in the past, in your *personal/private life* with the theme of post-separation family conflict? Have you, your siblings, your parents, your children or your friends had real-life experience of this theme?
2. What experiences do you have now, or have you had in the past, in your *professional life* of post-separation family conflict? What do you think you have learned from these experiences?
3. Which of the experiences you have noted in your responses to questions one and two made the strongest impression on you, and why do you think this is the case?

THE CHANGING SHAPE OF FAMILY CONFLICT AFTER SEPARATION AND DIVORCE

The experienced mental health professional assisting families in post-separation conflict will have an intuitive awareness of the many transitions that have impacted that entity we still call 'the family'. These transitions relate in the first instance to the ever-expanding ways in which the notion of *family* is defined. Since the turn of the century, most Western societies have been marked by a developing spirit of inclusiveness when they consider which different 'units of intimate belonging' (Sheehan, 2013a) may avail of the different societal benefits and protections afforded to the family and its members. The traditional Western concept of the family as comprising a heterosexual married pair occupying a single dwelling with their own biological children has gradually given way to a notion of family which points to a rich tapestry of differently constructed relational units among which this traditional 'nuclear' family finds its place as one type among many. Hence, this chapter commences with a consideration of some of the very different units that now comprise our evolving understanding of family, as well as an examination of some of the newly emerging grounds of conflict arising when these units are struck by relational strife and breakdown.

The chapter also considers some of the ways in which changes in the broader social landscape are gradually restructuring the interior worlds of these many different families in both their material and psychosocial dimensions. Central among these changes are the ever-expanding range of digital media and communications that appear to be commanding the attention of individuals at all points in the life cycle for increasingly longer periods each day. One of the consequences of this development is that it marks a change in the permeability of the boundaries around something we still call 'family life'. This ongoing development has also led to changing experiences, for both children and their parents, of the phenomenon we still call 'childhood', with consequences for the performance of both parent–child and parent–adolescent relationships. The Internet has also facilitated and accelerated a change in the part the sexual bond plays in uniting the contemporary couple. It has done this by making available to individual couple members a wide variety of other sexual opportunities beyond the boundary of the couple relationship itself. However, the boundaries around family life have also been impacted by a phenomenon referred to by North American social psychologist Gergen (1991a) as 'saturation', a process by which an ever-increasing range of external demands, activities and opportunities bring family members away from the centre of family life for longer periods of time between waking and sleeping. The greater connectivity between people across the globe that digital media allows has also facilitated changes in employment patterns, which now require more and more adults to travel long distances to work, necessitating different kinds of absences from home, with different consequences for the management of family functions. One of the functions impacted is the daytime care of dependent children who are increasingly likely to have their needs met by a range of non-parental, non-familial childcare/minding professionals. In examining the various changes mentioned above, the aim is to highlight the newly emerging grounds on which family conflict may appear, as well as to consider the way these grounds impact the way family conflict can be performed.

Expanding Variety of Family Forms

Although there are many factors giving rise to the expanding variety of family forms, one group of these factors concerns developments in medicine which have facilitated the emergence of new kinds of parenthood (Varga and Budinayte, 2015). Developments in in vitro fertilisation (IVF), surrogate motherhood and sperm donation, as well as the prolongation of the fertility age of women, have all given rise to new parenting configurations which have embedded in them their own unique grounds for later conflict should separation and/or divorce become part of the family's evolution.

An Irish couple, Lisa and John, met when he was 36 years and she was 27 years, while both were teaching at the same school. They lived together from six months into the relationship and tried to have children from about the same time. Following a three-year period without a pregnancy, Lisa persuaded a rather reluctant John to avail of fertility assistance together. Investigations revealed that because of testicular surgery in his pre-adolescence, John was not producing any sperm at all. They fairly quickly decided to avail of sperm donation from a Scandinavian fertility clinic, and subsequently had three children, two girls and a boy, over a five-year period. Although both were devoted parents to the children, the couple's relationship eventually broke down when the eldest girl was seven years and the youngest child was three. The couple struggled post-separation about the amount of contact John should have with the children, but the issue which catapulted their struggle about child contact into the family court was a conflict about when to tell the children about their biological origins, and about who had an entitlement/responsibility to take control of this issue. Lisa had sought independent advice from a psychologist who advised her it was best to tell the children before they were ten years old and before someone else in the extended family and social network might tell them; John, on the other hand, felt quite threatened about the possible consequences of the children knowing he was not their biological father. John felt at that point that 'what they don't know won't hurt them' and that the matter should be left alone until they were at least 16 years, and then considered again in the light of the adolescents they had become. The ground of their conflict concerned specific critical information about biological origins, and the relational dynamics through which the conflict was performed involved a group of people that extended beyond the parental relationship itself to include adult members of the extended families as well as close friends who had been present years earlier to celebrate both the birth of the children and the means of their arrival in the family.

Same-sex couples are another group who face relatively new sets of dilemmas when separation occurs. Western societies are by no means uniform in their attitude to the families of same-sex couples when they separate. The slow pace of changing attitudes towards homosexuality means that a typical same-sex family pattern in many Western societies involves a gay or lesbian couple where one or both members of the couple have been heterosexually married before and have been jointly parenting children from their respective prior relationships. Different legal frameworks provide different levels of protection for the post-separation relationship between children and their nonbiological parents who may have been parenting them for several years.

Joan and Sue had been living together for five years before Sue met another woman through her book club and decided she wanted to separate from Joan so that she could pursue this new relationship. Joan, who had left her husband to be with Sue when her two girls were five and three years old, was devastated by the breakup and did all she could to keep her girls, now ten and eight years, well away from the woman who was leaving her. Sue, who had neither been married nor a parent at the time of meeting Joan, had built up a strong attachment to both girls, but to one of them in particular, whom she brought to her swimming lesson each week. The couple were neither married nor in a civil partnership, as Joan was only now finalising a problematic divorce from her ex-husband. The grounds of their post-separation conflict concerned the future of the relationship between the two girls and their mother's ex-partner with whom they had no biological connection. Sue's only claim to an ongoing relationship with Joan's children rested upon her attachment to both girls and her belief that the girls wanted a continuing relationship with her. The process of their post-separation conflict performance involved angry scenes in front of Joan's ten-year-old at the local swimming pool, where Sue continued to attend lessons despite Joan having taken over the role of bringing her daughter to and from the lesson.

The Mobile Telephone and Social Media

Within the last decade, this writer has heard many stories from family therapists who report coming to meet families for the first time, whether in their office or in the family's home, only to find all family members engaged with their own pieces of technology. Mothers may be on mobile phones, fathers on computers, and adolescent and pre-adolescent children on iPads and a variety of game apparatuses. Such families reveal themselves in the moment of meeting with their therapists as embedded in a very contemporary kind of paradox. Whether gathered around the kitchen table at home or huddled together on one or two pieces of furniture in a therapist's office, waiting for the therapy to begin, their physical proximity speaks strongly of their togetherness and shared community structure at the same time that a variety of electronic media position each of them in a number of other worlds.

This evolving picture of family life as a place where physical proximity is combined with different kinds of psychological retreat is summed up by Polish sociologist Bauman (2003, p. 64), who suggests that homes 'have turned from shared playgrounds of love and friendship into the sites of territorial skirmishes, and from building sites of togetherness into the assemblies of fortified bunkers'. This pattern of homes becoming new sites of a kind of separated togetherness is well captured by Schluter and Lee (1993, p. 37) who describe how we 'have stepped into our houses and closed the door, and then stepped into our separate rooms and closed the door'. They go on to tell us how, in this transition, the home 'becomes a multipurpose leisure centre where household members can live, as it were, separately side by side'. The following vignette illustrates some of the dilemmas created for parents and children where technology makes parents available to other worlds at the same time that they officially belong to their children.

Lawyers referred separated parents, Barbara and Tom, to me for media-tion assistance following Barbara's refusal to allow their nine-year-old son and eight-year-old daughter to continue their midweek contact with their father on Wednesdays from 6 p.m. to 8 p.m. They had been unable to discuss the matter on the telephone without screaming at each other, and the impasse triggered Tom to request his lawyer to initiate proceedings for breach of orders relating to contact. His lawyer had persuaded him to attempt to mediate a resolution in advance of initiating proceedings. When giving her justification for her cessation of the mid-week contact event during our first meeting, Barbara described how the children were coming home complaining that their father never really spoke to them that much when they were with him for the two hours. The children told her how their father would collect a family-size pizza from a pizza takeaway, having picked them up from home. Following their arrival at his apartment, Tom would settle the children, with their pizza, in to watching a movie on TV in the living room before he withdrew to his bedroom to work on his computer and his mobile phone. Tom responded to these descriptions by saying he could not see what the big deal was if he had some additional work to do when he got home. As far as he was con-cerned, the children loved pizza and loved the movies he found for them to watch. He further stated that he 'popped in' to the living room every 20 minutes or so to see if they were okay. From his perspective, it was not as though he was neglecting the children, and he suggested that Barbara might consider going back into the workplace at least part-time, where she might learn how people lived in the 'real' world, where you had to make a living. Following some further 'discussion', both parents agreed to my suggestion that the children be invited to participate in the process. Both children responded positively to this invitation, and I subsequently met them together. Although somewhat frightened by the conflict between their parents, they told me that they looked forward to seeing their dad on Wednesday evenings and missed him a lot now that they were only seeing him every second weekend. They enjoyed the pizzas and the movies, but they felt 'a bit lonely' when their dad was in his bedroom, and had spoken to their mum about this. They wanted to tell their dad about 'stuff' they were doing at school, but he did not seem to have time to talk. I wondered how they would feel trying to talk with their dad about their experience, with some help from me, and they thought this was a good idea. They agreed that I should talk things over again with their mum and dad and give dad a 'heads up' about their experiences before we had the discussion together with him. When I met with the parents the following week to discuss my meeting with the children, Tom seemed completely surprised that they should feel lonely on the Wednesday evenings when he was 'less than ten feet away'. It transpired that 'loneliness' had also been a central theme for Barbara during the couple counsel-ling which they had attended 18 months earlier, prior to her decision to separate. When the children met with the father and myself, they worked out the outline of *a possible resolution to the impasse, based upon a suggestion of the eight-year-old girl that on Wednesdays they have an eat-in pizza with their dad in the restaurant, where 'he couldn't use his computer and we could just talk and eat before going back to mum'. The parents both agreed to this adjustment to the mid-week contact arrangement, which saw the period reduced from two hours to one and a half hours. A final meeting with parents and children a month later found the children much happier with their experience of the revised contact arrangements and both parents content that a resolution had been found.*

The above dispute reveals some of the features arising in people's experience, which often accompany the extraordinary possibilities created by our contemporary communications technologies. Mobile phones and computers allow us to do business with people who are far away and live in time zones different from ours. They allow us to hear the voices and see the faces of those we love who live on the other side of the globe from us. As we move about during the day, the mobile is clutched tightly by most of us, as though our lives depended upon it. For Tom, in the example above, his own and his family's livelihoods were very dependent upon his mobile and computer; these were the means by which he managed the business of the company he owned, which had clients in different places throughout the world. His mobile and computer had the function of bringing his New York–based clients close to him in Dublin. But at the same time that the voice of his client sounded loudly in the bedroom of his apartment, he was distanced from his children who were 'less than ten feet away'. The mobile has that strange capacity to make present to us that which is far away while distancing us from that which is near. A certain kind of loneliness seemed to strike the children in the example above as they occupied the topographical space between the TV, which was eight feet in front of them, and their father on his computer and mobile, who was eight feet behind them.

The mobile, which is usually as close to us as the clothes we wear, is the key symbol of a virtual proximity rendered possible by our advancing communications technologies. Bauman (2003, p. 62), however, argues that the arrival of virtual proximity 'renders human connections simultaneously more frequent and more shallow, more intense and more brief'. This kind of proximity allows us to be part of an extensive range of contacts where we can do our business briefly as we keep focussed on the central purpose of our connection. Connections, however, he reminds us, 'tend to be too shallow and brief to condense into bonds'. What virtual proximity has brought about above all else is 'the separation between communication and relationship'. Our advanced communication technologies facilitate us to be connected in a way that doesn't need the prior establishment of a bond with those whom we contact, just as a bond does not necessarily result from our repeated connections to those we contact. Relationship requires us to be 'engaged' and signifies a process that is more costly for the individual in terms of time and effort than 'being connected'. Although 'being connected' may be less costly than 'being engaged', it is 'also considerably less productive in terms of bond building and bond maintenance' (Bauman, 2003, p. 63).

A further consequence of this supremacy of virtual proximity within our culture of communications concerns the way in which the skills associated with direct face-to-face communication are either inadequately acquired in the first place or lost along the way as individuals put an ever-increasing amount of their time and effort on a daily basis into communications governed by a virtual kind of proximity. This observation has profound consequences for mental health professionals assisting family members in contexts of post-separation conflict. We would do well to ask ourselves in particular professional engagements whether the problematic communication we observe between parents or between parents and children is an *effect* of the participants' conflict or is rooted in an *absence* of skills associated with expressing something important about one's own needs or inquiring about the needs and experiences of others. With a focus so firmly on conflict and its possible resolution, it can be easy to miss the need for a development of certain skills in the parties to the conflict without which resolution may remain a remote possibility.

Facebook and Twitter have also become almost universal modes of communication for many parents and adolescents. The possibility of sharing with your 'friends' events from your life almost simultaneously with their occurrence can be a very enriching and exciting experience for those geographically removed from one another. We can post messages about ourselves and/or others on our Facebook page, which can be seen by all our 'friends'. The downside to this is that Facebook can be used in conflict scenarios to post negative, critical and harmful messages about an ex-partner and/or her behaviour in a manner that can inflict psychological damage on adults while also impacting the interests of their children.

Shaun and Mary had been separated for four years, and Shaun was having three hours supervised contact every Saturday afternoon with their only child, a five-year-old boy called Josh. The contact was occurring at a supervision centre, following the court hearing professional evidence concerning a history of physical and psychological abuse on Shaun's part towards Mary. In order to avoid any direct contact with her ex-partner, whom she feared, Mary brought Josh to the centre on a weekly basis 15 minutes before Shaun arrived and collected her son 15 minutes after Shaun left. Out of the blue, Mary received calls from two different female friends who were part of a friendship network to which she and Shaun had formerly belonged. They wanted to alert her to messages about her that Shaun had posted on Facebook. The tone of these messages alarmed them. Mary felt extremely threatened and publically embarrassed by the messages which were forwarded to her by her friends. In addition to thinly veiled threats to her physical integrity, the messages contained some information about her from the past which she considered very private and outside the bounds of their conflict over the extent and character of Shaun's contact with Josh. Mary responded by no longer bringing Josh to the supervised contact centre, thus making it more likely that Shaun would have to initiate legal proceedings to try to have his time with his son restored.

Although the grounds of the above conflict are not particularly unusual – that is, conflict over paternal child contact in the context of a history of intimate partner physical and psychological abuse – the means by which Shaun chose to perform the conflict involved a very public display of what he knew his ex-partner had always regarded as very private. Posting messages on Facebook is a way of ensuring an audience for your conflict-promoting manoeuvres. Many ex-partners react to such provocation by responding in like manner, thus bringing a Facebook 'war' into being. Although post-separation conflicts have always had ways of becoming more public as more and more friends and family members are drawn in to the 'news' of the conflict, what is unique about 'Facebook war' is the ease and speed with which potentially large numbers of individuals are drawn in to the role of unwitting witnesses to the conflict. The allure of the speed with which communication can take place via social media often outweighs the need to reflect for even five minutes about the wisdom of making the communication at all.

The Pathway to the Postmodern 'Saturated' Family in Conflict

The family is a form that has always experienced change and transition, as it is both influenced by and influences the other social institutions that are its primary context. In each of our societies, the family is interlinked with economic, educational, political and religious institutions in a manner that is unique to that society. When we look at contemporary families and the conflicts they experience, both on the path towards separation and divorce as well as after 'breakup', we always see a multiplicity of different attitudes and perspectives at work in the individuals in conflict. Some of these perspectives seem utterly contemporary and postmodern, whereas others have had their genesis within past historical moments in our Western cultures but survive well in the psyches and personalities of our contemporary post-separation conflict participants.

During a recent court-ordered evaluation concerning the post-separation residence and contact arrangements for a ten-year-old boy, a 38-year-old mother, who had been a very successful financier employed by an international bank since she was 25 years of age, struggled to ensure that the court awarded her 80 per cent of the post-separation care of the separating couple's only child. Notwithstanding the fact that her work had taken her away from home four nights a week in the previous seven years, and that her son's Monday to Friday care had been shared equally over those years between a childminder and her 40-year-old husband, she based her sense of entitlement to the major portion of her son's care solely in the fact of her motherhood. At first glance, her presentation seemed filled with paradox. Her life as a worker/employee enabled her to earn a very large salary which gave her family many material opportunities, but had brought her far away from any kind of daily maternal role in her son's life. Hence the agreed historical facts concerning the child's past care seemed to offer little support to her claim. Yet, her very belonging to the category of 'mother' immersed her in a set of long-standing cultural discourses about motherhood and its entitlements which provided their own logic and coherence to support her claim. As a very talented woman, partner, worker and mother, she belonged to a multiplicity of different contexts which placed competing and incompatible demands upon her.

In a recent family mediation consultation, the separated parents of two girls, aged ten and eight years were in conflict over the extent of the father's midweek contact with the girls. The parents had been separated for the previous four years, and the mother had cared for them during the week, with the father having a 24-hour period of overnight contact each weekend. The mother argued that because they lived about an hour's drive away from the father, that midweek contact, which the father had not requested until now, should be confined to a two-hour period in the father's home on a Wednesday evening. The 48-year-old father, in making his claim to midweek overnight contact, argued that because the girls were now the age they were, he wished to have an appropriate level of 'influence' on their development and to bring his 'moral guidance as a father' to bear on this development. His presentation was a unique mixture of contemporary perspectives on shared responsibility and cooperative co-parenting after separation in addition to a rather old, Victorian-like perspective on fatherhood which underlined the father's unique role as moral guide in the developing life of the young person. In both the case of this father and that of the mother referred to in the previous example, a combination of highly contemporary and more historical discourses seemed to be the key edifices shaping their contributions both to family life as well as to the attempted resolution to post-separation conflict.

The contemporary mental health and social care professional assisting the family with post-separation conflict is, first and foremost, observing a particular instance of a social institution in transition. 'The family', separated or not, must be seen by the professional as a unique expression of a changing phenomenon. And it is the job of the social historians of the family, among others, to shed some light for us on the way this phenomenon appears to have changed over time in particular locations, and why. Indeed, it is an important assumption of this text that a historical focus on both our own lives as individuals as well as on the phenomenon we are dealing with – the family in conflict after separation and divorce – is an important underpinning of a reflective professional practice (Schon, 1991) that was mentioned towards the conclusion of Chapter 1. Sensitivity to the changing history of the family in the societies to which we belong can release us from the prejudices arising from present times as we observe and make judgements about the behaviour, interactions and desires of those we are engaged to help.

Perhaps one of the richest histories of the family in Western societies to emerge over the last 50 years was that provided by the Canadian social historian Edward Shorter (1975). This history provided an account of the processes that went in to the making of the modern family over the last 400 years approximately. His work traced the development of the institution of family in the Western world, from 'the traditional family' as it appeared in traditional societies to the emergence of 'the nuclear family', which in turn gradually gave way to a form he called 'the modern' or 'postmodern family'. The traditional family, he suggested, 'was held firmly in the matrix of a larger social order', where ties in space to the extended family network and the wider local community were matched by ties in time to future and past generations of the family (Shorter, 1975, p. 3). Shorter traced the dislodgement over time of the traditional family form to what he called 'a surge of sentiment' in three different areas: in the area of courtship, where romantic love displaced property and lineage as the basis for couples coming together; in the area of the mother–child relationship, where the welfare of the infant began to be 'a priority in the mother's rational hierarchy of values', where previously the struggle for existence required that she spread her attentions more broadly; and, finally, in the area of the boundary line between the family and the local community, where 'a shield of privacy' in relation to the extended family and wider community was erected, which strengthened the ties between members of the immediate family while weakening the ties to the outside world (Shorter, 1975, p. 5).

By the eighth decade of the twentieth century, Shorter was already seeing the outlines of the postmodern family in view. The reshaping involved in this transition appeared to him to have two key elements. The first of these was an inherent instability of the couple itself, which he saw as the result of 'replacing property first with sentiment and then with sex as the bond between man and wife'. This instability could also be traced to the paring away of the couple's ties with the community, extended family and lineage that had commenced in the transition from the traditional to the nuclear family. The second element he saw as pivotal in ushering in this new 'postmodern' family was 'a loss of control of parents over adolescent children'. Shorter traced the emergence of this element to the nuclear family's gradual disengagement from the larger lineage to which they belonged. Where once young people could comfortably answer the identity question ('Who am I?') by pointing to the generations behind them and to those certain to come after them, adolescents in postmodern times no longer see themselves as 'links in a familial chain stretching across the ages'. They make their identity largely independently from who their parents are. In the process of identity formation, the chain of generations no longer serves any moral purpose for adolescents. This pathway inevitably leads to the collapse of parents' moral authority over their adolescent children (Shorter, 1975, p. 8).

If Shorter provided us with us with broad hypotheses concerning key transitions in the phenomenon of the family as it appeared in the Western world, and of the elements that brought us to the doorstep of 'the postmodern family', it was the North American social psychologist Kenneth Gergen (1991a, 1991b) who sketched out the description of the family form as it was emerging in the final decade of the twentieth century. The term he utilised to capture the 'emerging character' of this form was 'saturated' (1991a, p. 27). The postmodern family, he tells us, is a place whose members 'feel their lives scattering in intensifying busyness' (Gergen, 1991a, p. 28). By the final decade of the twentieth century, family members had become embedded in a multiplicity of relationships at different times throughout the day which bring them into contact with a diverse range of cultures, attitudes and ideas. With the aid of all the contemporary technologies, such as the car, the mobile telephone, the TV and the jet plane, we have the means to engage in a host of different activities in locations far removed from one another. And at the level of our social relations, Gergen suggests that 'we ingest myriad bits of others' being – values, attitudes, opinions, life-styles, personalities – synthesising and incorporating them into our own definition of self' (p. 28). However, because we gather so many different bits from the outside in the making of ourselves, we find that when we look inward, we run the risk of seeing 'a maelstrom of partial beings in conflict' (p. 28). The inward glance is likely to reveal 'a realist co-existing with a romanticist, a lover of tradition mixing with a revolutionary, an advocate of commitment at odds with a free adventurer' (p. 28). It is this experience of the world and of self that Gergen refers to as 'social saturation'. Despite strenuous efforts to coordinate hectic schedules, the family and its members end up in varying degrees of turmoil with one another, and with a sense of fragmentation and chaos marking their lives as each is pulled outwards from the family towards an ever-expanding, and seemingly exciting, set of activities and relationships within which they are embedded. From the perspective of assisting the postmodern/contemporary family in post-separation conflict, however, an important point to remember is that the level of the conflict needing to be addressed is not confined to that between the adults themselves, or between adults and children, but to the level of the individuals' relation with themselves. This sense of chaos and fragmentation was certainly reflected in 45-year-old Joan, who asked for a therapeutic consultation alone in recent times.

Belonging to an intact family with her husband and two children, Tom, aged nine years, and Lia, aged ten years, Joan had recently had an experience which had unnerved her. She had returned home from her work the previous Tuesday at 4.45 p.m. with many things on her mind about the preparations she had to make for an early-morning work meeting the next day; as well, she was trying to figure out how she was going to get her 85-year-old mother to a consultant medical appointment for 12 noon later the same morning. Her only sister, who worked part-time, normally looked after the task of transporting her mother to medical appointments, but she was away in London for two days, celebrating her 15th wedding anniversary with her husband. Joan had come in the door at home and said a quick 'Hello' to the childminder before ushering Tom and his bag into the back of the car and driving away swiftly. She was halfway to her destination, and only half-attending to Tom's mumblings from the back of the car, before her son, in a raised voice, said: 'Mum! Stop! Where are you going? You are on the way to the School of Music, but I have football training in 15 minutes.' She heard her son, stopped the car, pulled over to the side of the road and burst into tears. She realised she was bringing Tom in the direction of his sister's piano lesson at the School of Music, which wasn't on until the next day, while her daughter at that moment was happily involved in her Irish dancing lesson at another venue. She felt overwhelmed and was panicking about the possibility of not being able to cope with the different demands of work, the children's schedules and her responsibilities for her own mother. She feared talking to her husband because she knew it would start him worrying about their capacity to pay the mortgage if she felt unable to continue her work.

Nor is this feeling of being overstretched and torn in different directions confined to adults. It places great demands on children as well. Denzin (1987) noted that the postmodern child is required to make continuous flexible adjustments between spheres. Children have to constantly adapt as they move between childminders, parents, after-school care, sport and recreational contexts, as well as grandparent care if it is available and has become one of the spheres to which the child belongs. The following example tells us something, I believe, of the conflicts that can arise for a not untypical postmodern child subtly caught up in the conflict between his separating parents.

Three years ago I met eight-year-old Jack in the context of a court-ordered evaluation in which his parents, both in their early forties and both very successful lawyers, were struggling over who should have the major portion of his care after their impending residential separation. Both left for work at 7 a.m. in the morning and were rarely home before 7 p.m. from Monday through Friday. The reality was that from 7 a.m. in the morning Jack was in the care of a childminder, who got him up for school some time after his parents had left for work, brought him to school at 9 a.m., collected him from school at 2.15 p.m. before transporting him to, from and between a very large number of interesting afternoon activities. A second childminder took over at 5.45 to give Jack his tea at home before his mother and father came home, independently of each other, between 7 p.m. and 8 p.m. Each parent argued for being the one to have Jack most of the time in post-separation care because each believed him- or herself to be more tuned in to their son's needs than the other parent. Part of the 'evidence' they presented to support their 'case' was the number of after-school and weekend activities that each had organised for Jack.

When I met with Jack alone, we went over the different activities he was involved in on a weekly basis outside of school. We counted twelve activities. He was doing swimming lessons, tennis lessons, an art class, piano lessons, children's chess, soccer, Irish football, Irish dancing, Tae Kwando, athletics, rugby, and Speech and Drama. When we had counted them out and he had helped me understand his weekly schedule around all of the activities and who brought him to and from each one of them, I commented to Jack 'Isn't that wonderful that your parents have organised so many different exciting things for you to do after school and at the weekend? How do you feel about all this?' Jack looked a little strangely at me before sinking down in the chair opposite me and replying: 'Jim, I am knackered!'. He went on to tell me about how really tired he was and that the only time he had 'off' during the week was Sunday afternoons. I wondered what he did then, and he told me: 'I lie on the bed with Mum. She is tired too.' I did an initial evaluation with Jack about the activities he would like to drop, and he felt that he would like to drop chess and Irish dancing. However, he did not want to hurt either his mum or dad in suggesting this because his granddad on his father's side of the family had been an Irish international chess player, and he knew his mother wanted him to do Irish dancing. When I inquired why he thought this was important to his mother, he told me: 'Mum thinks boys shouldn't just do things like soccer and rugby and sporty things.' Our further evaluation found Jack identifying four activities he wanted to stop and two additional 'activities' he would like to start. These additions were 'messing around a bit in the garden on my own' and 'sitting on the couch and reading a book'. The parents, despite their extremely adversarial approach to the conflict over their son, were able to hear his 'voice' on these matters and were able to engage with me in a parallel evaluation of the work/life balance within their own scheduled lives.

The busyness of postmodern lives to a large degree predetermines the ground on which some post-separation conflict naturally emerges today. The name of this ground is *scheduling*. Some of the scheduling challenges I have observed with postmodern separating families are closer in complexity to the challenges associated with scheduling in the London Underground Transport System than their family members realise. It probably speaks volumes about the developing skills of these same members and their paid helpers that there are not more 'accidents' as they go about their routines. In post-separation family life, a variety of variables are likely to lead to conflict around scheduling. These include varying work schedules where employees can be required to travel for different periods of time during the week as part of their contracts, work schedules that comprise three full days on followed by three full days off and bear no relation to the ebb and flow of children's lives, intermittent ongoing education and training with respect to adults/ core work-related skills, the demand from children themselves for involvement in a range of extracurricular activities, regular responsibilities for aging or ill grandparents, as well as coordinating an already overly busy family schedule with the schedule of another household to which one of the adults may now belong. Requests and demands for 'flexibility' from each other within these contexts naturally give rise to an increased sense of vigilance with respect to fairness and equity. These 'flexibility' requirements often lead to the need for the generation of an additional clause called 'Rules Governing Flexibility Requests' within post-separation parenting plans. In assisting parents with the negotiation of these plans and their attendant 'rules', the mental health professional must be able to coordinate a discussion between the parents concerning their views about who should be responsible for what within complex interlinked daily and weekly schedules. Hence, if *scheduling* is the ground of many post-separation parenting conflicts, focussed conversation about *responsibility* can be a vital element on the path towards conflict resolution.

Sex and the Cyberworld in Post-separation Family Conflict

Earlier in this chapter, we noted how the kind of communications technology (mobile telephone, computer) we now have available to us has changed the relationship between communication and relationship, with a world of connections achieved through a mode of virtual proximity beginning to displace the world of relationship based in real face-to-face communication. This displacement has reached the point which allows Bauman (2003, p. 63) to suggest that 'All proximity is now bound to measure its merits and shortcomings by the standards of virtual proximity'. Sex is one arena where virtual proximity appears to be having a profound impact on family and couple life. The Internet has increased the level of availability of different kinds of sexual opportunities to anyone who has the technological skills to gain access. Couples therapists in some parts of the Western world (Goldberg, Peterson, Rosen and Sara, 2008) report significant increases in couples seeking assistance because one or both members of the couple are shunning 'real-world' sex opportunities with each other in favour of 'webcam' sexual experiences with an unknown other or others. In the mid-1970s, Shorter (1975) noticed that as the postmodern family was beginning to come into view, the inherent instability of the couple could be traced to the replacing of property first with sentiment and later with sex as the bond between man and wife. It is quite possible that 40 years later we are beginning to witness, by means of a weakened norm relating to couple sexual fidelity and a much easier Internet-linked availability of extra-couple sexual opportunities, a dislodging of sex as the bond uniting the couple.

Contemporary couple and family therapists will have seen an increasing number of couples over the last decade whose relationship has come into crisis as a result of one or the other member of the couple being caught availing of the sexual opportunities flowing from access to the Internet. Although cyber-infidelity (Maheu and Subotnik, 2001; Subotnik, 2007) shares some of the same features as the 'real-life' affair it also carries many differentiating characteristics, such as the possibility of meeting a large number of other individuals over a short space of time as well as a reduced chance of discovery. Following cyber-infidelity, some couples, often with great difficulty, manage to repair their relationship and move forward again with a clarified set of norms and commitments. Others do not manage such repair or don't want repair. Depending upon the kind of sexual transgressions, these issues can have a profound consequence for rebuilding the level of trust necessary for negotiating satisfactory post-separation parent–child/adolescent relationships and contact arrangements. In particular, a parent who feels profoundly wronged and hurt may seek an alliance with a child or adolescent 'against' the unfaithful parent. Such cross-generational coalitions can sometimes have a long-lasting destructive impact upon a previously good parent–child/adolescent relationship (Brown, 1991b; Lusterman, 2005).

Pam, a 43-year-old mother of three boys aged eight, six and four years had been suspicious about the level of her husband's online activity in his study and managed to get access to his computer password, which he had told her was confidential to his work setting. Her 42-year-old husband, Peter, had not wanted any sexual activity with her for the previous two years. Her own investiga- tive efforts uncovered a private sexual life that he had been engaged in, he told her later, for the previous four years. The couple parted at her request and came some time later to see me to attempt to mediate a solution to their conflict over Peter's post-separation contact with the boys. For the first 18 months of the separation, Pam would not agree to the boys having any overnight or holiday contact with Peter because she did not trust in his capacity to refrain from Internet-related sexual activity while the boys were in his care. Her trust in him was so damaged that it was a full year post-separation before she allowed Peter to bring the boys to his apartment for their tea. The paternal child contact had been confined up to that time to two three-hour periods of time each week in his father's house in conjunction with meals at McDonald's.

In a world of rapidly changing attitudes towards sex and sexual expres- sion of different kinds, most mental health professionals will find within themselves and their clients a wide spectrum of opinions and beliefs about what constitutes acceptable forms of engagement in this area. Many adults experience profound shock and trauma when they discover the covert sexual practices of their partners, and it is not uncommon for such 'rev- elations' to be the immediate precursor to decisions to separate. However, the hidden aspect of these eventually discovered sexual practices can have major consequences for trust levels between parents in the post-separation context. Although the 'betrayed' parent may in time take the view that her ex-partner is entitled to engage in whatever adult sexual practices he wants to within the confines of the law, she may find it hard to trust his assurances that their children will not be exposed to these practices in any way while on contact. Sudden separations based upon traumatic discoveries relating to sexual themes such as an affair or sexual practices foreign to the couple's own sexual life tend not to augur well for the minimal levels of trust required to negotiate within mediation a satisfactory post-separation parenting plan. Mediators and other mental health professionals assisting the family in these contexts need to give consideration to the possibility of a therapeutic referral for the traumatised partner.

The Daytime Care of Children

A hallmark of the contemporary, postmodern, 'saturated' family is it's high dependency on a range of non-familial childminders and care profession- als at different points throughout the day. The continuing presence of both parents in the workplace following the arrival of dependent children is, more often than not, a necessity rather than a choice for most parents. In the transition to a post-separation family configuration, choice in this matter seems to have evaporated for all but a small number of families. It is no easy task for separating parents to achieve a financial survival that incorporates the capacity to pay for the additional accommodation that separation requires as well as securing the best possible additional care for their children at an affordable price.

The nature of this additional daytime care for children encompasses a very broad range of possibilities fulfilling a very broad range of functions. At one end of the spectrum are those arrangements whereby parents ask a sibling, friend or neighbour to mind children for them for a couple of hours a few times per week in return for a similar favour being returned in respect of that person's children at different periods of the week. No money changes hands in these situations, but children must adapt to having a parent other than their own involved in their care for predictable periods during the week, while also learning to be in the company of that parent's children for the same time periods. At the other end of the spectrum are those children, a little like Jack in the earlier vignette, who have a group of paid childminders to care for their needs during the day from the time they get up in the morning until one of their parents returns from work in the evening to resume their care. In these situations, children may just have one professional 'nanny' who will give them their breakfast, bring them to school or crèche, pick them up from school or crèche, feed them and care for them until their parent arrives back from work. Or children may have a number of carers during the day who take up their care for different parts of the day – for example from waking time to school commencement; from school pick-up to 5 p.m., when some carers must pick up their own children; and from 5 p.m. to parental return time. In this writer's jurisdiction, increasingly schools extend the range of services they offer to include a before-school care service, which can commence up to an hour before the school day formally commences; and an after-school care/activities service, which can continue until after 6 p.m. in the evening. Such schools seem to be making a very creative response to the dilemmas many parents face in coordinating their own complex work schedules with the care needs of their school age children. By offering a sequenced series of daily care/activity opportunities (breakfast clubs, arts and crafts classes, homework clubs and sports activities) under one roof throughout the day, these schools do away with the need for parents to piece together their own jigsaw of care for their children whose formal schooling is often finished by the midpoint of the working day. They also do away with the need for children to be transported between one care/activity venue and another throughout the afternoon and early evening. This spectrum of additional childcare also includes live-in and live-out nannies and au pairs, grandparents as paid or unpaid childcare assistants, as well as crèches, pre-school centres and independent after-school care services.

Separation can often seem like the event which will surely burst the bubble in families whose work/education/leisure/care schedules are already bursting at the seams. When the mental health professional is invited in to assist in managing conflict around the separation passage, it is an opportunity for parents to review the total schedule they have been living and to assess with the professional the demands and stresses this schedule places upon each member of the family as well as upon their paid assistants. The mental health professional also needs to consider with the separating parents whether the voices of one or more of their professional care assistants need to be heard, and under what conditions, within the family mediation process or within the child residence and contact evaluation, if the level of their post-separation conflict requires such court-related intervention.

Skills and Interventions

Throughout this book, many different skills and interventions are named that mental health and social care professionals will require among their repertoire as they attempt to assist families and their members in the context of post-separation conflict. Some of these skills are broad in nature, and others are quite focussed and specific. In this section, the skills and interventions named and described are those linked with the central themes of this chapter, which has concerned itself with the way in which changing definitions of the family, changes in our communications technologies, as well as changes associated with the way large numbers of people live their postmodern, 'saturated' family lives, have altered both the grounds of post-separation family conflict and the processes through which this conflict is performed. The following are five skills/interventions relevant to the changing shape of post-separation family conflict:

(i) *Promoting family members' evaluation of their relationship to communications technologies and the social media.* This skill is about promoting awareness in family members about the relationship that has evolved among them and the different communications technologies they use in their daily lives – for example mobile telephones, computers, iPads and social media. The skill usually has three associated elements: firstly, the encouragement of individuals to make either a written record or a mental note of the purpose and frequency of different kinds of usage; secondly, to assist them to reflect on how well their pattern of usage is serving their individual and relational purposes; and thirdly, to assist them in noticing the choices they have with respect to their usage and to make new choices when they consider it is in their interests to do so.

(ii) *Promoting family member's evaluation of their relationship to the amount of activities they undertake.* Like the previous skill, this skill is about encouraging awareness in individuals of the level of activity they undertake, reflection on how well their activities pattern serves themselves and their relationships, and identification of new choices that might be open to them in this regard.

(iii) *The capacity to appreciate the complexity and variety of parenting schedules in the post-separation family context.* In order to be a useful conversational partner for parents engaged in post-separation conflict, the mental health practitioner needs to acquire an appreciation of the different kinds of complexity attaching to different kinds of parenting schedules. This skill also involves a capacity to perceive levels of elasticity attaching to these complexities that parents themselves may not perceive. In other words, we need to be able to help parents see that they may have more choices open to them than they realise in the context of conflict management conversations.

(iv) *The capacity to assist parents in conflict to have a grounded conversation about the way their relationship with the adult world of cybersex interfaces with the world of their parenting in the post-separation context.* Establishing a manageable family existence following the emergence from a painful, and often very unsatisfying, couple experience can be a big challenge for many parents. It is not uncommon for a certain kind of blurred vision to occur in parents who feel a strong sense of entitlement around the meeting of their own sexual needs in the context of trying to evolve new patterns of parenting in unfamiliar living spaces. The mental health practitioner must always foreground the protection and welfare needs of children in these conversations with parents and help them to develop agreed rules concerning the degree of separation required between the adult world of cybersex and the world of their children's experiences and care.

(v) *Helping parents evaluate the jigsaw of care that is in place for their children in the context of their post-separation world.* This skill is not simply about helping parents assess the childcare plan they have in place from the perspective of its pragmatic fit with their own schedules. Nor is it just about helping them to assess the quality of the personnel and services they have engaged to assist them with the care of their children throughout the day. It is also about trying to help them step into the shoes of each of their dependent children and imagine how they are experiencing the jigsaw of care that surrounds them every day. It often means encouraging parents to have a different kind of conversation with each of their children in which they listen to their children's experience with a little more depth.

Personal and Reflective Exercises

The following questions and exercises relate to some of the themes in this chapter. They are an opportunity for you, the reader, to reflect on both your personal experiences in certain areas as well upon your values, positions and preferences in relation to some of the themes mentioned. Write some notes or paragraphs in response to each of the questions. If you are doing this exercise as part of a group, share as much or as little as you like of what you have written with other members in the group.

1. Make an evaluation of your own relationship to contemporary communication technologies and social media. Include in this evaluation some estimates of how much time you spend every day or week on these technologies, the context in which you spend this time and the purposes for which you use the technologies. When you have completed this brief evaluation, ask yourself if there are any changes you would like to consider making to your relationship with these technologies and media.
2. Write a note about the different activities you undertake outside of your work on a daily/weekly basis. Consider the range of different activities you undertake and the frequency with which you engage in them. When you have completed this 'inventory', ask yourself if there are any changes you might like to make to your daily/weekly activity pattern.
3. Write a note about what you know about the different ways that adults use the Internet to gain access to sexual opportunities of different kinds. Make a note about the different feelings and attitudes you may have about these different opportunities. Make a note about your own experiences, if any, of using the Internet to gain access to sexual opportunities.
4. Try to name as many different family forms as you are aware of. How many of these family forms have you come across in your own personal life through friends, relatives and neighbours, and how many other forms have you come across in the context of your work? How many different family forms have you been a participant in during your own

life so far? Make a note about any feelings or reactions you notice in yourself as you name these different forms.

5. What was your experience of being cared for as a child outside of your school-going hours? What choices did you make, or feel compelled to make, about the care of your own children during their dependant years? Write a note about any strong feelings you may have when you consider the range of care arrangements for children that you may be aware of through your own personal or work-related experience.

6. How do think any of your experiences recorded in your answers to the questions/exercises above might impact upon your work with families in the post-separation/divorce context?

THE SEPARATING FAMILY AND ITS CONFLICT MANAGEMENT

Throughout this book, the reader will meet a central idea about the phenomenon of separation itself. This idea concerns the character of separation as *a process that occurs over time*. When we look at that process from outside, and retrospectively, we can often see the gradual loosening of the bonds that hold the couple together. This loosening may or may not be accompanied by a certain amount of dialogue (which can include therapy) between the couple members about their changing situation and the possibility of either relational amelioration or separation. We then see the announcement of a decision by one person (although it may in time become a mutual decision) that he intends to leave the relationship. This 'declaration' usually marks the first transitions in the behavioural patterns of the couple members in relation to each other, at the same time that it ushers in a further period of dialogue and/or negotiation (which can include mediation) about how they are going to manage this new context. As the separation idea gains some level of acceptance, the couple or one of their members makes a decision about the manner in which their shared residence should come to an end. In whatever way that co-residence comes to an end, a new beginning to their separated lives occurs at that moment. Parents and children begin to re-form and perform their relationships in a physical space whose boundaries have dramatically altered and in an emotional space marked by an experience of absence and loss at the very least.

The reader will be aware that the description of the process in the last paragraph, notwithstanding its attempt to point to certain sequences within the separation pathway, reads like a set of unfolding steps and decisions that are governed ultimately by rationality and reflection and where reason trumps emotion as the basis for decisions along the pathway. Although such a description may have much validity for as many as a third of separating couples, it does scant justice to the large majority of separating adults, for whom separation can be experienced as profoundly distressing, an unwanted trauma and/or a kind of catastrophe. For many in this larger group, the steps are accompanied by a high degree of emotional expression, the intensity of which may never have been witnessed in any earlier period of the relationship. For many, the whole unfolding process is experienced as an injury to, or a wounding of, their deepest adult attachment (Crittenden, 2008; Howe, 2011) and can evoke feelings of rage and anger as their sense of abandonment grows. Once the separation process is underway, the emotional field of the family begins to be transformed as both adults, and often their children as well, enter a time of great uncertainty. Hence, if invited in to assist at this point, the mental health or social care professional needs to be aware that she is stepping in to an emotional arena marked by crisis and an anticipation of impending rupture, and where the key adults, the separating couple members, begin to look to others and themselves like caricatures of the persons they once were.

This chapter focuses on three key areas relevant to the early phases of the separation process. It first gives some consideration to the *context of the separation decision*. By the context of the decision, I am referring to 'who' appears to be making the decision, 'when' the decision is made, and 'how' the decision comes about. The second area of concern is *the management of the in-house separation process* as the couple members alter family interaction patterns in the time period prior to residential separation. The third area to which the chapter attends is *the management of family conflict in the time period immediately following residential separation*.

The Context of the Separation Decision

The impact of the separation decision on the family's relational environment varies enormously depending upon whether the process of decision-making has involved both members of the couple (even when one person wants the separation and the other doesn't) or has been the result of a private, inner reflection on the part of one person whose fruits are simply announced to the partner as a fait accompli. Consider the position of a couple who have spent a period of time in therapy together because of one person's uncertainty, for whatever mixture of reasons, about his desire to continue in the relationship. Let us imagine that this time period in therapy was long enough to allow for careful joint review of each person's perspective on the problematic issues in the relationship and for efforts directed towards amelioration. Let us further imagine that the 'uncertain' person gradually gains 'certainty' about his desire to separate and asks his partner to consider coming to family mediation when she is ready. Although the partner may be extremely hurt and deeply saddened by the unfolding decision-making in the other person, the process she has been through will probably have enabled her to absorb to a certain extent the idea of separation as one possible outcome of their dialogue. Although she may subsequently be in dispute with her partner about several matters relating to the management of post-separation family life, her very involvement in a therapeutic process as well as the transparency with which her partner dealt with his doubts, unhappiness and desires will usually position her differently with respect to a mediation dialogue than if such transparency and therapeutic process had not taken place.

Contrast the above picture with that of a woman who arrives home from work to her partner one day who announces, without warning, that he has been involved with a colleague at work for the last three years, that he loves this person and wants to go to live with her as soon as arrangements about the children, money and their accommodation/housing have been worked out. His partner will be shocked, possibly traumatised, and will, in all probability, feel significantly betrayed. This kind of emotional positioning leaves her with neither the capacity nor the desire to respond to the request to work out matters relating to the children, finance and residence in the context of mediation.

In considering interventions at this early juncture in the separation process, the mental health professional needs to be familiarised with each of the adult participant's perspectives on the *processes* that have led up to the decision as well as with any particular *events* or incidents that have occurred as antecedents to a separation decision. Five different, but typical, contexts of the separation decision are described here, and in each case the likely processes and events underpinning the context will be noted as deserving of the intervening professional's attention. These five typical contexts can be named as follows: deciding to separate following a 'falling out of love'; deciding to separate because of domestic violence and abuse; deciding to separate following an affair disclosure or discovery; deciding to separate because of the ongoing addiction of a partner; and deciding to separate following significant changes to the financial balance in the relationship.

One of the more common contexts of the separation decision in our Western contemporary societies is when one member of a couple reports experiencing a lack of, or disappearance of, feelings of love within himself for his partner. Those words so familiar to the couples therapist – 'I still love you as a person, but I am no longer in love with you' – can be experienced as the event which heralds an oncoming decision to separate. The process leading up to the 'event' is often a gradual disengagement over time by one of the partners from a variety of previously shared couple and parental activities. The range of scenes from which disengagement may occur can include the sexual relationship, family meals, socialising with friends and extended family as well parent–teacher meetings. Although the partner may be deeply distressed by both the declaration concerning a lack of love as well as the decision to separate, she may not be hugely shocked by the unfolding events, having already noticed and experienced many different types of disengagement by her partner. However, where the emotional and practical investment in family life is extremely high in one partner, this can lead to a massive denial of the significance of the other person's disengagements, and the decision to separate can be received as a total shock. One of the factors the intervening professional must consider in this context is the psychological state of the adults as the crisis unfolds. Although the person who has 'fallen out of love' may be feeling some relief because he is finally naming and addressing his experiences, his partner's shock may quickly deteriorate into depression (Cano and O'Leary, 2000) and suicidality. Hence, an assessment of psychological and emotional risk, with the possibility of referral to the local mental health team, should always be part of professional considerations during the early phase of such separation contexts.

A second important context of the separation decision is where there has been a history of domestic abuse or intimate partner violence. Within this context, the decision to separate is often taken with the advice and assistance of domestic violence services and/or friends and family members, and the process leading up to the victim's departure from the home often contains a series of threats to leave by the victim. Such threats are often not carried through for some time because of fears concerning the consequences. The consequences may be perceived as the likelihood of physical abuse by the perpetrator, or financial destitution leading to an inability to support children or themselves. Because the theme of domestic violence in the context of post-separation family conflict receives further attention in a later chapter of this book, the general complexities concerning post-separation professional intervention in these situations are not addressed at this point. Suffice to say that such contexts are filled with risks of different kinds for both adults and children. These risks can include not only risks to the physical integrity of adults and children but to their actual lives as well. One of the most important skills required by the intervening mental health professional in these separation contexts is the capacity to liaise effectively with a range of other professionals and services (police, mental health, child protection, domestic violence services, refuge accommodation, etc.) in the interests of a safe passage for parents and children into the space and time of a separated family life.

A third context of the separation decision concerns the affair disclosure or discovery (Sori, 2007). Depending upon the degree of prior trust between the couple members, the emergence of information regarding an affair of one of the couple members may constitute a profound shock for both individuals (where the level of mutual trust was previously regarded as high by both) or be experienced by others (where there is a poor level of mutual trust impacting several areas of couple life) as simply 'the straw that broke the camel's back'. In the former instance, it matters a lot whether the affair is disclosed or discovered. Although there is normally a massive breakdown in trust in both situations, the breakdown is normally more significant in the context of affair discovery. The research on couple infidelity (Peluso, 2007) tells us little about the extent to which either affair discovery or disclosure leads to decisions to separate immediately after the event (disclosure or discovery) or at some distance after the event. Brown (1991a), however, in her typology of affairs, refers to one of five different kinds of affair as an *exit* affair. The exit affair occurs when one of the partners who has a difficulty with endings uses the affair as a way of bringing the relationship or marriage to an end.

Whatever the relational background to an affair might be, the discovery or disclosure of infidelity inevitably brings to many couples' lives either a decision to separate or the possibility of such decision. Sometimes a decision to separate appears to be made relatively quickly following disclosure, only to be reversed after some time and following consideration of the consequences of such a decision for all involved. Even when a decision to separate is made very quickly following disclosure, and time proves that this decision is not reversed, there is a lot of couple and family life to be lived or endured between the time of decision and actual residential separation. And there is a great deal at stake for all family members in the way this time period is managed. It is not unusual for couples to present for family mediation very shortly after affair disclosure, and the mental health professional acting in the role of mediator needs to be aware of, and sensitive to, certain matters. Summarising the broad range of negative emotional and behavioural effects of affair revelation on couple life, Snyder et al. (2007, p. 102) remind us that research includes in these effects such phenomena as 'partner violence, depression, suicidal ideation, acute anxiety, and symptoms similar to post-traumatic stress disorder'. The mediator needs to be aware that just because the couple have managed to get themselves into a context of dialogue does not mean that they are protected from any or all of the above effects.

The wounded partners in these situations often describe moving in and out of extreme feelings of rage, experiencing overwhelming powerlessness as well as a sense of victimisation and abandonment (Atkins et al., 2001; Brown, 1991a; Cano and O'Leary, 2000; Lusterman, 1998; Spring, 1996). The mental health professional/mediator has to be alert to the importance of securing the necessary mental health and therapeutic supports for both individuals, particularly in contexts where the wounded person is demanding the immediate departure of the offending individual from the shared residence in situations where the latter either has nowhere to go or does not wish to leave the residence.

A fourth context of a separation decision relates to the presence of an addiction in one member of the couple. In these contexts, the relational processes leading up to the decision may vary depending upon the nature of the addiction and the manner in which it is performed by the person with the addiction. The relational history may have included a great deal of patience on the part of the non-addicted partner, as well as approaches to recovery followed by setbacks on the part of the addicted person. Decisions to separate are often taken with the greatest reluctance and only after the addiction has done a great deal of damage to the partners as individuals, and to their relationship, their children and parent–child relationships. The triggering event for the decision may simply be one more substance-related, time-limited disappearance from family and couple life or one further unapproved removal of finance from family funds for the purposes of gambling where that is the particular addiction involved. In the above type of contexts, the decision happens at the end of a road where the couple relationship has survived on the back of their shared hope in recovery. The decision to separate marks the disappearance of this hope in one of the partners. Intervening mental health and social care professionals need to be aware of the length of time over which the addiction struggle has occurred, as well as the amount of hope and emotional investment the partners had maintained in the relationship prior to the separation decision. Where there are children involved, the professional must consider the degree to which they have been exposed to the addiction behaviours and their consequences, and whether the children require any additional therapeutic support in their own right. The above process descriptions refer to what might be considered the milder end of the addiction range, where addiction is the key aspect defining the context of the separation decision. Addiction can be, and often is, an integral part of a domestic violence context and can pose unique challenges for mental health and social care professionals trying to secure the physical safety and integrity of abused adults and their children as they leave the family's residence. The concluding chapter in this text places some emphasis on the way a three-cornered relationship between addiction, mental health concerns and domestic abuse provides the ground for a whole group of post-separation family conflicts.

A final context of the decision to separate, worthy of mention at this point, concerns the impact of a significant financial change on the experience of couple life. An unexpected legacy, a job change or a job promotion that dramatically improves the earnings and/or income of one of the partners relative to the other may sufficiently unbalance the power dimensions of the relationship such that one or the other member of the couple may feel disinclined to continue in the relationship. The imbalance in financial power in a relationship may also come about through the unexpected loss of employment and income for one partner either through redundancy or illness. The decision to separate may centrally belong to an individual who cannot tolerate the idea of being more materially dependant on his partner in the future than he had ever envisaged, or it may belong to the now 'wealthier' person who experiences the new level of inequity in financial contributions to the relationship as too challenging of his assumptions about how a personal relationship should operate. The mental health professional assisting such groups, following a decision to separate, needs to be aware of the range of feelings that can dominate their conflict as they try to put a new shape on their family and parental life. A mixture of jealousy, resentment and a sense of abandonment can be the emotional underlay of both pre- and post-separation dialogues oriented towards conflict management.

Managing Conflict in the In-house Phase of the Separation Process

The in-house phase of the separation process carries many challenges for parents and children while also being a time that carries opportunities for learning conflict management skills that can have positive implications for all family members as they make their way into later phases of the process. Most of the challenges arise from the fact that the couple have entered a new phase of detachment from each other while many familial and parent–child patterns remain unaltered. Although residential departure of one of the partners may be relatively immediate, depending upon the context of the separation decision as well as upon the availability of other residential opportunities, it is not uncommon for many separating couples that this phase might last anywhere from one month to four or five years. Many adults look back on this phase of their separation process as the worst period of all and recount something of the enormous strain they felt as they tried to keep some semblance of normality in the household for their children's sake as they attempt to negotiate the future with their now estranged partner. As they live on the edge of their wounded wits, they must manage potential or actual conflict about the use of household space, responsibility for their dependent children, and the use of their financial resources, as well as the degree to which the outside world should be informed about their unfolding separation. These are massive challenges that arrive at a time when the family's emotional field has been dramatically altered. Before considering the task facing the mental health professional who has been engaged to assist the family with this phase, it is necessary to understand just what is at stake for family members during the management of this time period.

A start should be made at the darkest end of the challenges facing the partners in their new context. The practitioner must be aware that, even for couples who have had a violence-free history up to that point, the strain of sharing household space with an estranged partner in the context of the upheaval of emotions that has already been described can lead to the emergence of physical aggression in the relationship for the very first time. The aggression can emerge over what would have previously been experienced as tolerable infringements deserving nothing more than mutual rebuke.

James and Deirdre had been together ten years and had two children, aged seven years and five years, before Deirdre discovered for the second time in their history that James was having an affair. She made a fairly immediate decision that she wanted their relationship to end. Two weeks after they had commenced their initial appointment for mediation, there was an incident in the morning at the bathroom door. Deirdre was in the bathroom, washing her teeth in advance of going to work, when James entered the bathroom to get his razor and shaving cream—a conjunction of events that would have happened many times in the course of their relationship. On this occasion, Deirdre screamed at James to get out of the bathroom as she was using it. He ignored her scream and went to get his razor. Before he was successful in getting his razor, she physically blocked his way, and there was a pushing and shoving incident between them before he withdrew. Although there was no physical injury incurred by either James or Deirdre, they were both devastated by this occurrence when they arrived for their second appointment, which they had brought forward to an earlier date than originally planned.

The strongest expressions of anger the above couple had previously experienced in their relationship were considerably raised voices over some disputed matters which were always curtailed, they agreed, within a 15-second period because of the children being within earshot. Although each member of this particular couple, following a short period of mutual blaming for the occurrence of the incident, managed to accept some responsibility for the event, such is not always the outcome of such incidents. Sometimes one parent will take emergency applications in the courts to try to obtain an order for the exclusion of the other parent from the residence because of domestic violence. Where such orders for exclusion are obtained in contexts where the aggression has been mutual rather than one-sided, the dispute over who should leave the residence is resolved in the short term. However, when this type of resolution is experienced as unfair by one party, as it often is, it can sow seeds of bitterness and resentment which can impact negotiations between the ex-partners for years to come. Hence, great care needs to be taken in all negotiations about family space.

The above example brings to light two of the intervention skills needed by mental health professionals as they assist with the mediation task in the early phase of the separation process. The first skill is that of providing support and emotional containment to the adults as they commence the task of restructuring their family interactions and responsibilities in the light of the decision made. The second task is educational and preventive. It involves alerting the couple members to the possible unanticipated effects of the emotional storm they find themselves in. Practitioners need to remind themselves that, although they may have assisted many sets of estranged partners through such troubled periods, this territory, in all probability, will be completely new for the couple in question. Calling their attention to the possibility of unforeseen aggression in either of them towards his or her partner or themselves in the context of newly experienced emotional depths can, at best, have an inhibiting effect on the expression of aggressive feelings, and at the very least make it more likely that the couple will seek the assistance of the mental health professional should such events occur in their midst.

If the risk of domestic violence is one of the challenges dominating this period, so also is the risk of a larger family 'split' on the back of the couple split. The loss of a partner can lead to such intense feelings of anxiety and abandonment in some adults that they draw very close to some or all of their children for comfort in the face of this anxiety. This can mean drawing some children into an alliance with one parent against the other parent. Systemic theory (Haley, 1976) refers to this type of alliance of a parent with a child *against* the other parent as *a cross-generational coalition*. The operation of such a coalition often involves speaking inappropriately and negatively to a child or children about the other parent. Such 'badmouthing' sometimes succeeds well in commencing an alienation (Gardner, 1985; Kelly and Johnston, 2001) process of a child or children from the other parent. Chapter 7 of this text deals more extensively with this phenomenon of parental alienation. Sometimes, however, a parent simply intensifies a bond with a child that was already strong in advance of the crisis and starts to build up a mutual dependence between himself and the child such that the young person becomes gradually disaffected from the other parent and from other siblings with whom a close bond was formerly enjoyed. Research (Bank and Khan, 1982; Cicirelli, 1995; Coles, 2006) has shown us how important positive sibling bonds are for individuals as they make their way through the life cycle. In particular, they appear to offer some protection and promote resilience with respect to mental health vulnerabilities in adulthood. Hence, mental health practitioners have to be alert to the importance of doing all they can to protect such bonds for young people when they come under threat from a particular kind of splitting process that can occur when adults feel extreme levels of threat, anxiety and anger in the early phase of the in-house separation process. These family splits can also result from an intensification of pre-existing family alignments based upon gender with mother and female children on one side of a family divide, and father and male children on the other. When such splitting processes go unchallenged for any lengthy period of time, the new pattern can prove extremely resistant to intervention. Hence, practitioners have to be alert to the development of these splits during the in-house separation phase of the separation process and should initiate preventive therapeutic interventions as soon as possible.

An example of such preventive intervention relates to one of the earliest negotiations that partners make following the separation decision. This negotiation relates to the changing use of sleeping/bedroom spaces. In the immediate aftermath of the decision, it is not uncommon to find one partner sleeping with one of the children in that child's bedroom and another child sleeping with the other parent in what was the couple bed. Such movements are rarely the result of open parental 'negotiations' and, more usually, just 'happen' in an unconscious kind of way. That they just 'happen', of course, may reflect an unacknowledged pattern of strong alliances already operational within the family. The mediating mental health professional needs to keep a close eye on the interests of children from the earliest stages of mediation, even when parents are focussed on other matters about which they are in conflict.

Pauline and Tom came for mediation four months after Pauline decided to separate because of what she experienced as unrelenting disputes and arguments about the management of their two children, aged eight and six years. Since the first night she left the couple's bedroom, she had slept with their six-year old daughter in her daughter's bed and bedroom while their eight-year old son had joined his father in the couple's bed and bedroom. Further inquiry revealed that the boy, who had a close relationship with his mother up to the time of her decision to separate, was doing less and less with his mother during the week and weekends and had refused to eat with his sister and mother at any time. He would only eat with his father, when the latter returned from work at 7 p.m. The daughter, who was normally accompanied to her Saturday morning swimming lesson by father, had been having stomach aches on Saturday mornings and had signalled that she did not want to go swimming anymore. She no longer watched television on her father's knee, which she had done daily in the past, and now watched television with her mother in her own bedroom from about 6.30 p.m. each evening. Following some reflection with the mediator/mental health professional and some advice on what appeared to be evolving for the children with respect to their relationship with each of them, they agreed to handle the sleeping arrangements differently and put the children back sleeping alone in their own bedrooms as they had been before. Mother encouraged the girl to return to her swimming lesson with her father despite her stomach aches, and the father persuaded the boy that he wanted him to eat most of his meals with his sister and mother but could have breakfast with him during the week, as well as having some meals with him at the weekends. The parents decided to manage their challenges about space allocation by using their living room as an additional sleeping space, which they shared between them on a week-on, week-off basis, thus allowing each of them to have a fair share of the use of 'their' bedroom in the period leading up to residential separation.

In the above example, interventions in the early phase of an extended mediation process succeeded in offsetting what might have evolved into a full family split, where the future of both parent–child and sibling bonds may have been jeopardised. Negotiations over bedroom and sleeping space are usually only the first step in the process of boundary making, which prefigures processes that may emerge when the 'full' residential separation occurs. If the partners, or at least one of them, are unable to tolerate eating at the same table or sharing the living room, space negotiations will need to attend to how time in the living room will be shared, as well as to how and when the kitchen will be used by each of the partners. The allocation of space in the fridge and freezer may also need to be negotiated.

Meaningful and imaginative participation by the mediating mental health professional in dialogues about space allocation and space management depend upon his or her sound enough grasp of the nature and layout of the space in question. The offer to the partners of a professional home visit to get acquainted with the unique space that is being negotiated can be one way of ensuring that the parents know that the mediator really knows what is being spoken about. If such a visit is not feasible for whatever reason, asking the parents to draw a simple diagram of the space can be a useful option.

The negotiation of household space usage goes hand in hand with the need to agree a parental rota of responsibility for the general care of the children, their meals, and their leisure and friendship routines. In facing these dilemmas, the mental health professional is assisting the partners to learn how to negotiate the sharing of parental responsibilities and how to take into consideration, to some degree, the unique aspects of each other's life routines. Depending on the degree of threat that the impending separa-tion poses for the partners, these negotiations will be achieved with more or less difficulty.

A key area that needs to be worked out almost immediately for most sets of separating partners concerns the spending of personal and family income. This is a time period when the sense of threat can push individuals into hid-ing money, 'cleaning out' joint bank accounts or spending recklessly just to ensure that the other person does not gain access to the same funds before they do. It is critical that the mediator/mental health professional takes the initiative in raising this issue of regulating access to and use of family funds, as there is no issue more guaranteed to jeopardise the stabilising functions of a mediation process than a clear financial misdemeanour by one of the partners in a context where new rules have not yet been made. Whether the partners have a large surplus, a great shortage or an average amount of family funds, the importance of agreeing rules about spending is vital for the successful management of the in-house phase of their separation process. Because access to money can be so associated with a sense of basic survival, in a context of threat a breach of implicit trust in this area can be the catalyst for gaining revenge in other critical areas of the partners' lives.

Another facet of the in-house separation process that may need to be negotiated is the extent to which the outside world of family, friends and work colleagues should be told about the changing internal context of the partner's relationship with each other. Sometimes the partners will not want to impose any restrictions on each other with respect to who can be informed, but will struggle more over the kind of narrative that will accom-pany this news. Narratives have an explanatory aspect built in to their structure, through which individuals give an account to themselves and to others of the actions that are being taken by self and others (Polkinghorne, 1988). The partners cannot bring such momentous news to certain parts of their social world without offering some kind of explanatory narrative to accompany the telling. However, the telling of these stories begins a process of reshaping of the social world around each of the partners. Depending upon the kind of stories being told, these narratives may draw sympathy, support and concern around one of the partners, while the other partner may experience a degree of social withdrawal by friends and others who were previously close. It is unsurprising that separating partners often struggle with this matter more than any other as they anticipate the likely impact of certain ways of sharing the separation news on the social field around them. Mediation dialogues which address the 'public relations' aspect of the separation process need to encourage reflection within each of the partners about the impact upon themselves, others and their children of telling their preferred versions of the separation story. The support and emotional containment provided by the mental health professional within these dialogues has an important role to play in facilitating such reflection within the very troubled emotional field that the partners' relationship has become. The next chapter considers this matter in further detail when it is thought about as one of the 'symbolic' goods to be negotiated by the separating partners in the aftermath of the separation decision.

A further emotionally charged issue to be dealt with in the early phase of mediation dialogues concerns the timing and management of the partners' entry into new intimate relationships. Separating partners may vary considerably in their attitude to this matter. Some will easily make an agreement that new relationships will not be embarked upon until the residential separation has taken place, whereas others will not wish to impose any restrictions on themselves or their partners in this regard so long as the children are not made aware of such relationships until an agreed time later in the separation process. Some partners may even welcome the possibility as it can facilitate the absence of one or both of the partners from the accommodation a few nights per week, thus making the separate management of dependent children a more tolerable experience.

Although the negotiating partners may not want to draw up *written and signed agreements* relating to the in-house phase of their separation process, the mental health professional may need to point out to them the value of making provisional agreements relating only to the time that they remain sharing a residence together. Written, short-term agreements can provide a sense of security for participants in the short term. They can also give the participants an experience of making agreements that can be modified as circumstances evolve. Should the partners not wish to draw up a written record of what they have agreed, it is important for the mediator/mental health professional to keep her own careful record of agreements between the separating individuals.

The relative success of the conflict management dialogues relating to the in-house separation process paves the way for the continuing mediation dialogue to address the longer-term conflicts surrounding the shape the family's life will take once residential separation has occurred. The mental health professional needs to be aware that, although functioning agreements between the partners may reduce anxiety levels within all family members, the strain of sharing a residence with an estranged partner will continue to be felt as considerable by most individuals. This strain can have a distorting impact on negotiations about the longer-term arrangements, as the following example demonstrates.

Felicity and Michael were a full year into an in-house separation period following a decision by Felicity to leave the relationship caused by a gradual 'falling out of love' on her part. She worked part-time and looked after their three children (all under seven years) part-time. Michael had a very well paid job which required him to work until 8 p.m. three evenings per week. Felicity was finding the strain of continuing shared residence increasingly difficult to cope with. Michael had indicated that he was willing to consider leaving the home and getting his own separate and affordable accommodation so long as he got what he considered a fair amount of time with the children after he left. He wanted to be able to come to the house to see them every Wednesday evening, to have tea with them and put them to bed, and to have the three children with him in his own accommodation every weekend from Friday at 6 p.m. to Sunday at 6 p.m. Despite her clear reservations about the wisdom of this proposal, Felicity wanted to make this agreement with Michael as a way of bringing the strain of the in-house phase of their separation process to an end. The mediator brought to their attention that it appeared to him that it was their differential capacity to bear the strain associated with shared residence that was driving the kind of deal they seemed to be coming to, rather than the needs of their three young children. He involved them in a discussion about the likely impact on the two younger children of a two-day separation period at the weekend from their mother, whom both parents agreed was their primary attachment figure. He urged them to prolong this aspect of their negotiations a little longer in the interests of coming to an agreement that might have a better chance of working for everyone after the residential separation had occurred. Both parents were responsive to this plea from the mediator, and by the end of another mediation meeting had come to an agreement to divide the care of the children equally between them on each weekend, in addition to Michael coming in to the home on two evenings each week to have tea with the children and put them to bed. Michael made a relatively comfortable transition into his own accommodation a month after this agreement was made and made proposals to Felicity about the gradual easing in of the children to the overnight aspect of their agreed weekend contact with him.

During both the in-house phase and the phase subsequent to residential separation, the mental health professional must give some thought with the partners, who are becoming ex-partners, to the possibility of attendance at parent education programs relating to the separation process. Although research (Arbuthnot and Gordon, 1996; Bacon and McKenzie, 2004; Fackrell, Hawkins and Kay, 2011; Keating, Sharry, Murphy, Rooney and Carr, 2016;

Thoennes and Pearson, 1999) shows that parents benefit differentially from such programs, it is clear that some of the benefits accrue not simply from the reception of helpful knowledge content about the separation process but also from participation with a group of other parents who are going through similar experiences. Many parents will be anxious to get some assistance with how they might tell their children of different ages about the impending separation and to receive any other advice about what might help their children through the process. Some parents will be able to attend a parent education program during the in-house phase of their separation process, whereas others will be so troubled, anxious and overburdened that such attendance is more than they can manage at that moment in time. What the mental health professional needs to keep in mind is that what might be an unrealistic option at a moment in time for some parents may become an interesting and feasible option at a later date. Nor is the educational task the sole responsibility of parent education programs. It is a task that needs to be dispersed through the whole network of professionals who meet with the separating family and its members. This network includes not just the mental health and social care professionals who may carry most of the mediating functions with the separating partners but family doctors, health visitors, child protection social workers, judges, domestic violence workers and members of the police.

Managing Conflict Following Residential Separation

Conflict may be an enduring feature of family life for several years following residential separation; however, the remarks about conflict management made in this section of the chapter relate to the period of time which commences immediately following the leaving of the shared accommodation by one of the partners and concludes when a first level of equilibrium in the post-separation family relationships has been achieved. For some separating parents, it may be the first time that they engage the assistance of a mental health professional, and parents are regularly guided in that direction by lawyers as an alternative to using the legal framework as a dispute resolution process. The type of context governing the separation decision has much to do with the kind of conflicts that emerge at this stage. Where there has been little or no effective communication between the partners prior to the separation, the departure of one person from the home can come as a complete shock to the other person. A history of domestic violence can lead to one person's unannounced departure from the home, with the children, to a destination unknown to the other parent. Or a person who feels unable to articulate to his partner his decision to separate or to dialogue about his manner of departure may simply leave and inform his partner a day or more after the act. Such sudden, unannounced ruptures in the fabric of couple and family life can be traumatising for both the 'left' partner and the children. In both instances, and for different reasons, a mixture of panic and extreme anger can take hold in one of the partners when he is cut off from his children for a period of time and has no knowledge of their whereabouts. Likewise, young children can panic and grow very anxious and worried when they are separated without warning from a loved parent.

Whether the gap in parent–child contact has its roots in a history of domestic violence or in a lack of skills enabling participation in a dialogue about separation and its execution, the first task of the mental health professional must be to assess the manner in which these parent and child anxieties can be correctly and safely addressed. Where mental health professional intervention is performed at the request of the family court, such intervention, in contexts of alleged domestic violence, must make an initial determination regarding the needs of children for safe contact with the excluded parent, and it will probably be the task of the mental health professional to advise the court in the short term whether there should be contact, what the venue and time length for such contact should be and whether it should be supervised and by whom. Such initial determinations may lead to agreed frameworks for longer periods of assessment either within or outside of legal frameworks.

Where there are no background concerns relating to child protection, the mental health professional will need to facilitate the negotiation of renewed contact between parents and children. The first priority will be to secure a meeting of some kind between parents and children in advance of any dialogue about what a short-term framework for parent–child contact might be. Such meeting, following a period of uncertainty and anxiety, can calm the whole family system down considerably and pave the way for more manageable parental dialogue about the next steps in parent–child contact. An important element in the early part of this phase can be the type and quality of accommodation that the now non-resident partner/parent has secured. It is not uncommon, particularly where the residential departure has been swift and unplanned, for the nonresident parent to have to move accommodation several times during this phase until he finds a place to live that is both personally tolerable and affordable and meets his needs with respect to child contact. It is the role of the mental health professional in these contexts to continually moderate both the expectations of the non-resident parent and the anxieties of the resident parent around contact in a way that responds to the limitations and affordances of whatever accommodation the nonresident parent occupies at a moment in time.

In managing what are usually anger-filled conflicts about temporary parent–child ruptures and restorations, the mental health professional has to keep one guiding principle of intervention in mind. Part of the achievement of a 'successful separation' is the emergence or development in each of the partners of a capacity/skill to be able separate the conflicts they might have with each other within the couple domain from the exercise of their parental functions through which the needs of children can be realised. Practitioners in the area know that this is easier said than done and that the mental health professional role must incorporate an educative function in relation to this matter, as well a skill function wherein they are constantly trying to facilitate the emergence and enhancement of such capacity in each of the partners. It is the development of this skill, to whatever degree possible, that will safeguard children from being used as 'ammunition' or 'pawns' in the conflict manoeuvres made by their separating parents and guardians.

Whether the passage into this phase has been one of unanticipated rupture or a more planned transition, the goals of intervention during this period by the mental health or social care professional are clear. With respect to children, the goals must include the establishment of a safe, albeit provisional, contact routine with the nonresident parent; their return to school (or a school) where school-going has been interrupted; their reconnection at some level with their friendship network; and the consideration with parents of their need for either individual or sibling group therapeutic support. With respect to the adults/parents, the interventions must ensure that a level of financial support, however provisional, is paid where this is necessary, aim at the re-establishment of parent–child contact for the nonresident parent, and review the mental health needs of each of the partners individually, as well as considering with them their need for therapeutic support. In the course of achieving these goals, the mediating mental health professional may need to liaise with both the family court as well as the legal representatives of both parents. Many parents make their first entry to the legal system during this period to resolve some issues that they are unable to resolve through their own mediation-assisted dialogue. It is critical that the mental health professional accompany the ex-partners through this process to ensure that the necessarily adversarial aspect of legal proceedings does not swamp their capacity for assisted dialogue on other matters. During the exercise of these liaison skills, the practitioner's goal must be to protect and support this capacity for dialogue. It is this ongoing relational capacity that proves to be the main vehicle through which all future conflict resolution and management will be achieved.

Skills and Interventions

In the previous sections of this chapter, there has been an indication of the skills and interventions required by assisting mental health professionals in these early phases of the separation process. These skills will be named and listed again here in summary form in advance of an invitation to the reader to participate in the personal/reflective exercises relevant to the content of the chapter:

(i)   *Emotional containment.* The mental health and social care professional needs to have the capacity to offer empathic support to each of the separating adults in a manner that conveys her appreciation of the emotional terrain pertinent to the context of the separation decision.

(ii) *Fairness and balance in the co-ordination of mediation dialogues.* The professional needs to be experienced by the partners as fair and impartial in the management of conversations about disputed matters. This does not mean that the professional should restrain herself from making imaginative contributions to the dialogue that does justice to her experience, knowledge and expertise. It does mean, however, that she has an obligation to give due weight to each person's perspective on each matter under review.

(iii) *Mental health oversight.* The professional needs to be aware of the traumatic and disorienting consequences that a separation decision may have for some individuals and to be able to address with them, in an appropriate forum, their possible need for mental health review and/or counselling/therapeutic assistance.

(iv) *Recognising the differential strain accompanying the in-house separation.* The professional needs to be able to convey to the partners an appreciation of the strains accompanying the in-house period of their separation process and to acknowledge that these strains, for a variety of reasons, may be experienced as more burdensome for some adults than for others.

(v)   *Attention to safety.* Where necessary and relevant, the professional must convey to the separating partners that it is part of their role and function to attend to the physical, psychological, sexual and emotional safety of their dependent children within their problem-solving conversations and that they will also be concerned about their safety as adults.

(vi) *Educational interventions.* The professional needs to consider with the separating partners whether they and their children might benefit from the parents attending a parent education program which addresses matters relating to the separation process. The professional also needs to be able to impart to the partners/parents specific pieces of information relating to the likely impact of certain parental behaviours on each of their children given their age and developmental stage. The skill in delivery of such educational information is that it attends to the unique experiences of unique parents of unique children in unique situations.

(vii) *The identification and arrest of family-splitting processes.* The mental health and social care professional needs to be able to identify processes of family splitting that can occur early on in the separation process and to initiate interventions with both parents and children aimed at arresting these processes.

(viii) *Drawing up written agreements.* The mental health professional must be able to facilitate parents in the drawing up of written, signed agreements relating to the new provisional structures for living that they wish to put in place for a specific period of time. The professional needs to ensure that these written agreements have sufficient clarity to enable them to offer a degree of security to individuals in what is generally felt as a time period filled with uncertainty.

(ix) *Re-establishing parent–child contact following unplanned residential departure.* Prolonged and unwarranted absence of parent–child contact following a parental departure from the home that has not been negotiated can lead to a build-up of anger and resentment in the parent separated from his children. Such a build-up of emotion can fuel the extension of parental conflict into areas of family life previously protected from parental dispute. In these contexts, the mental health professional must work for the speedy, but safe, re-establishment of parent–child contact.

(x) *Keeping open possibilities for dialogue in the context of family court appearances.* The mental health professional must work to keep open the channels of communication and dialogue between parents even when they need the assistance of their legal representatives and the courts to resolve some critical disputes.

Personal and Reflective Exercise

Write some notes for yourself in response to the following four questions:

1. If you have ever experienced a separation process from a partner you were residing with for any length of time, try to describe what your experiences were in the time frame between the separation decision and

the residential separation and in the time period immediately follow-ing the residential separation. If you have never personally experienced such a separation, try to imagine what your priorities might be if you were to have such an experience in the future, and make some notes about these priorities.

2. Which particular contexts of a separation decision might most strongly challenge your capacity to remain balanced and neutral within the context of a mediation dialogue? Why?

3. Which aspects of children's safety needs during the separation process do you think you might be most attuned to? Why?

4. Which of your beliefs about post-separation parent–child contact do you think might be the biggest challenge to your neutrality in the context of mediation dialogues with separating parents negotiating this theme?

GOODS AND RELATIONSHIPS IN POST-SEPARATION/DIVORCE FAMILY CONFLICT

This chapter forms a bridge between the opening three chapters of the text and the remaining chapters of the book. At this point, we have examined the general territory of post-separation family conflict, the changing shape of such conflicts in our contemporary world as well as the role of the mental health professional in conflict management during the two early phases of the separation process. Following this chapter, the remaining chapters of the text examine the challenges for the mental health professional associated with specific issues arising in post-separation family conflict such as those associated with resolving disputes relating to child contact (whether through mediation or the family courts), addressing the phenomenon of parental alienation, and mental health professional involvement with families where post-separation parental communications are marked by a high degree of conflict over a long period of time. In this chapter, we take a step back to look at the broad 'spectrum' of what is involved in post-separation family conflict. We look at this spectrum from two specific vantage points. The first concerns the range of 'objects' or 'goods' that people struggle over as their couple relationship comes apart. By the term 'goods' I want to denote the range of different things that people consider desirable or valuable or that they want in the post-separation context. We are concerned with the way struggle over different kinds of 'objects' gives unique shape to couple negotiations through the different ways that couple members position themselves around these objects. The second vantage point concerns the kind of post-separation parenting relationships that underpin the negotiation processes that address the division of these 'goods'.

We draw, in particular, on two pieces of North American research (Ahrons, 2007; Hetherington and Kelly, 2002) as the background to a consideration of the different ways that parents appear to relate to each other following separation and divorce, and of some of the consequences for mental health professional interventions arising from such differences. Indeed, these differences become increasingly pertinent as our explorations in the chapters ahead reach the more challenging areas of mental health professional practice with families whose members perform their conflict with greater levels of frequency and intensity, which carry more serious consequences for all involved. The chapter concludes with a description of some of the practice skills required of the mental health professional arising from some of the key distinctions emerging in the chapter and a small number of reflective exercises aimed at deepening the reader's own relationship to the chapter's themes.

The 'Goods' at the Heart of Post-separation/Divorce Family Conflict and Negotiation

Despite the statistical prevalence of separation and divorce in most societies around the globe, ending a relationship with an intimate partner remains one of the most profoundly distressing experiences that can happen in an individual's life. Whether an adult feels she has, at some level, 'chosen' to separate or perceives the parting as an event thrust upon her by a decision of her partner, the experience as a whole involves the loss of what is, in all probability, her most significant adult attachment bond (Howe, 2011). For many individuals, the loss of such a bond ushers into their lives a mixture of different feelings such as anger, grief and sadness; a sense of isolation and abandonment; and a general feeling of threat to their sense of safety and well-being in the world. A central consequence of this threat to safety for many parents is an anxiety and fearfulness about how they will or will not cope with their life and responsibilities in the future. It is often the case that it is only within the experience of the loss of this attachment figure that individuals come to realise something of what participation in couple and family life provided for them. Enduring relationship, notwithstanding the unique challenges attaching to unique relational circumstances, provides individuals with a secure sense of identity and a confidence about where they primarily belong. At the levels of the relationship itself, the extended family, the wider local community and society, the culture provides myriad ways in which daily social interaction confirms a positive sense of personal identity for individuals based upon their participation in an enduring relationship. In a previous chapter, we noted how this sense of personal identity has a narrative underpinning (Ricoeur, 1991; Roberts, 1994; White and Epston, 1990). Our sense of personal identity emerges from the host of different stories told about us over time by ourselves and by others.

Personal Identity Transformation Following Separation and Divorce

When separation occurs, it brings with it a major rupture to the life and identities of the separating individuals. The ending of the relationship reveals how critical the presence of the relationship has been to a relatively stable sense of personal identity for both individuals. With this stability removed, individuals are challenged to fashion a new sense of personal identity over time. In the context of their changing relationship with self and others, they must forge a new narrative of who they might become in the future, a narrative that maintains a degree of continuity with the past but proposes a liveable life for the years ahead. Although many individuals may experience this challenge as exciting, others will find the challenge daunting and be gripped with a considerable degree of fear and anxiety about the future. The last chapter alluded to the significant mental health challenges that can arise in both the pre- and post-residential separation phases of the total separation process, but it can be noted here that the rupture to personal identities is a key element in the psychological health vulnerabilities that accompany the separation transition.

Why is it important to advert to this story of personal identity in advance of a consideration of the great range of 'goods' and matters that must be negotiated by family members in the context of separation? It is important because the mental health professional assisting the family and its members in the context of a formal mediation process, or in less formal professional settings, or in counselling and psychotherapy settings, needs to be aware that this great drama of personal identity transformation is the hidden backdrop to all the different kinds of negotiations that occur in the family post-separation. Indeed, personal identity transformation is much more than the 'backdrop' to all other negotiations but is, in fact, the first 'good' which is substantially impacted through the negotiation of all other 'goods'. Nor is this drama of personal identity transformation the domain of adults alone. Children and adolescents of separating parents also struggle to make a new story of their changing lives and to have some impact on the shape these stories might take. Although a father's struggle with his ex-partner to gain and maintain a certain level of contact to his children post-separation can reflect his anxiety about the kind of fatherhood he can continue to exercise in his post-separation world, his eight-year-old daughter's request of her parents that her school not yet be informed about the family breakup might be understood as her struggle to maintain some control over the timing and manner in which her school-based identity might be transformed over time in the context of her relationship with teachers and peers. Both the father's 'fatherhood' and the daughter's 'pupil-hood' are likely to be important elements in their respective post-separation personal identities.

The Place of Mourning in Personal Identity Transformation

When we speak about 'personal' identity transformation, this does not mean that this challenge is faced alone by the individual child or adult. Indeed, personal identity transformation is a genuinely interpersonal and social achievement which contains both cognitive and psychological/emotional components for the individual. When we say of an individual that she just cannot yet get her *head* around her separation, we are certainly pointing to her need to develop a new perspective and new thoughts about her future. But this cognitive task is intimately bound up with the emotional challenges that the loss of a primary adult attachment figure presents to an individual. Foremost among these emotional challenges is her need to both recognise and respond to this loss. Since the time of Freud (1957), the place of *mourning* in response to loss has been recognised as a key element in the psychic health of those who have endured significant loss. However, when we move towards that part of the continuum of post-separation/divorce parenting which seems marked by ongoing and repetitive conflict, we see many individuals who appear to 'refuse' to mourn or seem incapable of grieving their profound loss. Conflict appears to remain in the place where mourning might have led to a kind of psychological resolution which would allow the individual to move forward in life and make new attachments and bonds that might sustain her into the future. Conflict, it must be remembered, is a mode of communication and connection for these parents/individuals. The weekly, and often daily, grind of conflict-laden relating to an ex-partner over some predictable themes such as money or contact to children provides a way of remaining connected to a now departed attachment figure, but in a manner which often repeats experiences of psychological injury. For many individuals at the more 'high-conflict' end of the post-separation parenting spectrum, the 'refusal' or failure to mourn is evident in the way their faltering attachment to their ex-partner becomes *replaced* by an attachment to the patterns of conflict themselves. Notwithstanding repeated psychological injury, it is as though the predictable pattern of moves and countermoves, along with intermittent periods of apparent quiescence, forms a dance that provides reassurance to the conflict participants that the objects of their attachment have not completely disappeared.

So how are we to understand why some adults successfully 'mourn' the loss of an intimate relationship and 'move on' in their lives while some others seem to remain entrenched in repetitive patterns of post-separation conflict for many years? Attachment theory (Bowlby, 1969, 1973, 1980; Crittenden and Claussen, 2000; Howe, 2011) provides a window into this puzzle by suggesting that those with insecure attachments in their own childhood are likely to experience separation as a much greater threat to their sense of security than those who were securely attached to their own parental figures in childhood. But the picture is more complicated than that. We said earlier that the work of personal identity transformation post-separation is a social achievement. In the context of any particular individual, the outcome of the effort to achieve personal identity transformation post-separation is fully bound up with her relationship to her immediate social network, which includes her children, her extended family and her wider community of friends and neighbourhood relationships. Culture (Crittenden and Claussen, 2000) plays its part at the heart of these relationships, and cultural attitudes to separation and divorce often have either a permissive or inhibiting effect on the individual's capacity to mourn the loss of a significant attachment figure that an intimate partner usually is.

Material, Psychological/Emotional and Symbolic Goods in Post-separation Conflict Negotiation

So what are the different 'goods' that must be negotiated as part of post-separation conflict negotiation and management? They are essentially of three different kinds: *material* goods, *emotional/psychological* goods and *symbolic* goods. Included in the category of material goods are a home or homes (including the family home, holiday homes, mobile homes, caravans and camping vans), income, savings and investments, debts, pensions, cars, bicycles, household furniture and other possessions. Whether the separating family have a lot of material goods or very little, they will still have to negotiate a place for each of the adults to live as well as some income to support both themselves and their dependent children during the time they will be in their care. For all but the extremely wealthy, the arrival of separation means a materially diminished existence for everyone in the family. However, the degree of this diminishment can vary greatly from family to family depending upon their relative wealth/poverty, and from individual to individual depending upon the manner in which the diminishment is apportioned between family members. Repeatedly in post-separation negotiations, mediators and mental health professionals witness parents doing their utmost to protect the material benefits built in to their children's lives while remaining in conflict over the degree to which such protection is feasible in their new context.

Family mediators know how all the material elements in negotiations are interlinked and how these are also linked, in turn, with emotional/ psychological as well as symbolic goods. Although ex-partners will feel the necessity of making short-term agreements in response to the immediate demands of their evolving life context, there is often a very explicit understanding between them that nothing is finally agreed until everything is agreed. Principal among emotional/psychological goods are access to both biological and nonbiological children, continuing contact to the pre-separation friends of the couple, continuing contact with childminders and portions of their employed time. Contact with family pets is also often experienced as an emotional/psychological good. Negotiating the share each adult will have of these goods is a very different task from negotiating the share of material goods such as property, savings and income. When you have successfully negotiated the division of an agreed amount of money available, each partner is likely to receive exactly what has been agreed. The one hundred dollars, pounds or euros you have in your hand today will have much the same value the next day, and there is nothing your partner can personally do to either diminish or enhance the value to you of this amount of money. The reality with emotional/psychological goods is quite different. If a father negotiates with a mother that he will have eight days contact with their dependent children each month in his new accommodation, the expected emotional/psychological 'enjoyment' of this parenting time does not necessarily have a stable value. If the mother sends the children off to their father for these periods with the clear message that she wants them to enjoy themselves with the father and looks forward to hearing about their new adventures with the father during their shared time, and if father treats them appropriately while in his care, it is likely that the value of the parenting time with the father will remain at the levels anticipated during the negotiations. However, if their mother conveys to the children, either explicitly or implicitly, that she is not really happy that they are spending so much time with someone she cannot trust as a co-parent and that she only wants them to 'go through the motions of contact' in order to protect her from her ex-partner's complaints, it is likely that their father will meet disgruntled, disengaged children during 'his' parenting time, if he does not meet with a reluctance to come with him in some of the children or a request to go 'home' early from others. In other words, the value of the agreed share of emotional/psychological 'goods' such as parenting time with children can vary greatly over time depending upon the way a parent, grandparent or other persons relate to children about spending time with their other parent. The value of these 'goods' may even be wiped out altogether, as happens when a child or children are fully alienated from one parent by the other parent. Indeed, one problematic manner of performing post-separation parental conflict is when one of the ex-partners attempts to increase the value to them of some material good – financial support for themselves and the children, for example – because they feel that what had previously been agreed no longer seems fair or adequate, and in failing to achieve an altered level of this good – that is, more money or by attempting to get the partner to pay for some child-related material necessities that were previously regarded as their liability – decides to alter the value of the agreed parenting time for the other parent by withholding the child/children for part of this time. The partner then often acts in some way to diminish the value of some material good – financial support, for example – as a way of protesting the change in value of the emotional/psychological goods described above. This type of negotiation through action usually involves the accusation by one parent that the other parent is using the children as 'pawns' in the financial negotiation, and the responding accusation is that the former parent is materially neglecting the children. At this point, the conflict is on a path of escalation that will be very familiar to family mediators, family lawyers and family court judges. Indeed, it is the task of mediators and mental health professionals to help the parents approach the negotiation of each of these areas again in a discrete rather than a fused manner. Financial support must be looked upon and examined in its own right, just as the needs of the children in relation to parenting time with the other parent need consideration in their own right. And a prerequisite for this is the mental health professional's capacity/skill in convening the parents and containing their evolving emotional worlds sufficiently to enable them to begin negotiations afresh without further escalation. The professional efforts must be directed towards the containment of the emotional responses of the persons in conflict while encouraging dialogue and dialogue-based negotiation as a replacement for the continuation of escalating actions.

The final set of 'goods' that the ex-partners may wish to negotiate are *symbolic* goods. Chief among these nonmaterial goods are matters like the reputation of each of the partners within the extended family circles and the wider community. It may also extend to include the reputation of the ex-partners in their workplaces and leisure/sports associations or clubs. These are very important 'goods' to protect and negotiate in the aftermath of separation, and the tarnishing of these goods for either of the partners can have significant impact on their capacity for social participation, with resulting problematic effects on mental health. The tarnishing of reputation in the workplace can have serious longer-term effects on the future well-being of the family as a whole because of its potential to impact a parent's income-producing capacity. The impact of a damaged reputation can be even greater on individuals who reside in small, rural communities, where the opportunity for alternative employment or to join alternative clubs and associations may be severely limited. Making an agreement not to share all the stories about the separation can be a very constructive step for the ex-partners, and an indicator of likely success in the other negotiations to come. However, when individuals have been very hurt in the separation process by the behaviour of their ex-partner, this 'information' may feel like too big a weapon not to use. It is the function of the mental health professional as family mediator, however, to offer sufficient *emotional containment* and acknowledgement of wounds received to enable reflection upon the consequences of sharing stories in a way likely to severely diminish the reputation of one of the ex-partners and have a knock-on effect upon the whole family.

Another important symbolic good to be negotiated concerns the level of responsibility to be assigned between the ex-partners for the breakdown of the relationship itself. Although the primary beneficiaries to this negotiation appear to be limited to the separating partners themselves, the benefits of experiencing a relatively fair outcome to the negotiations about this symbolic good are likely to be felt by a wide circle of others, principally the children, into future years. Some mediators may take the view that negotiation about such a symbolic good is more appropriately the domain of a separation/divorce counselling service; however, this writer's experience suggests that these three levels of 'goods' are so intimately intertwined within the negotiation process that 'hiving off' the symbolic area – which usually means that it will remain unattended – has the potential to 'load' the other hard-won agreements in the material/emotional-psychological arena with a certain vulnerability. The ex-partners in the vignette below exemplify a whole group of separated parents who remain in intermittent conflict many years after separation without ever actually needing to bring their disputes to the family court for resolution.

Monica and Terence had separated in their mid-thirties, following Monica's traumatic discovery that Terence had been having an affair for the previous two years with a colleague at work. They had two young boys aged five and three years at the time. They came to see me for mediation eight years later in the context of being unable to agree on the secondary school their eldest boy should attend. They reported a history of relatively frequent attendance at different mediation services during that time over a range of issues that seemed relatively minor.

They had experienced deadlock between them in their efforts to negotiate such issues as extending the return time for midweek evening contact by 30 minutes as the boys got older, the range of summer camps the boys should attend, as well as how each of them should be involved in preparing the boys with school books and clothes for the start of each new school year. Mediation had always succeeded in bringing about a resolution with respect to the immediate issue at hand, but they both reported a continuing 'unease' in their infrequent contact with each other and a lack of confidence in their own capacity to work out any difficult issue concerning the boys between themselves. When I invited them to step back from the school choice negotiation for a week to allow us to have a broader discussion about their history as a couple and as parents, what emerged was a very strong feeling in Terence that Monica had always made him feel that he was '100 per cent responsible' for the ending of their relationship and for bringing about a situation in which the boys 'had to be reared by separated parents'. He felt Monica had never acknowledged the part she played, through her very considerable personal neglect of him and of their relationship after the boys came into their lives. Monica listened carefully to Terence in the context, and told him how her own subsequent reflections made her see that there was a certain amount of truth in what he said about her neglect of him, which she regretted, but that she had never felt inclined to say this to him because she felt he had never sufficiently acknowledged the 'horrendous' thing he had done to her by having an affair for so long. This led to further exchanges in which Terence said that although he had apologised to Monica for his betrayal of her at the time, it was only later that he began to see what a horrific experience the whole thing had been for her, and he wanted to apologise to her again now in a new kind of way. She was appreciative of the new apology and followed up by saying that she was sorry for her neglect of him and realised now that she had become overly engrossed in every 'cough or sneeze' in the boys in a way that had been unnecessary. When I saw Monica and Terence the following week, with a view to addressing the school choice decision, they told me they had worked the matter out on the phone themselves and had decided to bring the two boys out together for half a day to get clothes and other school-related items, and to have something to eat with them together, which had never happened since the separation. Terence felt something had finally settled much better within him about the separation, and Monica reported feeling 'a huge relief' following the discussion the previous week and that 'something' had finally resolved much better between them. They both wondered why they could not have had the conversation some years previously.

The negotiation of symbolic goods such as the above issue relating to the apportionment of responsibility for the separation is clearly not possible in all post-separation conflict negotiations. Those partners who have experienced a high degree of conflict for a long period prior to parting will be unlikely to negotiate these 'goods' successfully. Indeed, it may well be harmful to the negotiation of other matters to even try such a negotiation, as it may only re-evoke levels of hostility between the partners that make resolution of more immediate issues pertaining to children more difficult.

The Fate of Parenting in Post-separation/Divorce Family Life

In writing a book on post-separation family conflict, it is most important that we keep the size of this phenomenon in perspective. At one end of the post-separation parenting spectrum, we witness parents who struggle about almost everything and perform their conflict in a way in which every issue seems to continually feed into every other issue. At the other end of the spectrum are parents who, notwithstanding their different perspectives on many post-separation issues, manage to achieve a style of co-parenting that is marked by a necessary amount of constructive communication about their children, a preparedness to adapt their schedules in order to meet the contingent needs of their children's relationship with the other parent, and a cordiality in their parenting relationship that is witnessed by their children at 'handover' moments when they are moving from one home to another. At this end of the spectrum, both parents seem to have emotional and relational capacities that seem absent in those parents at the other end of the spectrum. Chief among these capacities is the ability to keep separate their interpersonal struggles and wounds relating to the fate of their own adult relationship from their desire and capacity to help their children to adapt in the best possible way to the demands and challenges of a new family organisation. This capacity includes an ability to keep an appropriate boundary between the information pertaining to the 'adult' world of their relationship breakdown – which information might be shared with close friends, extended family members and therapists – and the information that children might need to know that would assist them in making the best post-separation adjustment possible given their developmental stage. But these are merely two ends of a spectrum and in many ways don't do sufficient justice to parenting profiles that display variations over time. There is no such thing as perfect parenting either before or after separation and divorce. Even the 'best' post-separation parents have moments when they let slip some of their negative feelings about the other parent in front of the children or fail to send a text or call to the other parent to let them know that, because of unexpected traffic, the arrival of the children to the contact handover point will be 20 minutes later than agreed. Likewise, even those parents who seem to occupy the 'persistently' high conflict end of the spectrum enjoy periods of time, however brief, where the exercise of parenting goes according to a plan that has some measure of agreement. And what about all the parents that fall between these two end points on the spectrum? How many are they, and are they differentiated from one another? And how might they be differentiated from one another and from the parents at each end of the spectrum.

Two pieces of research throw light on this broader picture of post-separation parenting. The first is the research of Hetherington and Kelly (2002), whose study of a large cohort of separated parents suggests that the whole group of post-separation parents can be broken down into three reasonably distinct groups, all of whom can be regarded as co-parents, albeit in different modes. The first group, which comprises 25–30 per cent of the sample cohort, are those involved in cooperative co-parenting. This is the group who communicate effectively with each other for the sake of their children and can make appropriate adjustments when needed to parenting schedules without always insisting on the letter of the law. Indeed, it is likely that within this group there are many who have successfully used mediation services to make an agreement about parenting plans, or who have worked out their own parenting plan without the need for mediating assistance.

The second group, comprising 50 per cent, or half, of the total sample cohort, are those engaged in what the researchers call *parallel co-parenting*. This is the group of parents who, as the description suggests, parent their joint children in parallel, rather than in cooperation, with each other. These parents tend not to be in communication with each other unless they absolutely have to, and even then may do so through a third party. However, they rigidly adhere to whatever parenting plans have been put in place either through mediation or family court proceedings. This gives a good deal of security to their children who, despite quietly complaining to mental health professionals that their parents 'never talk', benefit greatly from the predictability surrounding their movements between parental homes. The downside of this co-parenting pattern from a child's point of view is that when adjustments in the parenting/care schedule are necessary, particularly around the time of late childhood and early adolescence, the children are often reluctant to make such requests to either parent for fear of igniting a conflict that they sense lies not far beneath the surface of the calm, incommunicative waters of their parents' non-relationship. Clinical impressions would suggest that the meaning behind this parental pattern varies. For some parents, the experience of their own conflict around the themes leading up to separation is felt to be so horrendous that a strategy of avoidance of each other seems to be the best insurance against the possibility of sinking back into the mire of a conflict that traumatised both of them. The pattern remains because neither parent feels safe enough to deviate from the avoidance strategy. For others, the pattern seems to have been built upon one person's determination not to have anything to do directly with the other parent after separation. The pattern can also originate from the extreme hurt and sense of rejection/abandonment of one parent at the hands of the other. For that individual to communicate in any manner with her ex-partner would be a kind of acknowledgement of the other person that seems undeserved following his 'crime' of rejection. The ex-partner/parent eventually accepts the total silence, and the parallel pattern is born. It is not clear how many of this very large group of separated parents arrive in this pattern by the route of mediation, family court proceedings or other means.

Kelly (2007) points out that research shows that children in joint physical custody after separation/divorce fare better across multiple measures than those children who remain in the physical custody of one parent alone. This is likely to be a characteristic shared by most, if not all, of the children in both of these first two groups. It has also been suggested (Hetherington and Kelly, 2002; Maccoby and Mnookin, 1992)) that the children in this second group fare marginally less well than their counterpart children belonging to the first group, whose parents function as cooperative co-parents. Indeed, this may be one of the important research contributions to this area of professional practice insofar as it places a check on our beliefs regarding the extent of the added value for children arising from a cordial, communicative relationship between their parents after separation. It is also worth pondering the fact that, in the context of this study, this 'parallel' kind of co-parenting seemed to be the norm for post-separation parenting practice and that, regardless of its potential deficits, which have been mentioned above, appears to have the potential for creating the conditions sufficient for the ongoing development of children's lives while allowing parents to move on in most respects with their own.

In contrast to the 'parallel' type of post-separation parenting which appears in many respects to be 'good enough' parenting, the first category of 'cooperative co-parenting' is often held out by the media and some parent education programs as the 'gold standard' of post-separation parenting. In my view, this type of exhortation to parents to achieve what is 'best' for their children can place unrealistic demands on many parents who, for a variety of interpersonal and circumstantial reasons, cannot achieve the standards implicit in the 'cooperative' category. It is interesting to note that what seemed to be the norm emerging in this study reflected that group of parents who, notwithstanding their intense levels of interpersonal conflict, manage to substantially protect their children's relationships with the other parent. It is one of those areas in social life where reaching for what is 'best' may turn out to be the enemy of what is 'good enough'. Inexperienced mental health professionals can often fall into this trap when they encounter certain symptoms and difficulties in the children of separated parents and assume that a central plank of their treatment must be the restoration of parental relations to a communicative and cordial level. In failing to see the origins of these symptoms in other contexts, their attempts to unite the parents in a new kind of cooperation around the child runs the risk of re-igniting dormant parental patterns of conflict and unsettling an otherwise stable post-separation/divorce family system.

The third group of parents emerging from the Hetherington and Kelly (2002) study are those whose parenting is characterised as *conflictual co-parenting*. This group comprise 20–25 per cent of the total sample cohort and can be broken down into two subgroups. Although both subgroups demonstrate high levels of conflict, the smaller of these subgroups, which comprises about seven per cent of the total sample, shows patterns of very intense conflict. Although most members of this group are frequent users of the family courts, the group showing more intense conflict seem more persistently engaged in escalating cycles of action and reaction which tend to be performed without much pause. Indeed, when there are pauses in their cycles of conflict, these pauses seem to coincide with court hearings or court case management meetings. Eddy (2009) suggests that families where parents are engaged in high conflict are challenged by three common issues: they suffer from what he calls 'all-or-none' thinking; they are unable to manage their emotions; and their members exhibit extreme behaviours. In my experience, the parents in these families often eschew the opportunities to engage in mediation dialogues and use the family court system as a means of periodic regulation of their intense conflict. They approach court hearings with the 'all-or-none' disposition to which Eddy (2009) refers. Each time they hope and expect that the presiding judge will vindicate their position fully while punishing their ex-partner. They are always disappointed with the court outcomes, as the 'vindication' sometimes does not arrive in any measure, or the 'punishment' of the ex-partner is never sufficient.

The second piece of research that throws some light on parenting relationships post-separation and divorce is a North American study by Ahrons (2007), who looked at the phenomenon of divorced parenting through the lens of young adults whose parents had divorced during their childhood. This study threw up five typologies of divorced parenting. The first type were *friendly ex-spouses* who were referred to as 'perfect pals'; the second type reflected *cooperative shared parenting*, whose representatives warranted the abbreviated title of 'cooperative colleagues'; the third type of parenting was characterised by *conflict with cooperation*, whose pairs were referred to as 'angry associates'; the fourth group was marked by *persistently conflictual parenting*, which merited the relational name of 'fiery foes'; and the fifth type, called 'dissolved duos', reflected that subset of divorced *parents who have no contact at all between them*. When taken in the light of each other, these studies support an idea that separated and divorced parents probably fall into three categories, with the first being marked by cooperative parenting performed with or without a degree of cordiality, the second being marked by the complete absence of contact, and the third characterised by conflict performed with different levels of persistence. A great deal of more contemporary research needs to be undertaken on the shape of post-separation parenting in different societies, to allow us to determine whether the kinds of categories proposed by the research described in the paragraphs above continue to hold good and to discover what kind of variations might exist in the prevalence of the different categories in relation to one another. In particular, it would be interesting to know more about any impact that the availability and use of family mediation services in the immediacy of the separation event might have on subsequent more enduring patterns of post-separation/divorce parenting.

Skills and Interventions

This chapter has looked at the broad spectrum of post-separation/divorce family conflict and its negotiation through an attempt to answer two particular questions. The first question enquired about the range of things that people value which subsequently become the focus of post-separation conflict management. The second question concerned the nature of the post-separation/divorce parenting relationships that underpin conflict negotiation and management. Both themes point initially to a number of conflict assessment skills mental health practitioners must draw upon as they plan their interventions with a family, its constituent members and others in their context. Some of these assessment and intervention skills will be relevant to both family mediators and court-appointed child custody and contact assessors, whereas others will, perhaps, be more relevant to psychotherapists and counsellors working with those engaged in ongoing post-separation relational conflict. The following are six key skills that mental health professionals need to have within their repertoire if they are to respond helpfully to some of the themes mentioned in the current chapter:

(i) *Making an assessment of the full range of 'goods' to be negotiated in the post-separation family conflict.* When the mental health professional is in the role of mediator, one of the first skills he must acquire is the capacity to make, along with the separating partners/parents, a full inventory of the material, emotional/psychological and symbolic goods to be negotiated as part of their conflict resolution process. This is not always a simple task as it is not uncommon for the key participants in the process to disagree about what is included in the negotiation 'pot'. A partner who feels very wounded by being 'left' by the other person may insist that contact between their ten-year-old child from a previous relationship and the partner who is 'abandoning' them now is 'not on the negotiation table' despite the close bond built up between that child and the ex-partner over the previous eight years. The partner may insist that the child contact negotiations include this child along with the couple's other joint children not simply because of her close bond with that child but because of the close bond between all the siblings. Or one person may feel that a valuable painting left to her by a deceased parent is of such symbolic importance to her that it cannot be considered part of the material goods to be divided in some way between her and her partner, whereas her partner points out that the monetary value of the painting is so significant in the context of the separating family's scarce resources that it cannot be omitted from the material goods to be apportioned between them. Whatever differences there are between the mediation participants about the inclusion or exclusion of certain matters from the negotiations, the mediating mental health professional must be able to assess with the participants the full range of 'goods' to be negotiated, including those 'goods' whose inclusion remains in dispute.

(ii) *Making an assessment of the position of each of the conflict participants in relation to each good to be negotiated.* Embedded in the first assessment skill mentioned above is the related skill of finding out how each of the key participants is positioned in relation to each of the 'goods' to be negotiated. This may often be accomplished in private one-to-one conversations with each of the partners, as they may not wish to reveal their personal priorities in front of their separating partner lest it weaken their 'hand' in the negotiations. The skill in conducting these one-to-one conversations involves the ability to assist each participant (parent or a child/adolescent) to work out what his or her priorities really are. It means assisting adults to step back momentarily from the maelstrom of swirling emotions that often accompany the separation process to consider what is most deeply important to them about the future and what values they are trying to uphold for themselves and others by having the immediate future organised in a certain way. The mental health professional will also try to facilitate these individuals to identify what the second-most important thing or issue is for them and to try to say why they think this is the case. They might also facilitate the individual to identify which 'goods' might have very little importance for them.

(iii) *Fostering a negotiating attitude in conflict mediation.* The mental health professional, whether in a formal mediating role or a counselling/ consultative role, will need to have the capacity to foster 'a negotiating attitude' in the individuals participating in conflict resolution processes. This capacity means being able to point out to individuals that it is extremely rare that individuals in a negotiating process like their own manage to get everything that they want and that it is important that they learn to yield on some matters while struggling hard to achieve certain other things that they really want very much or that they very strongly feel 'should be the case'.

Clare was a 13-year-old adolescent girl who was seen alone as part of a mediation process in which her parents seemed locked in a bitter dispute over financial and child contact issues. Her parents had just commenced living apart, and her mother was consenting to nothing more in relation to her father's contact with her and her ten-year-old brother than an arrangement for every second weekend and a couple of hours each Wednesday evening. Her father was insisting upon every second weekend and every Wednesday overnight for herself and her brother as 'the bare minimum' he might accept. Clare had a good relationship with both her parents and was already showing signs of considerable social independence. Although she had articulated in an open whole-family mediation session that what she wanted with regard to contact was the very same as her mother had proposed – that is, every second weekend and a couple of hours every Wednesday evening – she told me during an individual meeting that it did not matter that much to her whether she spent overnights on Wednesdays with her father or not. It was no 'big deal' for her one way or another. She told me that what she really wanted most of all from the negotiations was to be sure that both her parents would allow her to spend an hour or two with a school friend up the road each evening once her homework was done. I encouraged her to explore this question with both her parents, and each of them in turn confirmed for Clare that, while she was in their care, they would not stop her from spending time with her friend once her homework was complete. Armed with this promise from both sides of the parenting fence, Clare told her parents that she was fine with spending a single midweek overnight with her father every week in addition to every second weekend. Her mother did not struggle against Clare's offer once she was satisfied that her daughter was not being 'forced into this offer', and her father seemed pleased at the prospect of securing what he had earlier termed 'the bare minimum contact' he would accept. The opportunity for Clare to work out her priorities had clearly paved the way for a resolution to the contact issue for herself, her brother and her parents. Clare's behaviour in the mediation dialogues exemplified a negotiating attitude which spread to her parents.

(iv) *Assessing and respecting adult choices in the making of post-separation parenting relationships.* When conflicts emerge in the post-separation/ divorce parenting relationship about child issues, the mental health professional needs to find out how this particular parental relationship has been working up to that point and to respect the preferred ways that adults have chosen for the performance of those relationships, including the avenues they have chosen for conflict resolution in the past. This means not always assuming that it is the right thing to do to try to convene the parents for a joint meeting to attempt resolution of whatever issue is in dispute. It means not only consulting both parents about their perspective surrounding the disputed issue but also consult-ing them, prior to meeting up, about the way in which they would like to participate in the resolution of this particular dispute. Parents may have had very bad experiences of mediation dialogues in the past and be extremely wary of any offers of assistance which include sitting in the same room together. Or they may not wish to engage in face-to-face negotiation dialogues because of the fears and anxieties that such suggested dialogues evoke. The mediator needs to consider with each of the ex-partners the different means that each of them would find acceptable as a conflict resolution pathway in this instance. This means being patient with each of the participants while reassuring them and oneself that there are always different pathways to the same goal of dispute resolution.

(v) *The capacity to assist people to look realistically at the future in the middle of conflict negotiation.* When people have been very wounded by the events leading up to separation, as well as by the reality of the separa-tion itself, it is often very difficult for individuals to get a sense of any possible future that might offer them something like an acceptable life in the time ahead. Their gaze seems firmly fixed upon the past and all its traumatic events. Yet, despite the weight of their wounded past, it is the job of the mental health professional to keep an ear open for the time when the same adult might be ready, with support and encouragement, to look towards the future and what it might hold for her. Once the mental health professional succeeds in facilitating a new kind of narrating in the separated individual – a type of narrating that spreads its focus between the past, the present and the future – the work of personal identity transformation has begun. Often this type of individual therapeutic work, which awakens a sense of hope for the future, is a necessary step for some individuals before they can engage meaningfully in the conflict resolution efforts that mediation provides.

(vi) *The capacity to facilitate and support individuals in mourning the loss of an intimate relationship.* In the face of the anger and hostility that the mental health professional often observes both in and between the ex-partners emerging from an intimate relationship, he needs to remind himself of the significant loss the partners are both experiencing in their own different ways. The mental health professional must be able to listen in to the ex-partners in whatever context that might meet them for the moment when it might be right to acknowledge this loss and to invite them to recognise this experience in themselves. Facilitating individuals in the emotional work of mourning associated with the loss of an intimate relationship can be an important element in assisting ex-partners move from a position of complete stand-off with respect to the negotiation of certain post-separation 'goods' towards a place where they feel more motivated to negotiate for the sake of a future which beckons slowly but surely. For the mental health professional, the facilitation of the mourning process in post-separation contexts means moving with a person in the emotional space where despair and hope often seem to overlap (Flaskas, McCarthy and Sheehan, 2007). It can mean carrying hope for the person while she remains in despair, or containing her despair in a way that makes it possible for hope to make an appearance.

Personal and Reflective Exercises

Write some notes and reflections for yourself in response to each of the following four questions. I suggest that you take as much time as you need to respond as fully as you can to each of the questions. Because each question is like a full exercise in itself, it may not be possible to respond to all four questions within the classroom setting within a single meeting of the class. For some readers it may be more comfortable to do some or all of this exercise at home.

1. Imagine you are going through a separation in the context of your current life circumstances (if you do not have a partner, give yourself an imaginary partner, imaginary children and an imaginary life context) and that you are separating because you have met someone in your work context with whom you want to pursue a longer-term relationship. Make a complete list of all the different 'goods' that might have to be negotiated in the context of your engagement in mediation with your partner, and try then to make some notes on what your relative priorities might be with respect to these different 'goods' to be negotiated.

2. Using the real or imaginary situation you described in your answer to the first question, try to imagine how your partner would position herself in relation to each of the different 'goods' at stake in the mediation. Given the different ways that you imagine each of you would be 'positioned' in this context, where, in your view, would the biggest challenges be for the mediator in this situation? How might the 'positioning' of your partner in relation to the different goods impact the way you approach these negotiations?

3. Imagine you are commencing a mediation process with a couple who have been together 15 years and have two children of ten and eight years. You are the mediator offering a service from a governmental family mediation agency. What words or sentences might you actually use near the beginning of the process with the couple to cultivate a positive negotiating attitude and culture?

4. Try to recall a significant past romantic relationship where you had to endure a lasting separation, whether you feel you chose it or not. Describe for yourself the process you went through in mourning the loss of this relationship. How did this mourning happen? Who else, if anyone, became involved with you in this mourning process? How long did this process take? Do you think this mourning process is complete?

PART II
INTERVENTIONS IN ESCALATING POST-SEPARATION/DIVORCE PARENTAL DISPUTES

PARENTAL CONFLICT OVER POST-SEPARATION CHILD CONTACT

Although parental conflict after separation and divorce can focus on any of the 'goods' mentioned in the previous chapter, some of the most intense post-separation conflicts are about child contact with a parent who has become nonresident through the separation process. These conflicts, depending upon their underlying psychological and relational bases as well as upon their management, can result in a range of different outcomes. Some conflicts are strongly related to the phase of the separation process and to the developmental stages of the children involved. These conflicts can be short-lived once the right kinds of interventions are made available in a timely fashion. Other conflicts can become more serious when they fail to respond to educational, therapeutic or mediation interventions or when one of the parents refuses to engage with any of these processes. In these latter conflicts, the nonresident parent has nowhere to go but the family courts to find a resolution he thinks is more in line with his child's best interests and in keeping with what he feels is an acceptable level of contact with his child. However, many practitioners and writers (Fidler, Bala and Saini, 2013; Kelly and Johnston, 2001) have noted the potentially detrimental effect on conflict management arising from the transitioning of the conflict scene into the adversarial process of the family courts. A third group of contact-related conflicts develop into protracted disputes in which the courts, with the assistance of family lawyers and court-appointed assessors and therapists, are required to play an increasingly significant role in conflict containment and management. Among this group are a subgroup of separating parents who go on to acquire the description 'high-conflict' (Eddy, 2010) separated/divorced couples/parents. Systemic theory (Bateson, 1972), however, invites us to be wary about the labelling of any group of parents in this way without reference to the growth of certain professional contexts around them. Although this group of separating parents certainly contribute significantly to the performance of 'high-conflict' dramas that are staged daily in family courts in a host of different jurisdictions, they do not appear alone in the cast lists of such conflict dramas. Judges from different level courts, family lawyers, court-appointed assessors and other professional and lay witnesses all occupy important roles in process-driven dramas which can unwittingly push parental conflict over time to levels that would have been unimaginable to participants at the commencement of legal proceedings.

This chapter does not deal directly with the last-mentioned more serious, prolonged and intense parental conflicts over child contact. Many, but not all, of these conflicts transform over time into disputes over child residence as well and often involve allegations of child abuse along with counter-allegations of parental alienation. This group of conflicts is the subject of Chapter 7, which deals extensively with the challenges for conflict management arising from parental alienating behaviours as well as from conflict histories dominated by a mixture of parental alienation and domestic abuse allegations. Nor does this chapter address that group of contact-related disputes that are associated with either alleged or acknowledged parental histories of domestic abuse and violence. The place of domestic violence in contact disputes is the central focus of the next chapter. The decision to address such disputes in a separate chapter mirrors the trend in many jurisdictions where the hearing of such matters belongs either to specialist 'domestic violence' courts or to special sittings of regular family law courts.

Following an overview of the multiplicity of different child contact disputes, the focus in the first part of the chapter is on the less intense, less prolonged contact-related conflicts and how they can be managed in the context of therapeutic, educational and mediation interventions. In turn, the parts played in contact disputes by perceived difference, separation anxiety, affinity and alignment are considered. The chapter then moves in its middle section to a reflection on the way the gendered dynamics of power can underpin many of the apparently less intense contact-related disputes. This is followed by a consideration of the dilemmas faced by parents when their dispute is at risk of transitioning into the arena of the family courts. The final part of the chapter examines some of the issues faced by mental health professional mediators as they attempt to achieve an appropriate level of child and adolescent participation in mediation dialogues concerning their post-separation life with each of their separating parents and their siblings.

The Multiplicity of Child Contact-related Conflicts

Conflicts over child contact can be of many different kinds and can commence as early as the first weeks of a child's life. Where a child is just a couple of months old and the parents have separated early in the pregnancy, and perhaps don't know each other very well, a dispute may arise about whether contact should happen at all. The child's mother may be unwilling to allow the father contact with the child except for very short periods of time and infrequently. She may be unwilling to have the father remove the child from her home and also unwilling to have the father inside her home to see the child. I have known many young fathers and infants who commenced their parent–child relationship in the context of 30-minute contact events in a front garden or side yard, in a car parked in the mother's driveway, or in the hallway of a neighbour's home. Typically, young parents whose relationship has been of short duration often need a mixture of therapeutic and mediation interventions to assist with the commencement of both the parental relationship and the parent–infant relationship. Such interventions often benefit from the inclusion of grandparents or older siblings, once it can be ascertained that they will support the stabilisation of parent–infant contact patterns that respect the infant's developing routine. Such interventions should include an appropriate level of educational input where this might be necessary. Educational interventions should not necessarily be limited to the parents, but may need to include grandparents and any adult siblings involved in the child's management and care. The main goals of intervention in these contexts are threefold: first, to facilitate the growth of both the parental and parent–infant relationships; second, to assist young parents with the acquisition of parenting skills and capacities; and third, to contain conflict and prevent it from escalating into the adversarial arena. Although attendance at group-based parent education programs can be of great value for some young parents, such attendance may not be feasible for others for a variety of reasons. In these latter contexts, mental health professionals should incorporate an educational dimension into their routine meetings with parents.

As the post-separation process gathers momentum, parental disputes can arise about whether child contact needs to be supervised and where the location of contact should be. Many first-time fathers resent the idea of supervised contact and point out that they have not done anything wrong. They may sometimes agree to have contact *accompanied* by their own mother or a sibling for a period of time which can just be long enough to allow the infant's angry and anxious first-time mother to be reassured that nothing harmful will happen to 'her' child. It can be a huge step for some mothers to allow paternal child contact in the father's own home, and successful mental health professional interventions often depend upon the capacity of the professional to facilitate the growth of patience in frustrated fathers, while fostering risk-taking in small steps in understandably protective first-time mothers. Such balancing interventions must always be contextualised by the growing infant's need for predictability in her routine and protection from exposure to conflict between her parents.

Conflicts over child contact can relate to a whole set of other contact-related variables. Conflict can focus on any of the following matters: whether and when daytime contact should extend to overnights; what clothes should be worn by the child on visits to the nonresident parent; who should wash these clothes; whether handovers should happen at the parental homes or at some neutral venue; whether handovers should be managed directly by the parents or through some intermediaries; whether there should be telephone or Skype contact between the child and the parent she is away from at a moment in time; who should take the child to and from meetings with the nonresident parent; what are acceptable modes of transport for a child to and from contact venues; who should pay for contact-related travel if there are costs involved; who should specify a child's diet while on visits to the nonresident parent; who else may be present while a child is on contact visits; what activities a child may engage in while on such visits; what a child's sleeping arrangements should be during overnight contact; whether a child should have any clothes bought for her or get a haircut during such visits; and whether a child should be allowed to have play dates while she is in the care of a nonresident parent. Mediation or therapeutic dialogues will usually reveal what is driving these different kinds of conflict on both sides of the parental 'fence'. Anxiety about the child's welfare while out of sight can drive some parents to over-control and over-specification of the whole circumstances of contact. For other resident parents, it is the memory of past moments when it seemed to them that the other parent neglected the interests of a child that drives their efforts to prescribe specific activities for the child while they are in the care of the other parent. A not uncommon conflict is generated by the resident parent making plans for a child's activities during the contact period without consulting the nonresident parent. Much of the resolution of these different conflicts in the arena of mediation or therapy involves the parents learning the skills of listening to each other, trying to understand the reasons why the other person is taking up certain positions, trying to articulate their own position on any matter and the reasons and justifications for this position, and learning the art of negotiation, which makes space for some of both their own and their ex-partner's desires to be met. Ironically, these are often the very skills that were so difficult to acquire during the parents' previous life together as a couple.

Difference and Power in Parental Disputes over Child Contact

One subgroup of post-separation parental disputes over child contact is generated through various kinds of differences that emerge for parents, and how these differences come to be perceived by one or both of them and by the institutions to which they belong. Cultural differences in parenting practices, perceptions about the impact on parenting of a separated parent commencing a same-sex relationship, differences between separated parents regarding child participation in religious services and parental differences regarding the management of children who are 'different' by virtue of their chronic illnesses are just some of the bases for evolving parental dispute over post-separation child contact. Such disputes sometimes find resolution between parents themselves; others require mediation or family court intervention as vehicles for safeguarding the continuity of parent–child relationships. Some of these disputes may not resolve and may escalate to the point where a child's contact with one parent breaks down fully and finally. The following two vignettes reflect something of the way varying kinds of difference can lie at the heart of post-separation conflict over child contact. Cultural difference is the focus of the first vignette, whereas transitions in the sexual preferences of a nonresident father constitute the difference at the heart of the second vignette.

A separated heterosexual couple in their forties came to mediation one year following their breakup because of a dispute over the post-separation care of their four-year-old twin girls. The father was from a Mediterranean culture but had resided in Ireland for some years, whereas the mother's primary cultural identification was Asian. Following their relatively amicable parting, the parents had negotiated with ease the mother's primary role in the children's ongoing care while the father had a secondary, but substantial, part in the girls' management and care. A dispute had arisen between the parents after the father had learnt from the girls that they were spending long periods of time in the home of the maternal grandparents and regularly slept in a double bed with them rather than in a room of their own in the mother's home. When the father heard about these relatively constant sleeping arrangements while in their mother's care, he refused to return the girls to their mother at the end of a contact period. A number of angry telephone 'conversations' failed to resolve the matter. The mother was finally forced to make an emergency application to the family court to have the children returned to her under their previously agreed arrangements. The court, during the hearing of the emergency application, persuaded the parents to attend mediation on the understanding that their prior agreement regarding the girls' care would be reinstated while mediation efforts were ongoing. During the formal mediation process, which the mother initially experienced as somewhat alien, she described how the children were rarely left alone in her parents' care and that when they slept over with the grandparents, she was always in their home in a different room. She explained that it was quite normal for her brothers' and sisters' children to stay over with her parents and that the younger ones quite regularly slept with their grandparents. She did not want her children to be any different from their cousins. The father, for his part, said that he was shocked to hear what was happening and that mother was not only facilitating these sleeping arrangements but seemed to be arguing that they contributed something positive to the girls' relationship with their grandparents. He pointed out that when he stayed over with his own parents during holiday periods in the country where they resided, he always slept in the same room with the girls, who were always in beds of their own. His parents had built up a very good bond with the girls but had done so by bringing them to special places for outings of different kinds, but not by sleeping with them. The mediator introduced the idea of culture as a framework for exploring and understanding some of their different experiences and perspectives. Both parents responded positively to this suggested exploration and found that, although there seemed to be some clear differences between them with respect to how both their cultures understood certain family relationships, their cultures also had a lot in common in the way they both saw children's relationships with grandparents as very important. It became clear from the discussion that the father felt a little jealous about a kind of intimacy the maternal grandparents had with the girls that he could not allow himself. Following two extended culturally focussed conversations with the mediator around the themes of trust, intimacy and boundaries attaching to different family relationships, both parents expressed a desire to reposition themselves as parents in relation to their girls. The mother decided that she wanted to be a little more independent from her parents with respect to daily decisions that had to be made about the twins, and the father decided that he wanted to have a closer relationship emotionally with the girls than he had seen his father have with his sisters. By the end of their third mediation appointment, they both felt that they had reached a better understanding of each other's evolving positions, and they did not need to have further meetings or further court assistance.

Cross-cultural comparisons of parenting practices suggest that there is almost no aspect of parenting that is not informed by culture (Bornstein, 2013). In the above vignette cultural differences played their part in the evolving conflict through the somewhat different assumptions each parent held concerning the respective roles of parents and grandparents in the care of young children. The cultural assumptions held by the father seemed to locate the central responsibilities for the children's care firmly at the feet of both parents within a nuclear family, separated or not. Grandparents had a place in this set of assumptions, but this place operated more as a type of bonus for children's well-being rather than a central plank in their day-to-day care and welfare. The assumptions held by mother and her parents, emanating as they did from their belonging to a unique part of Asian culture, saw responsibility for young children as held collectively by the extended family's adults, which included parents, grandparents, aunts and uncles, with the grandparents having a special role as elders in the family. As can be seen from the type of resolution that emerged, the role that culture played at the point of conflict generation did not remain static. The mother's positioning in relation to her own family's culture of origin was beginning to shift, at the time of conflict resolution, in the direction of adopting a more independent and autonomous stance in relation to her own parenting. It may well be that this repositioning, which made its contribution to the resolution achieved with her ex-partner, would prove to be the seed of a new conflict for her with her parents. Perhaps the character of the repositioning of both parents was more impacted by the Irish host culture than any of the mediation participants realised at the time.

About 25 years ago Mary, John and their two children (a girl of ten years and a boy of eight years) were the central participants in a court-ordered evaluation relating to contact of the children with John, their nonresident father. Both in their late thirties and Irish, the couple had separated two years previously after John had revealed to Mary that, although he 'loved' her, he was no longer 'in love' with her. Despite her anger and desolation at John's relatively sudden abandonment of her, Mary agreed to a set of post-separation contact arrangements which saw the children spending every second weekend with their father, as well as one midweek afternoon and overnight. This contact appeared to have gone well for the children and provided them with a degree of continuity for what had been a very engaged and involved pre-separation relationship with their father. However, following this strained but uninterrupted two-year period of post-separation shared parenting, John told Mary that he was in the process of coming out as a gay man and that he had recently commenced a relationship with a man he met through his work. He told her that he had very strong feelings for this man and that the evolving relationship might well prove to be long term. Additionally, he told her that he was not planning to introduce this man to the children for at least six months. Mary reacted to this news with a mixture of shock, anger and disgust. She immediately withheld the children from any type of contact with their father and spoke to them directly about what was happening in their father's life. During the subsequent court-ordered evaluation, she told the assessor that she would never allow her children to have any contact with their father during their childhood. She felt that what John was now involved in was utterly immoral, even if homosexuality was no longer a crime under Irish law. As a parent and a Roman Catholic, she could not allow her children 'to be exposed to that kind of thing in any shape or form'. During the evaluation, both children refused to be seen with their father and told the assessor that they did not want to see him anymore because he was doing things that were 'evil' and 'sinful'. They had clearly been well informed by their outraged mother of the 'correct' way to think about and respond to the elements that made up the crisis. Following an extensive court hearing of the matter, in which lawyers for both sides expressed different ways of thinking about the themes at the heart of the conflict, the judge, opposing the assessor's advice regarding management of the situation, decided that no pressure of any kind should be put on the children to see their father within the changing parental context and that no orders for parent contact would be made. The children's contact with their father did not resume during the years following the court decision, and their relationship with him was reduced to the receipt of unacknowledged cards and gifts throughout the calendar year.

Let us consider now the mechanisms through which the 'differences' at the heart of the above two vignettes found particular responses from the contexts in which they appeared. When we speak of a situation, or a context, as constituting a difference, we normally mean that it heralds a difference from something else. This 'something else' is the normal or more usual way a phenomenon appears to those in a particular context. Within any specific culture, privilege or dominance is accorded to certain ways of thinking about and knowing phenomena of different kinds. Thinking about the two vignettes above within a poststructuralist framework (Derrida, 1981; de Shazer and Berg, 1992; Dickerson, 2014) and, more specifically, within Foucauldian terminology (Foucault, 1980), we could say that dominant *discourses* within the Irish host culture regarding grandparent–grandchild relationships and adult same-sex relationships were the means through which *power* and power relationships in the respective contexts in which difference emerged made certain outcomes more likely than others. The two ideas/concepts of 'discourse' and 'power' are italicised here because, along with the concept of *knowledge*, they form a triangle of interrelated Foucauldian terms that, together, can throw light on the processes enfolding the actors described in the vignettes. But what do these terms mean within a Foucauldian framework?

At the risk of oversimplifying a very complex set of concepts and their interrelationships, we can say that discourses for Foucault are bodies of knowledge that preside over a whole period of time in human history. This concept of discourses as 'bodies of knowledge' has less to do with language and more to do with knowledge we receive within particular 'disciplines'.

94

For Foucault, a discipline referred both to the knowledge contained in and by *scholarly disciplines* such as science, medicine, psychiatry or sociology and to the *disciplinary institutions* of social control such as the prison, the hospital, the confessional and, we might add in the context of our current study, the family court (McHoul and Grace, 1995). Much of Foucault's own scholarly energies were directed to an understanding of the historically specific relations between disciplines, considered as bodies of knowledge, and disciplinary practices within specific historical periods. Disciplinary practices, for Foucault, were not just mechanisms of social control but also operated as vehicles of social possibility.

What then of Foucault's use of the concept of power? Within the Foucauldian framework, power and knowledge are so closely interrelated as to be almost indistinguishable from each other at times. One thing power does not refer to within this framework is one individual's domination over another. For example, a Foucauldian concept of power would not be focussed at all on any alleged power of the judge over the gay litigant in our second vignette. Nonetheless, both the family law judge and the assessor would be viewed as important persons through whom power passes within a specific field of power relations.

Foucault's work, however, was not just focussed on the functioning of power relations through dominant or official bodies of knowledge but also attended to what he called 'subjugated' or 'marginalised' knowledges, which are those knowledges which have either been disqualified, thought to be inadequate, or ranked very low down in a hierarchy by official knowledges. In this more critical phase of his work, Foucault was concerned with the way official knowledges were constantly at work as instruments of 'normalisation' which were 'continually attempting to manoeuvre certain populations (bearers of marginalised knowledges, for example) into 'correct' and 'functional' forms of thinking and acting (McHoul and Grace, 1995, p.17). In his thinking about knowledge, Foucault removed himself completely from any conceptions of science and knowledge as moving us ever closer, and in a cumulative way, towards the something called the truth. Dominant and official discourses, however, operated to enable subjects to accept their knowledges as true and to accept the versions of themselves, as they were framed by these knowledges, as true reflections of who they were.

Drawing upon a Foucauldian poststructuralist framework, a mental health professional considering the two vignettes described above would be interested in the way dominant discourses in the Irish host culture concerning grandparent–grandchild relations and parenting in the context of adult gay relationships produced a set of power relationships in both mediation and family court contexts that favoured resolutions of particular kinds. In the second vignette, for example, the mother's perspective and the judge's decision-making drew upon a dominant discourse concerning adult sexuality which sees heterosexuality as the only correct and morally acceptable context for continued parenting. Through the processes of court hearing and judicial decision, the position of the mother was confirmed as 'correct' in that it was fully aligned with the dominant discourse concerning adult sexuality and parenting at a time in which alternative knowledges concerning positive parenting of children in the context of adult gay relationships remained marginalised and devalued.

In summary, what a poststructuralist framework offers the mental health practitioner in this context of practice is an invitation to a particular kind of critical reflection. This reflective work, engaged in collaboratively with others, attempts to identify those discourses which have shaped the thinking, speaking and actions of both professionals and clients alike, with a view to revealing hidden or alternative knowledges about key matters at stake in their conversation. Such critical reflective thought and the 'other knowledges' it brings to light function as points of resistance to the power of dominant discourses while offering participants new and more positive descriptions of who they are.

Separation Anxiety in Parental Disputes over Child Contact

Our earlier explorations in attachment theory (Bowlby, 1969, 1973) have alerted us to the way the separation process and event has the potential to undermine the sense of security and safety of adults and children alike. For some, particularly when the event is unanticipated, separation is experienced as a trauma (Herman, 1992) which requires its own recovery time. Even when children are prepared for the event by their parents and given a lot of time and support in coming to terms with the new family reality, separation can 'hit' some children harder than others for reasons that are not always obvious to their parents or assisting professionals. Separation-related anxiety can present either as a psychological phenomenon in a child or as a relational phenomenon in which a parent and child participate. In the following vignette, the mediating mental health professional was challenged to locate with and for parents the sources of a child's anxiety, to consider what else might be fuelling such anxiety and to devise a shared plan for its management in the child.

When Robert was seven years of age, his father announced to his mother that he wished to separate from her because of an absence of any feelings of romance for a number of years. Although she was shocked and very hurt at his decision, she responded constructively in the mediation sessions they attended. These sessions allowed them to work out the key elements of the separation, which involved father moving into an apartment nearby, with mother remaining in the family home with Robert and his nine-year-old brother, Tom. The parents agreed that the boys would go to father for three hours on two midweek late afternoons in addition to one 24-hour period each weekend. However, when it came to the implementation of the plan, both parents discovered that Robert was highly resistant to accompanying his father with his older brother for the first midweek contact period. He became extremely clingy to his mother, who seemed unable to persuade him to go with his father with whom he had never had anything but a very good relationship. Subsequent efforts to encourage him to go with his father met with the same result. Further mediation meetings, requested by the father, revealed that Robert had been in hospital on three occasions in the 18-month period after he had been knocked down by a car in the neighbourhood shortly after his fourth birthday. He had been very 'tied' to his mother after these hospitalisations, and he found it difficult to attend school for a period of time after his final stay in hospital. However, with some patience and reassurance on his parents' part, he began to achieve an uninterrupted attendance pattern at school, and in the year before his father's separation decision, he had let go of his 'clinginess' to mother and appeared to be enjoying the ordinary routines of a normal seven-year-old boy. During the time of the contact 'failures', however, Robert's father's best friend, also separated, had convinced him that it was probably his ex-wife's anger about the separation that was the crucial element in these resistances in his son, and he had given him a book on the theme of parental alienation to assist his understanding of what might be going on. Robert's participation in the mediation dialogues confirmed an excellent relationship with his father, but also showed that his resistance to contact participation according to parental plans was associated with a heightened sense of anxiety and fear about being separated from his mother for even short periods of time. The mediator suggested to the parents that they might understand Robert's responses in the light of his previous hospitalisations and subsequent fears, rather than in the context of any commencement of an alienation process (for which there seemed little or no evidence). The father was persuaded to explore this idea, and both parents decided to slow down the contact transition for Robert through the father spending an hour with him in the family home on each of the two midweek evenings and two hours in the company of both his parents at the weekend while his brother Tom was playing his football match. Within a six-week period, Robert had fully settled in to the routine of his parent's plan for himself and his brother and appeared to be helped in the management of his anxiety by his mother joining himself, his brother and father for tea in his father's apartment on a couple of occasions. The mother reported feeling very relieved to see exactly where the boys would be sleeping while away from her for the weekend night, and the father managed to keep at bay the critiques of his friend, who wondered what kind of separation this really was 'when you are having your ex-wife over for afternoon tea in your new pad'.

In the context of the emotional turmoil of the separation process, it is easy for a mental health or social care professional to miss the fact that some child and adult responses have much more to do with the heightened sense of anxiety provoked by the context of child contact, rather than being located in consciously held motivations by a resident parent to withhold a child from the care of the other parent. In the example above, the outcome might have been very different had the strength of parental engagement with the mediator arising from the initial meetings not provided sufficient leverage to allow for the exploration of different ideas and behaviours when the crisis came.

Children's Affinity with One Parent: A Scene for Conflict Containment or Escalation

Another type of less severe contact-related parental conflict involves situations where a child, for reasons of age, gender or shared interests over a long period of time, simply wants to spend a lot more time with one parent than another or seems to have a greater *affinity* with one parent than another. These affinity-based parent–child relationships in no way imply a rejection or dislike of the other parent. However, in the immediate aftermath of a painful and contested separation decision, it is unsurprising that such child preferences are experienced by one of the parents as a rejection. Such affinities can often transfer from one parent to another over time as the 'child' goes through preadolescence and adolescence.

Trevor is an only child who 'lived in his father's pocket' since he was six years old. He had played a nightly game of draughts, and later chess, with his father since he was eight years old. Father and son had followed Manchester United football team together since Trevor was seven years and had made several excursions from Dublin to see the team play in Manchester in the company of other boys and their fathers. His mother, a hospital-based nurse with a challenging duty roster, was initially overjoyed to see such bonding between her husband and their son. However, later she felt deeply wounded when, following the couple's separation when Trevor was 12 years, her son wanted to live with his father and spend minimal time with her on her time off. Trevor tried to reassure his mother that he loved her very much, and he spoke with her on the phone several times a day. In the privacy of the broken parental relationship, his mother accused his father of 'not doing enough' to encourage Trevor to spend more time with her, and seemed inconsolable in the context of their first mediation dialogue. The mother's fluctuating expression of intense anger and sadness brought her to the point of making a court application for increased contact, only to withdraw such application at the 11th hour following telephone contact with the mediator, which led to a resumption of the mediation dialogues. Although such continuing dialogues led to a minimal increase at that time in mother–son contact (a one-hour Sunday lunch date squashed in between Trevor's own Sunday morning football and his Sunday afternoon football viewing with father and friends), he made a request to return to live with his mother two years later when he sensed he might have greater freedom to spend more time with his friends while residing with her. Both parents consented to him making this move, and he maintained a very positive relationship with them both as he negotiated ever-increasing amounts of autonomy.

Trevor's parents were on the brink of finding their dispute enter the adversarial process, where others speak on their behalf and they find themselves speaking less and less to each other. This is fertile ground for the development of parental suspicion and with it the possibility, as has been noted (Fidler et al., 2013), of affinity-based disputes developing into alienation or 'justified rejection' (Kelly and Johnston, 2001). Early and effective interventions, including educational interventions and counselling support, are essential if such a conflict development pathway is to be avoided.

Children's Alignment with One Parent: A Scene for Conflict Containment or Escalation

A different kind of contact-related conflict finds its origin in the *alignment* of a child with one parent. Fidler et al. (2013, p. 23) suggest that alignments 'between the child and the preferred parent may develop before, during or after separation because of the other parent's non-existent, interrupted or minimal involvement, or inexperience, or poor parenting, even if these shortcomings do *not* reach the level of abuse or neglect'. Alignments are not about the rejection of a parent by a child, but usually result in a child wanting to spend little or no time after separation in the company of one parent. There is much about contemporary life in the West for some families that gives rise to the possibility of post-separation alignment-based contact disputes mushrooming into extended court-assisted conflicts. I am thinking in particular of those families where one parent's work requires that he travel a great deal and that he has to be 'online' during many of their leisure hours at home to maintain links with colleagues on the other side of the world. Such parents often earn large incomes for their families, who pay an equally large price in terms of parental absence. When separation happens, usually at the initiative of the lonely, left-behind, other parent, what becomes apparent is that the reason the child or children want to spend little or no time in the company of one parent is largely the same reason that the other parent wanted the separation – that is, the travelling partner/parent has had almost no time to nourish or be nourished by the adult–adult or parent–child relationships, and family life increasingly looks like a graveyard of broken promises. One of the reasons such conflicts can have a greater likelihood than affinity-based conflicts of developing into court-assisted 'alienation' cases is that many of the wounded parents have the financial means to engage in protracted court-based struggles, which foster suspicion and hostility between ex-partners. This is the fertile ground in which an alignment with one parent, with its strong emotional base, can transform into a cross-generational coalition (Haley, 1976) against the other parent. Early intervention is critical in these contexts if they are not to deteriorate very rapidly into extensive and long-lasting conflicts. Both therapeutic and mediation initiatives will be needed to assist the parents in making a realistic appraisal of the historical state of parent–child relation-ships in the family and to make modest plans for the maintenance of those relationships in the future.

Gendered Power Dynamics in Contact-related Parental Dispute

Because mental health professionals, for the most part, only enter the arena of a family's post-separation life when a breakdown of some kind occurs within agreed or ordered parent–child contact, it is understandable that professionals focus on finding a solution to the issue as quickly as pos-sible before exiting the situation. The danger of this 'quick-fix' approach, often justified by the issue of cost containment for the family and by being minimally intrusive for the professional, is that mediators or therapists can facilitate a return to the status quo of parent–child contact while failing to address the interactional dynamics between parents that led to the break-down. Regularly these dynamics reflect the power attaching to the parents' respective genders as they attempt to negotiate some matter pertaining to child contact. Elizabeth, Gavey and Tolmie et al. (2012) remind practition-ers that a dynamic of gendered power is always operational in these con-texts regardless of whether practitioners attend to it or not. The following vignette reflects the operation of such a dynamic within a contact handover scene that is so typical that there is unlikely to be a practitioner in the area who does not recognise it.

Ethel and Graham were separated for two years following an eight-year relationship and a seven-year marriage. They had one son, Stuart (six years), who was the subject of a court-ordered contact schedule with his father following his parents' inability to agree contact arrangements after their separation when Stuart was four years. Part of the court-ordered contact schedule involved Stuart coming over to his father's apartment for a two-hour period every Wednesday evening from 5.30 p.m. to 7.30 p.m. The court ordered that Ethel was to bring Stuart over to his father by 5.30 p.m., and Graham was to return him to his mother by 7.30 p.m. Following Graham's repeated lateness home from work on Wednesdays over a four-month period, Ethel decided that she had had enough of waiting lengthy periods (up to 40 minutes) with Stuart in her car, outside Graham's apartment, for her ex-partner to arrive for the commencement of the contact period. Graham had regularly, and without negotiation, extended his contact time beyond 7.30 p.m. to make up for the fact that he had missed some time with Stuart at the start of the period. He never contacted Ethel to let her know he was running late and never answered her calls or texts inquiring where he was when he didn't arrive on time. When Ethel stopped bringing Stuart for the Wednesday contact period, Graham immediately asked his lawyer to re-enter proceedings on the basis of Ethel's breach of the contact order. Following a brief hearing, the family court judge proposed that he would put the matter back for three months on the basis that Stuart's contact period with his father was restored straight away, and he asked both parents if they would be willing to discuss the issues with a mediator in the meantime. Both consented to the court's proposal, and as the weekly mediation dialogues got going in the period immediately following the initial court hearing, Ethel was always present for Stuart to be received by Graham at 5.30 p.m., and Graham was always back from work in time to take Stuart into his care at 5.30 p.m. In the course of the mediation dialogues, the mediator asked Graham why he had been late for the start of the contact period so many times in the past, why he had not made contact with Ethel about either the possibility or probability that he would be late, and why he felt it was okay to extend the contact period beyond 7.30 p.m. without Ethel's agreement and without regard for Stuart's regular midweek bedtime. Graham, whose earnings from his full-time work were about four times the part-time earnings of Ethel, who looked after Stuart once he had completed his school day, replied that he was paying for the roof over Stuart's head and that his work responsibilities had to come first. He went on to assert that it was Ethel's responsibility to make Stuart available to him from 5.30 p.m. and that he was quite entitled to keep Stuart in his care beyond 7.30 p.m. because the court had ordered that he could have Stuart for a two-hour period on Wednesday evening. When the mediator asked Ethel why she felt she had tolerated Graham's lateness for

15 weeks before she stopped bringing Stuart on Wednesday evenings, she replied that she wanted to make it work for Stuart's sake and that she had been afraid of the very thing that did happen – Graham bringing the matter back to court – because she could not afford to pay for legal representation but was not eligible for legal aid. She had only stopped bringing Stuart when she saw how upset he was getting when his father didn't arrive for a long period of time. Further discussion of the issues with the mediator revealed that it was the same kind of interpersonal dynamics that had led Ethel to leave the marriage two years previously, notwithstanding her fears of being unable to cope financially.

In the above vignette, the deployment of differential power attaching to the gendered positions of the mother and father seems clear. The father drew upon discourses of male privilege and entitlement associated with higher levels of income provision within the separated family, to justify having it his own way with respect to the midweek contact period and to keep his partner in a position of subservience. These same discourses allowed him to place his own Wednesday evening contact with his six-year-old son in a superior position to either the child's need to keep to a midweek bedtime routine or his ex-partner's possibility of being able to plan some recreational opportunities for herself in relation to the designated time slot in which the child was not formally in her care. Her assumption, by agreement, of the central role in the ongoing care of their son had implications for her already lesser earning power than that of her ex-partner, who played for four months on her fear of a court hearing she could not afford. Through his non-communication, his persistent lateness and the implied threat of court proceedings, he controlled his ex-partner's sense of herself as a parent who is worthy of the respect of others in her daily management of the child's needs.

It is very likely that busy family law courts addressing a situation such as that described above will take minimal interest in the gendered dynamics of power lying behind the breach of contact orders which brought the matter back to its attention. Indeed, the court and the lawyers representing parents such as those in the vignette are likely to consider the matter resolved once the court's own unaltered orders are once again being complied with, and a child continues to have a relationship with both parents. Information and feedback from mediators and other mental health professionals is unlikely to be sought by courts in the face of apparent resolutions achieved. Both Cooper (1994) and Elizabeth et al. (2012) suggest that what makes fathers' exercise of power possible in situations like those described in the vignette are the continuing gender differences in access to economic power as well as the operation of a patriarchal sociolegal context which facilitates men to exercise power in ways not similarly available to women. An example of this is the way a number of nonresident fathers with orders for child contact exercise their power and control over ex-partner parents by remaining unpredictable with regard to their take-up of such contact on a weekly basis. They may confirm their attendance, but not show up; cancel full weekend contact at the last minute, thus obligating the other parent to cancel his own plans at the last moment; or bring the child back to his primary residence earlier than scheduled. Given that most of such parents have never been physically violent to their ex-partners or their children, many courts are reluctant to suspend the contact that existing orders provide, as they feel such suspension may be injurious to the interests of the child.

So what might assisting mental health professionals do when they observe the exercise of gender-based interactional power at the heart of the production of contact disputes? In this writer's view, the mental health professional should invite participants in the dispute to consider those wider discourses on gender and parenting which shape them both, and to critically reflect on the implications for themselves and their children of continuing to relate to each other under the spell of such discourses. Such dialogues, when they can be realised, are exercises in shared critical reflection (Foucault, 1980) which hold the promise of identifying new and potentially more satisfying ways of relating to both children and ex-partners.

Dilemmas Attaching to Family Court Applications

The separating family in which one parent feels it necessary to make a court application in relation to child matters faces a number of dilemmas. It is easy to forget in the context of ongoing court proceedings that many such parents perceive their post-separation familial conflicts as private matters that are best managed by private resolutions. It is usually when the more 'private' efforts of direct interpersonal negotiation and confidential mediation have failed to achieve resolution that the more 'public' arena of family court hearings becomes the reluctantly chosen route towards settlement of the dispute. However, in making a decision to invoke the assistance of the courts, two key things happen. The first is that parents depart from their shared role as problem-solvers in their own dispute and enter a new arena as adversaries before the court who will impose a settlement in the disputed matter following a hearing in which both 'sides' have the opportunity to put their case. The second thing that happens is that the parents, who have now become the 'parties' to the 'proceedings', begin to have gathered around them a system of judges (there may be more than one judge as the proceedings go up and down different levels of a court system), family lawyers, professional witnesses and other 'lay' supporters. This is a group of individuals who all have their own legitimate interests and roles both in relation to and within the proceedings. The whole process of involvement in this now wider system of conflict management fosters a 'black and white' approach to matters in dispute. Often the disputed matters are written about for the first time in legal 'affidavits' which are exchanged between the two sets of legal teams. These affidavits constitute a particular type of legal narrative which selectively 'remembers' some events while 'forgetting' others (Ricoeur, 2004). Ney, Blank and Blank (2007) have examined the way that a language emanating from a privileged legal discourse is used in affidavits to both construct and escalate conflict between parents with long-term consequences for family relationships. The opposing perspectives, now fixed for the first time in such legally written documents, generally foster an immediate sense of anger and outrage in both parents, who turn further away from each other, while they turn more and more towards others for support and representation in the face of developing hostilities.

The term *juridogenic* has been used by a judicial participant in a recent study (Fidler et al., 2013, p. 26) of child resistance to post-separation parental contact to denote 'the damage the court process can do without any intention of doing harm, simply because the procedure goes on too long or because wrong turns have been taken along the road'. A less benign perspective is offered by Ney (2015), who challenges a key assumption embedded in many of our different Western practices for engaging conflict – namely, that the disputants are responsible for their own conflict. Following the perspective of Cloke (2001), she suggests that in many situations it is the 'rational-legal institutions we rely on to do our conflict business', rather than individuals, that may be causing and sustaining our conflicts (Ney, 2015, p. 177). Whatever levels of responsibility we apportion between the parties to a dispute and the legal/judicial systems that surround them for the promotion of family-specific conflict cultures, it is clear that entry into the family court system as a dispute resolution framework further polarises the parties in conflict and raises the intensity levels through which conflict is performed by several degrees. In the short term, however, the very setting in motion of proceedings can act as a brake on the further escalation of family conflict as parents are warned by their lawyers to be 'on their best behaviour' in advance of the court's hearing of their case. Such conflict containment effect can be short-lived, however, once parents realise the modest amount the court system has to offer dispute resolution.

Managing Child and Adolescent Participation in Family Mediation

Several writers (Folger and Jones, 1994; Windslade and Cotter, 1997) over the last 25 years have noted the growing popularity of mediation as a preferred avenue for post-separation family conflict resolution in many contemporary Western jurisdictions. Some jurisdictions impose a level of no-charge mandatory mediation before entry to the family court system becomes admissible, whereas in others the provision of no-charge voluntary family mediation services is available on a wide basis. Alongside this societal impetus towards mediation is a growing appreciation that childhood and adolescence are changing phenomena. Children and adolescents have become the bearers of rights and entitlements of different kinds. One of these entitlements gradually being written in to the legislation of many Western states is the right to have a participatory 'voice' in the decision-making processes about matters where their interests are at stake. Family post-separation conflict resolution processes are one example of an arena in which professionals have become increasingly obliged to find ways to facilitate child and/or adolescent participation. Where 50 years ago children were seen and not heard, now they are heard often and not seen as much. However, if child-inclusive practices (McIntosh and Long, 2006; McIntosh, Wells, Smyth, and Long, 2008) are becoming more the norm in family mediation, this does not mean that the pragmatic achievement of such practice norms is without its challenges and dilemmas.

Assessing Parental Positions Regarding Child Participation in Mediation

Family mediation can be regarded as a series of differently connected dialogues between different groups of family members in which different kinds of negotiation take place (Sheehan, 2016a). And the pragmatics of a child-inclusive family mediation process is necessarily linked to the way in which the mediation participants 'position' themselves around the question of child participation. One of the first tasks of the mediating mental health professional in this context is to assess and acknowledge the positions of each parent and child/adolescent about the question of their inclusion while being clear with everyone involved about their own position. In this writer's practice experience as a mediator, five basic but different parental positions about the inclusion of their children and adolescents in the mediation process emerge. It must be emphasised that these are commencing positions that can, and often do, alter as the dynamic process of mediation evolves.

The first position is where *both* parents *want* child participation. The second parental position is where *neither parent wants* this participation. The third position is where *one parent wants* child participation while the *other parent doesn't want* this participation. The fourth position is where the parents *want some children* involved, but not others. The fifth position is where the parents are open to child participation, but not during the early phases of the process. There are, perhaps, variations on each of these positions that readers will note for themselves.

Whatever positions the parents take up about this question of child participation, the early part of the mediation dialogue with them will aim to clarify both with them and between them the meaning of the positions they have taken up. This stage of the dialogue can also provide an opportunity for them to reconsider their positions on the matter. It is also a time for the mediator to confirm for the parents that although mediation is not a therapy, it is not without its therapeutic characteristics and that as mediator he or she has a responsibility to protect, contain and support all participating family members in the context of their age, developmental stage and unique set of concerns. This initial phase of the dialogue normally includes, where parents are open to this, a negotiation of contact for the mediator with the child/children for a consultation about their possible participation. The mediator also recognises, with the parents, that the process at that point is just at the 'talks about talks' stage. This phase of the dialogue also gives the mediator an initial flavour of the form and structure of the family as they approach conflict negotiation efforts. In other words, parental reports about the post-separation family dynamic provide the mediator with an indication regarding where the strong relational alliances currently exist within the family and whether such alliances are of relatively recent duration, perhaps having grown out of the conflict dynamics associated with the separation, or reflect much longer-standing patterns of family relationship.

Child Consultation about Participation in the Mediation Process

Meeting with children to discuss their possible participation affords the mediating mental health professional the opportunity to engage the children and offer them some initial support in the process. It is also an opportunity for the mediator to assess the children's perception regarding the safety of their possible participation and a beginning opportunity for them to express something of their experience within the unfolding family conflict and about their wishes and fears regarding the future. The central purpose of the child consultation, however, is to help children clarify what their position might be about their participation. Allied to this clarification is a 'negotiation' about the kind of confidentiality they require in order to feel safe and protected in the process.

In this writer's practice experience with a child-inclusive mediation process, *eight* different child/adolescent positions about their participation emerge. These positions can, and often do, evolve over the course of the mediation process. The *first* of these positions is where the child/adolescent wants involvement from the beginning and expects her 'voice' to be the basis of future reality. The mediator will already be assessing whether such positioning has been promoted in the child by one of the two parents or represents a sense of entitlement that has grown out of a certain kind of joint parenting. The mediator might attempt to moderate this expectation in the child by noting the difference between her having a 'voice' in the process, which is her entitlement, and having a 'choice', which might have to be negotiated with both her parents. A *second* position is expressed by the child who *fears* involvement because she fears rejection by one of her parents if her views and wishes were to become known. A *third* position is reflected in a child's wish to be involved *so long as her parents never hear her views*. These two positions are closely connected to each other, and the second can evolve into the third once the child receives some reassurances from the mediator. In the *fourth* position, the child wants to be involved because she wants to know what is going on so that she can prepare herself for the future, but she is not really sure she wants a voice in the process. A *fifth* position is reflected in a child who wants to be involved with the specific intention of trying to stop the separation process. The following case vignette exemplifies a child in this position and demonstrates how mediation dialogues can have a skill-building focus deployed in the interests of satisfactory resolution.

Sue and John were both in their early forties and sought the assistance of a mediator in the context of the breakdown of their relationship. They both were high-income earners working in the area of financial services. John's work brought him regularly from his work base in Dublin to New York, where his employing company had another base. He developed a relationship there with a work colleague and announced to Sue that he intended to live in New York with his female work colleague and her two children, whose father also lived in the New York area. Sue and John had told their 11-year-old son, Jack, about the impending separation and had sought the mediator's assistance in trying to work out an agreement between them regarding Jack's future contact with his father in both Dublin and New York. John wanted to have Jack visit him in New York almost immediately following the date he had planned to take up co-residence with his new partner, which was three months from the date of the first mediation dialogue. Sue was not in agreement with the timing of this visitation schedule but was not, in principle, against Jack having contact in New York at some point in the future. Both parents were in agreement with the mediator's proposal to have Jack participate in the dialogues if he wanted this. Jack was very clear with both parents that he wanted to participate. At the first child consultation, Jack told the mediator about how shocked and upset he was that his father was going to be leaving. He described how close he had been to his father, who brought him to his football training every week when he was in Dublin and always came to his Sunday football matches while his mother had a Sunday morning rest in bed. They had had this routine for the previous six years. His father had also brought him to school two mornings per week. He told the mediator that he felt the whole thing was really unfair and that he didn't want his father to go. The mediator asked Jack if he would be willing, with his help, to express some of his views in a way that his parents could hear. Jack agreed, and the mediator, in a session with Jack and his parents, asked the parents just to listen carefully to Jack as he facilitated him in the expression of his shock and his fears. Both parents listened well to Jack, and when all three returned for a further appointment the next week, John reported that he had not anticipated Jack being so upset about the separation. In the light of this upset, he had decided to postpone for one year the date of his full transfer to New York, to give Jack more time to get used to the idea. He was, nonetheless, firm with Jack about the fact that he would be moving to New York. Jack was pleased and relieved at this development, and within a few weeks he was, at the mediator's suggestion, practising having Skype calls with his father between their respective bedrooms and beginning, at his father's suggestion, to make a weekly visit to his paternal grandmother who lived nearby and alone. He became an active participant with his mother and father in the plans for his ongoing contact with his father once New York became the place of his father's residence. When he had returned from a two-week summer holiday alone with his father, about seven months after the mediation began, Jack unexpectedly announced to his parents that he was now ready for his dad to go and live in New York. His mother was content with the plans all three of them had made together for the gradual phasing in of Jack's contact with father in New York and with his father's plan to ensure Jack would not feel 'swallowed up in a new family' by having to spend too much of his New York time in the company of his new partner's children.

In the above vignette, the mediator focussed on the additional skills (Skype calls) and resources (emotional support from paternal grandmother) some family members might need to help them come through the experiences they have to face. In the *sixth* position, most often taken up by adolescents, the young person says to her parents that she only wants to be involved in mediation to signal her own priorities. A regular presentation within this position is when the young person says that she does not really care how her parents work out the details of the separation so long as she is able to still see her friends four times a week. She has no real interest in participating beyond making this indication of her desires. A *seventh* position is where the young person is clear with her parents about not wanting to be involved at all. This can sometimes be a way of her saying to her parents: 'This is your decision to separate. So now take the responsibility yourselves for working out all the details'. An *eighth* and final position can be where a child or young person indicates that she wants to be involved, but not alongside her siblings. This position often alerts the mediator to the fact that the performance of the family conflict up to that point has brought about a split in the sibling subsystem, reflecting the depth of the split in the parental subsystem. Although the mediator will work towards an agreement between the central parties to the conflict, she will do so with a central eye on how the negotiated future contact arrangements protect both sibling bonds and parent–child attachments.

The Perceived Integrity of the Mediator: Negotiating Confidentiality

Successful mediation with families in post-separation conflict depends upon many different things. One of the most important of these is the continuing perception by different family members of the mediator as a person and professional of integrity. When child or adolescent participation occurs in mediation dialogues, one of the places where this perception can be most threatened is in the maintenance of the 'deals' the mediator makes with different subgroups of the family. If the mediator makes a deal with the parents that the voice of a child can be kept confidential from the parents, then the mediator must live up to that deal with both parents and child. That means being straight with a child that if she does not want her parents to know about her positions on different matters, there is a limit to how much the mediator can do to help her achieve some of her goals. It also means being firm with parents who may give several rationales for the mediator to breach their agreement with the child about confidentiality and to 'spill the beans' about the child's position to them. Parents need to be reassured that they are doing something positive for their child by facilitating her participation, even if they never hear directly the child's views. Very often a child just needs to express some of her feelings about the separation without the burden of having to cope with her parents' responses to those feelings. The issue remains, however, of how the mediator uses, in her dialogues with parents, information and views expressed in confidence by the child in child consultations while maintaining her integrity with all involved. One way of working out this dilemma facing mediating mental health professionals is to allow themselves to use the themes emerging from the confidential child consultation to provide additional foci to the parental consultations. This means asking parents to focus on some themes relevant to the child that they may have overlooked, without divulging the child's position on the themes in question. A further challenge arises should the child give the mediator permission not to retain confidentiality in relation to some matters, but insist that it be retained in relation to others. All of such challenges mean that the mediator must take great care of the agreed 'confidences' as they move from one mediation dialogue to another in the context of a total process aimed at workable resolutions for the future.

Skills and Interventions

This chapter has considered a broad range of themes that emerge for the mental health and social care professional when post-separation parental disputes occur over child contact. These themes suggest the need for a skill set that relates to such different settings as therapeutic intervention, mediation dialogues that are child-inclusive and family court-based responses to dispute resolution. This skill set includes a range of both assessment and intervention skills. The following six skills are central to the mental health professional's capacity to respond effectively to parents and children caught in contact-related post-separation disputes:

(i) *The capacity to assess the specific character of child reluctance to parent contact proposals.* This capacity refers to the professional's ability to tune in to the unique character of a child's resistance to a certain kind of parental contact proposed by others for her. In particular, it refers to the capacity to gain access to sufficient information about current and past family relationships to allow her to distinguish between child resistances/reluctances based upon separation anxiety, parent–child affinity and parent–child alignment. This skill is intimately connected to the skill proposed in Chapter 7, where the professional needs to be able to distinguish each of these three contexts of reluctance from reluctances which relate to parental alienation or to what has been referred to by Kelly and Johnston (2001) as 'justified rejection', which refers to a child's rejection of a parent based upon real experiences of abuse, neglect or poor parental behaviour.

(ii) *The capacity to identify different cultural discourses embedded in parental dispute about child contact and to consider how they themselves and the conflict participants are positioned within the sets of power relations flowing through such discourses.*

(iii) *The capacity to reflect on the gendered power dynamics operating within both the conflict participants' relationship around their dispute and the professional's relationship with the conflict participants.*

(iv) *The capacity to assess the history and nature of intimate partner violence or family violence in contexts of dispute about post-separation parent–child contact.* This assessment skill relies heavily upon the mental health professional's ability to facilitate different members of a family – adults and children – in the safe telling of their violence-related experiences and in the safe exploration of what these experiences have done to each of them, whether they were perpetrators of these acts or witnesses of different kinds to such acts. It also means exploring the positive sides of the history of parent–child and adult–adult relationships. The skill means having the capacity to assess the veracity of the different stories told and to keep the present and future safety and well-being of all family members to the forefront of professional thinking at all times. It means attempting to identify and distinguish the different types of violence and aggression that may have occurred and to assess the *risk* of reoccurrence of any such acts in the context of different child contact proposals being made. Embedded in this skill is the capacity to *listen well* to stories of real life events that may have had a traumatic impact on the narrators.

(v) *The capacity to distinguish between different parent and child positions in relation to child-inclusive mediation.*

(vi) *The capacity to articulate for parents and children the mediator's own position in relation to child participation and how this might evolve in response to the changing positions of family members throughout the mediation process.*

The mental health professional needs the capacity to move fluently between parent and child consultations at the commencement of the family mediation process and to facilitate all participants in clarifying the position they wish to adopt with respect to child participation. This skill implies facilitating the negotiation of confidentiality between the subgroups in the family during the mediation process and the capacity to recognise when issues of confidentiality need to be renegotiated.

Personal and Reflective Exercises

Write some notes for yourself in response to each of the following four questions. If you are doing this exercise alone, come back to your responses about a week after you have made your notes, and make some additional notes arising from any reflections you may have had in the meantime. If you are doing this exercise as part of a class group, you should allow yourself to share as little or as much as you want from your responses to the questions with a class colleague.

1. Were you ever a personal participant in a post-separation dispute about a child's contact with a nonresident parent? If you were, write an account of this dispute from the perspective of another person directly involved in the dispute – that is, from the perspective of a child or parent other than yourself. If you have never been a participant in such a dispute, try to recall your first experience, professionally or among your wider circle of friends and relatives, of such a dispute, and write some notes for yourself about this experience. What impression did this experience make upon you?
2. Imagine you are the resident parent of a ten-year-old girl whose nonresident other parent has her for a contact period every week, from Saturday at 6 p.m, to Sunday at 6 p.m, since you separated one year ago. Write some notes about what you most deeply fear might happen for your daughter in the context of such contact.
3. Imagine you are a 12-year-old boy, the eldest of three male siblings, whose parents have just told you that they are separating and that your father will be leaving shortly to live in the next town, which is one hour away from where you now live. Write some notes, as if in the personal diary of this boy, about the range of thoughts and feelings you imagine might belong to such a boy in this context.
4. Which of the vignettes described in this chapter moved you most? Why do you think this was?

DOMESTIC ABUSE/VIOLENCE IN THE CONTEXT OF CHILD CONTACT DISPUTES

The general approach in this text has been to offer the mental health and social care professional a broad overview of the whole sweep of themes, challenges and interventions relating to contemporary post-separation family conflict and its management. The advantage of this approach is that it provides a window on pathways of post-separation family conflict progression while revealing some important connections between many themes at the heart of the topic. The limitation of such an approach, however, is that it sacrifices something with respect to the depth and variation belonging to each individual theme. Such limitation is nowhere more evident than in the current chapter addressing the theme of domestic abuse and violence, as it relates to the management of post-separation disputes about child contact. What is offered here is an introduction to a theme that is revisited a number of times in the chapters ahead. The approach is to focus on the key aspects of the territory of domestic abuse and violence as it is met by mental health and social care professionals in the context of post-separation family conflict. Following a brief historical note, this chapter commences with a description of the range of behaviours that are part of different kinds of domestic violence and abuse. The chapter then moves on to consider some of the challenges met in the assessment of situations where domestic violence and abuse have been alleged in contexts of post-separation dispute regarding child contact, and concludes with a review of the outcome choices available to practitioners, judiciary and families arising from such court-ordered evaluations.

Historical Recognition of Domestic Violence and Abuse

In approaching this topic the practitioner needs to remind himself where his own society is located within the history of recognition of domestic violence or abuse. Many Western societies have gone through significant transformations in this process of recognition over the last 50 years. However, the pace of this transformation has varied in different societies. Despite these variations in pace, the last half century has seen domestic violence move from being perceived almost exclusively as a private family matter towards its contemporary status as a criminal offence. Fifty years ago victims were unlikely to report domestic violence incidents to law enforcement agents, as they would have had little or no expectation of receiving a sympathetic or protective response. This did not mean that there were no controls operational at that time. In some societies, the controls were informal rather than formal and often operated through the actions of extended family members who applied different forms of summary justice to violent spouses. In other words, domestic violence was responded to by extended family violence, which sometimes achieved its aim of halting the aggression and, at other times, merely drove violence and abuse underground.

As we approach the end of the second decade of the twenty-first century, a great many societies have evolved legislation which allows for the speedier protection of victims and prosecution of offenders. A mixture of increased awareness and training among police officers, judiciary, lawyers and mental health and social care professionals has led to the development of a range of emergency refuge and assistance programs, family courts dedicated solely to addressing contexts of domestic violence, therapeutic services for victims and their children traumatised by domestic violence, as well as treatment programs for violent offenders. Practitioners know, however, that cultural attitudes to domestic violence and its reporting change at a slower pace than it takes to erect buildings to house new services and specialist courts. For this reason, practitioners must keep in mind the range of emotions and feelings such as fear, shame and embarrassment that still make it difficult for victims of domestic violence and abuse to either report their experiences to authorities or to speak about them in the contexts of therapy, mediation or court-ordered evaluations. Adults and children who may have suffered domestic abuse of different kinds need to be able to speak about their experience in the knowledge that they will be supported and protected in the process and consequences of their telling. Whether in the context of counselling, mediation or evaluation dialogues, one way of making it more possible for adults and children to speak of domestic abuse events is for the professional to ask directly, but sympathetically, if any such events might have been part of their experience in times of family trouble.

The Range of Domestic Abuse Behaviours and Experiences

Domestic violence and abuse encompass a wide range of different behaviours in different contexts. Although there has been a recognition that a lack of consensus on definitions relating to a group of related terms (e.g. domestic violence, battering, intimate partner violence, family violence, domestic abuse) has slowed down the development of legislation, research and treatment services for victims and those who abuse (Barocas, Emery and Mills, 2016), the approach adopted here is to describe the range of behaviours practitioners are likely to hear reported in the contexts in which they meet this multifaceted phenomenon. The broad categories of these behaviours include physical violence, emotional abuse, sexual violence and coercion, financial abuse and coercive control.

The *physical abuse* of a partner can include striking with objects, punching, hitting, slapping, hair pulling, scratching and scraping, pushing, kicking, pinching, burning, slamming doors in their face, throwing objects at them, pinning them up against a wall, pushing them down stairs and dragging them out of a bed or along a floor. Victims can receive multiple and different physical and psychological injuries from any of these behaviours, and some victims pay the ultimate price of their lives. Violent partners, when asked to account for their behaviour, may either deny their aggression completely or minimise significantly both the extent of its occurrence and its possible consequences. Practitioners, however, need to keep in mind that it is not only physically abusive partners who deny or minimise the consequences of abusive behaviour; victims, for a different set of reasons, may also deny the impact of what they have suffered at their partner's hands.

In a session on her own with a family counsellor, Marie, a 40-year-old mother of four children under ten years, admitted that she had received 'a box or two' recently from her male partner who was the father of her three youngest children. When the male counsellor had clarified that she was talking about receiving punches to the face for which she had decided not to seek medical assistance, he asked her about the impact she thought receiving these 'boxes' had upon her. Marie replied as follows: 'Well, it wasn't too bad, really. Just the result of a few drinks too many. I didn't go out of the house for a couple of days. But it gave me a chance to finish the cardigan I was knitting for my mother. My mother had her cardigan for Christmas! Every cloud, you could say, has a kind of silver lining'.

Victims of physical abuse often feel a sense of shame, embarrassment and humiliation arising from their experience. This means that practitioners need to provide enough support, time and patience within the right setting (not with their partners!) to enable someone who has suffered the trauma of physical abuse at the hands of her partner to speak about her experience in her own way and at her own pace.

Although physical abuse carries with it the risk for victims of serious injury and even fatality, *emotional abuse* does its damage by assaulting the very spirit of a victim. It can, like physical abuse, be episodic in nature, and there may sometimes be lengthy abuse-free periods between incidents. Or it can be relatively unremitting in its presence as it gradually grinds down a victim by undermining her self-confidence, her competence and her self-worth. When making an assessment of parenting in post-separation contact disputes, practitioners need to keep in mind that poor parenting skills observed in a victim parent may be the result of prolonged emotional abuse by an ex-partner rather than a reflection of inherent parenting deficits. Some patterns of emotional abuse contain explicit or implicit threats of physical abuse such that victims live in a state of constant fear and anxiety for themselves and their children. Other patterns of emotional abuse contain no such threats. More regular forms of emotional abuse of partners include name-calling, shouting aggressively at them, giving them the 'silent' treatment by refusing to talk with them at all, or constantly criticising them in relation to their parenting practices, their lack of income generation, their physical appearance and weight, their cooking or their manner of completing household tasks. Emotional abuse can operate outside the household when one partner constantly puts the other down in front of others, friends or family, or repeatedly tells stories to others in front of her about her alleged ignorance or incompetence. It can also take the form of refusing to be accountable to a partner with respect to sharing the burdens of parenting or by refusing to let the other person know when he is available to assume his share of parenting responsibilities, thus limiting the partner's freedom.

Sexual violence and coercion is a third form of domestic violence and abuse. In cultures which strongly value the privacy surrounding couple sexual matters, and where adults generally find it challenging to speak about sex and/or sexual health matters even to healthcare professionals, it can be monumentally difficult for victims to report to any external authority rape or other sexual assault incidents from within their couple life (Clinton-Sherrod and Walters, 2011). The recognition of marital rape as a criminal offence has been on the statute books of different states for different lengths of time. Consequently, levels of awareness of sexual violence within intimate partner and spousal relationships differ from place to place and from one group of mental health and social care workers to another. Some writers (e.g. Augustine, 1991) have suggested that slowly evolving cultural attitudes to the private character of marriage have allowed it to function as a cloak behind which the sexually violent could hide.

The spectrum of behaviours underlying sexual violence and coercion within intimate partner relationships includes rape; forcing a partner to endure different kinds of physical violence and aggression while being raped; forcing a partner to have sex in ways that only satisfy the desires of the abusive partner; forcing a partner to engage in sexual practices experienced by them as degrading or humiliating; forcing a partner to engage in prostitution or in sexual activity that includes another person or persons; forcing a partner to observe them engaging in sexual activity with another person; coercing a partner into watching pornography or engaging in cybersex activity; or following them around the house, harassing them for sexual engagement. Readers will be able to supplement this initial list of behaviours for themselves. Where individuals report incidents of physical abuse by an ex-partner during court-ordered residence and contact evaluations it is important that the mental health professional makes a space for stories of sexual violence and/or coercion to be told if the person wishes to do so. Often a simple question like the following can give a victim of abuse the permission to report something more of their troubled experience: 'Can I ask you if the physical aggression and violence of your ex-partner that you have been speaking about ever spilled over into that intimate or sexual part of your lives?' Male professionals need to be particularly careful with female abuse victims, who may want to speak about experiences of sexual violence and coercion but may find it too difficult to engage in such telling with a male. Where the professional senses that this might be the case, he can follow up with questions such as the following: 'I am wondering, Ann, what it might be like for you to move into this conversation with me as a man? Would this have an impact on how much of your experience you would feel able to share or on the way you might like to share it?' Depending on the outcome of these initial exchanges about the topic, a male professional might discuss with the person the idea of having a female colleague present, having the abuse victim's own female support person present, having a female colleague conduct a single consultation alone with the abuse victim or simply proceeding with the conversation about this part of their experience.

Financial abuse is a further form of domestic abuse and can take on many different faces. It can operate through withholding information about family finances or giving false information about family finances such that a parent is constantly worried and anxious about the immediate and future material welfare of herself and her children. It can mean unnecessarily restricting a partner's access to money such that she doesn't have any resources to attend to her personal needs. Or it can mean leaving a partner/parent without any money on some days of the week while the abusive partner uses family income to take care of his own material and recreational needs outside the home. In such circumstances, the victim of financial abuse is often forced to borrow or beg from family members or friends to meet her own and her children's basic survival needs. At other times, financial abuse takes the form of spending significant portions of family income or savings without the knowledge and/or consent of the other person. It can mean forcing a partner to sign financial documents without giving her an opportunity to understand the consequences of what she is being 'asked' to do. For the parent/victim of financial abuse, the price exacted is often having to live with a constant sense of anxiety and insecurity regarding her own and her children's future.

The final form of domestic abuse is that of persistent *controlling behaviour*. Although this category of abuse has much in common with some other forms of abuse, it is distinguished by the abuser's attempt to restrict her partner's freedom to exercise choice in an ever-expanding number of life's spheres. It can take the form of controlling *where* the partner buys food for the family or insisting that only certain food items be purchased and setting the price level beyond which they should not be purchased ('I told you never to buy a packet of cornflakes for more than a euro'). It can mean forbidding the partner to bring their joint children to visit grandparents and extended family or controlling contact with siblings or friends. It can sometimes take the form of restricting the work-related socialising the partner is permitted to engage in, resulting in a gradual cutting off of friendships and relationships. It can mean insisting that the partner cut her ties with local sporting and community associations, thus fostering a growing social isolation of the victim. It can also mean forcing the partner to have a termination against their will. Although the intrapsychic aspects of the controlling person's motivation to control may be multiple and varied, the outcome for the victim is usually an evaporation of self-confidence and a gradual feeling of being unable to make choices even if she had the freedom to do so. Or she may deny the significance of her partner's behaviour and tell herself that the control needs to happen because she is simply not a capable parent and would not be able to make the 'right' decisions.

Assessing Reports of Domestic Abuse/Violence in Residence and Contact Disputes

One of the more challenging tasks faced by the mediator or assessor in both child residence and contact disputes is the understanding and assessment of allegations and counter-allegations of domestic violence and abuse. The work of assessing such allegations must be done carefully and methodically by the practitioner/assessor, as its outcome information is often relied upon heavily by the court in its decision-making process about child contact. It may be tempting, but is always an error to rush the completion of such assessment in the face of legal practitioners' anxiety to have a case fully prepared for a fixed hearing date. In making such an assessment, three questions are to the forefront of the assessor's mind. Firstly, the assessor will be interested in the *nature* of the incidents of domestic violence and abuse being reported by one or both adult participants and by involved children and/or adolescents. Secondly, the assessment will be oriented towards understanding the *pattern* underlying reported abuse behaviours. And, finally, an assessment must be made of the *risk* attaching to these behaviours given that some behaviours may be more closely associated than others with the possibility of serious injury and/or the death of a child or parent.

The validity of different claims is always at the centre of evaluation dialogues about alleged domestic abuse. Although the assessor may note that there is independent, corroborating evidence from police, hospital and medical records concerning some claims about which one of the partners may accept culpability, there are other claims which remain contested with respect to whether an incident occurred or not, the nature of the alleged incident and its severity. Where there is no corroborating evidence, and this is very often the case in many allegations of domestic abuse, the assessor must arrive at a conclusion regarding contested claims on the basis of probability. In other words, the assessor will be asking himself whether, in the light of the full range of information provided in the assessment, it is likely that an alleged incident happened at all or happened in the way it has been reported. In this process of assessing probability, the assessor may look for information from third parties connected with the participants, but the pursuit of such avenues brings with it the added responsibility to assess the reliability of these informants in the context of the positions they may continue to hold within the broader relational network of the separated couple.

Understanding the pattern of domestic abuse incidents may not always prove challenging for the assessor. This may be because the nature of the reported abuse was relatively mild and the pattern was of short duration, perhaps limited to one or two crisis points in the pre-separation period. It may be that both partners' description of incidents proves to be broadly the same. In such contexts, the information about domestic abuse may have little or no bearing on decisions about post-separation child contact, even when it may have a bearing on the recommendations made to a parent for addressing the manner in which she copes with personal crises. However, the practitioner assessor needs to keep in mind that patterns of abusive behaviour can change over time in response to different kinds of external stressors such as the loss of employment or the death of a parent. Under certain circumstances a pattern of episodic, highly infrequent, mildly abusive behaviours in the first decade of a relationship can later evolve into a pattern of more persistently abusive behaviours of a more serious kind. Understanding the linkage of such changes in pattern to possible changes in the levels of consumption of alcohol or other substances in one or both partners may be pertinent in some assessments.

The assessor must also guard against a too easy acceptance of a reported pattern where one parent tries to promote a picture of historical domestic violence as one of mutual violent combat (Howard-Bostic, 2013) in which both partners were equally responsible for incidents in which it is alleged that each 'gave as good as they got'. Although it may be the case that both partners committed acts of violence on each other, it may be that one of the partners was clearly the primary aggressor while the other partner's violence was quantitatively far less and, for the most part, emerged in self-defence. Busy family law courts can be encouraged by some lawyers to ignore the relevance of domestic violence on the basis that 'there's clearly two of them in it' and to proceed to foreground the importance for a child of having a continuing relationship with both parents. In determining the validity of claims around particular incidents, the assessor will normally accomplish this not just by listening to the contested reports of the incidents them-selves, but through a broadly based relational assessment of the partners across many facets of their shared life. This broadly based relational assess-ment is more likely to bring out features of domestic abuse that either one or both of the partners had discounted in the face of their demand that the assessor focus solely on one or two incidents that appeared 'to break the camel's back'. One important part of assessing patterns of abuse con-cerns mapping the timing of occurrence of abuse incidents with crises in the mental health of one or both ex-partners. Although the issues pertaining to mental health crises receive more specific treatment in the final chapter of this text, it needs to be noted here that the assessment of domestic abuse allegations must take account of the unique way in which patterns sur-rounding substance abuse and mental health crises in either or both parents may be linked to patterns of unilateral or bilateral domestic violence.

Hans, Haselschwerdt, Hardesty and Frey (2014), in the context of a large study (sample of 607 custody evaluators) examining the effects of domestic violence allegations on custody evaluators recommendations, found that evaluators are more likely to recommend joint custody where counter-allegations of violence are made by the second parent, who is often the father. They contend that mental health professionals, when acting in the role of residence and contact evaluators, need to be sufficiently sensitised to distinguish between situational couple violence and the more persistently coercive and controlling behaviour of one member of the couple. Their study found that most court-appointed evaluators were not equipped to make the distinction between these different contexts of violence, and that this gap was likely to jeopardise the post-separation safety of some parents and children.

Part of the assessment of pattern is the assessment of whether children have been exposed to the abuse and violence between their parents. A variety of studies have confirmed the negative impact that exposure to parental violence can have on many aspects of children's functioning and that this impact can continue to make its presence felt as the child grows into adolescence and young adulthood – in other words, often for many years after the violence has stopped. Sternberg, Caradaran, Abbott, Lamb and Guterman (2006), for example, have shown that children exposed to intimate partner violence exhibit higher than average rates of cognitive, psychological and emotional impairments and that those affected most frequently experience difficulties in their behavioural, emotional and cognitive functioning. Other studies show that children exposed to intimate partner violence show relatively lower levels of social competence than others in the same age group (Koutselini and Valanidou, 2014; Overlien, 2010). Yet other studies have shown that exposed children exhibit aggressive, antisocial, fearful and inhibited behaviours at higher rates than other children (Moylan et al., 2010; Sousa et al., 2011). With respect to more serious symptomatology, children exposed to intimate partner violence have been shown to exhibit higher rates of depression, anxiety and symptoms of post-traumatic stress disorder (Garrido, Culhane, Petrenko and Taussig, 2011; Overlien, 2010). Huang, Vikse, Lu and Silai (2015) note that the combined psychosocial effects of children's exposure to intimate partner violence often manifest later in negative behavioural outcomes that include violence, substance use and delinquency. However, they also point to important research findings which demonstrate that the negative effects of early trauma due to exposure are not necessarily permanent and can be moderated, if not reversed, by the provision of the right kind of support and education for both parents and children (Carpenter and Stacks, 2009; Cook et al., 2005; O'Brien, Cohen,

Pooley and Taylor, 2013). Such findings are a sign of hope in the middle of a very worrying picture about the impact on children and adolescents of exposure to intimate partner violence. But they also point to the important role mental health professionals can play in these circumstances through the accessing of appropriate educational and therapeutic opportunities for parents and children.

In assessing the risk arising from reports of domestic abuse, the mental health professional will be interested in such matters as the nature of the abuse reported, whether the abuse of one partner by another has been carried out without consideration for the presence of a child witness, as well as the nature of injuries already received by an adult or child as a result of abuse. In assessing risk associated with domestic abuse behaviours, the practitioner will also be looking for the presence or absence of factors in the context that may be closely associated with lethality. Jaffe, Crooks and Bala (2009), arising from their consideration of domestic violence research and the findings of domestic violence death review committees (Campbell, 1995; Campbell et al., 2001; Ellis and Stuckless, 2006; Hilton et al., 2004; Kropp, Hart, Webster and Eaves, 1994, 2000), suggest that factors commonly associated with lethal outcomes include separation where there has been a history of domestic violence, the availability of firearms, substance abuse, controlling and stalking behaviour, threats of murder or suicide, and noncompliance with previous court orders. Although the assessor must keep one eye on this research, they will always be oriented towards the assessment of risks arising for unique children and parents in the context of their unique histories, settings and relationships and in the context of uniquely projected contact situations.

Assessment Outcomes in Child Contact Dispute Where Domestic Abuse/Violence Is Alleged

Good assessments are like small pieces of qualitative research in that they must always be oriented by the questions in whose service they are made. In contact disputes where allegations of domestic violence and abuse are present, assessors should be asking themselves the following questions. Is there anything about the patterns of abuse reported that might make it physically, emotionally or sexually unsafe for a particular child to have contact with a parent seeking such contact? Might it be in the child's interest to have continuing contact with this parent even if there is some level of risk to their safety in certain dimensions? What might be done to make contact as safe as possible for the child should it be considered that it is in his interests to maintain contact with a nonresident parent? Might the risks to the child's safety under, any possible conditions be such that the risks outweigh the potential benefits for the child? How has the child processed his reactions to news, or experience, of domestic abuse between the parents? Who might have been involved in assisting the child to process this news and experience? Has the child memories of pleasant, nurturing experiences in the care of the parent seeking contact, and can these experiences be confirmed by any independent observers? It is the answer to these and other questions arising out of the assessment process that shape the advice offered to a court in any particular contact application.

When all the relevant questions have been explored through the lens of the assessment information and findings, there are only five basic outcomes for child contact. These include no contact; contact; supervised contact; accompanied contact; and therapeutic contact. Both assessor recommendations and court orders may be time-limited with respect to any of these outcomes. A court may decide that at the time of hearing there is no likely benefit to a child from contact with a nonresident parent with a significant history of abusive behaviour and poor parenting, but may indicate its willingness to reconsider the matter following participation by that parent in specified treatment and educational programs. Or it may decide that a normal level of contact should be maintained following an assessment that fails to confirm allegations of domestic abuse. Supervised contact may be ordered when it is judged that the child will benefit developmentally in the short and long term from a continuing relationship with a nonresident parent, but where the court retains anxieties about that parent's current level of parenting skill or about the possibility of the child being exposed to parental conflict at contact handovers. A later section of this chapter offers further reflections on the issues involved in recommending supervised contact. Sometimes a court may order accompanied contact for a period of time as opposed to supervised contact. It may do this when it wishes to indicate that it sees no dangers to the child from unsupervised contact with a non-resident parent, but recognises that both child and parent may benefit from some support as they become reacquainted with each other through contact activities where there has been no contact for a prolonged period of time. Or it may order accompanied contact as a reassurance to a child who has been exposed to parental conflict in the past at handovers. Finally, the court may order a number of therapeutic contact periods where a child and parent meet in the company of a therapist for therapeutic discussion of themes relevant to the parent–child relationship in advance of the court making a further order about child contact. None of the above resolutions to contact disputes preclude the court, with or without the advice of an assessor, from making ancillary orders for the attendance of either children or parents at educational or therapeutic programs of different kinds. A further ancillary recommendation or order, particularly where time-limited contact orders are made, may be for the monitoring of the progress of the contact in terms of its delivery of the intended positive consequences for the child.

Listening to the Voice of Children in Contact Disputes

The safety, in all its dimensions, and needs of children must remain of paramount importance to assisting mental health professionals within these considerations focussed on child contact. Very often parents who themselves have been engaged in intimate partner violence are unaware of their children's complex response to family violence events and falsely reassure themselves with the knowledge that none of the children them- selves were either struck in these events or were direct witnesses of the events. If a child is living after separation with a mother who has been a participant in intimate partner violence, her only concern may be whether the child's father might be physically aggressive to the child during any future contact that might be agreed between them. Both she and her ex-partner may be oblivious to the impact already suffered by the child from being an aural witness to the aggression and/or a visual witness to some of its consequences. When children participate in mediation or assessment dialogues in the company of their parents, they may be fear- ful to speak about their experiences in front of their parents for different reasons. For example, they may fear that speaking about their experiences will cause trouble between their parents or they may fear that one of their parents will express anger towards them for something they might say. The following vignette exemplifies some of the challenges associated with such dialogues.

Ten-year-old Thomas was the only child of his parents, who attended media- tion immediately following a residential separation which had been precipitated by a series of three late-night violent episodes between his parents. These three episodes apart, his parents' relationship had, historically, been without physical aggression. His father had moved out of the house after the third episode, and the parents had very quickly agreed that Thomas should spend one midweek night from after school and one 24-hour period with his father at the weekend in his father's newly rented apartment. The mediator persuaded the parents that it might be helpful for Thomas to participate in the mediation process and have a voice in the decision-making process about those matters that directly affected him. With some reluctance on the part of both parents, they agreed to Thomas meeting with the mediator alone. In dialogue with the mediator it became clear that Thomas had been an aural witness to two of the episodes when he had woken up from his sleep and gone to the top of the stairs, where he had heard a lot of screaming and shouting and a lot of noise from 'things breaking'. He was terrified that one of his parents was going to die. He went back to his bed on both occasions but could not sleep. He was too frightened to say anything to either of his parents on the day following the incidents, and they said nothing to him. He did see a cut on his mother's lip after one of the episodes he'd heard, and noticed that one of the kitchen chairs was partly broken. He remained frightened that something like this would happen again, even though his parents were now living apart. When the mediator spoke with him about his parents' idea for him to spend time with his father in his new apartment, he told the mediator that he would rather not do this yet, but was frightened to say this in front of his father in case he would be angry with him. He felt he would prefer to see his father in his own house for a while before he went to the new place with him. He did not want the mediator to tell his parents that he had heard the episodes, but agreed that the mediator could put his idea to them about his time with his father. He also agreed with the mediator that it might be good for him to talk with a counsellor a little more about the difficult experiences he had been through. When the mediator spoke with the parents again about Thomas's position and wishes, they agreed that for the next four weeks the father would come to the house for a couple of hours three times a week to see Thomas and that the mother would vacate the house for those periods. They also agreed to allow the mediator to source a child counsellor for Thomas. When the mediator had a further series of dialogues with the family six weeks later, Thomas was spending time with his father in his father's apartment a couple of times per week, but the parents had agreed that they would postpone the commencement of his overnights for a further month.

The above vignette is an example of a situation where there was very little dispute between parents over child contact, and the key issue was making space for their child's voice and interests to be heard a little more. Many contact-related disputes in which violence is embedded as a concern are not as easy to resolve. Some of the most intense and long-lasting disputes over contact occur when one parent has had to take the children and flee from a violent partner to a hidden destination or to a refuge where the whereabouts of the children is unclear to the other parent. These disputes often come very speedily to the family courts, where residence and contact evaluations are likely to be ordered along with child protection evaluations. Where the mental health professional is acting in the role of court-appointed evaluator, he needs to balance many factors when making a recommendation about child contact. In most jurisdictions, both parents and children have a legal right to 'enjoy' a relationship with each other, but this entitlement must be balanced by due regard for the emotional, physical and sexual safety of children. A violent parent may either be completely in denial about the violence he has perpetrated on his ex-partner and children or may minimise the impact such violence has had on their children. He may claim through his lawyers that his ex-partner is alienating him from the children, who are being prompted or 'coached' by their mother to say that they are afraid of their father and don't wish to see him. The evaluation professional needs to listen carefully to all the 'ordinary' stories from the family's life as well as to the details of the stories of violence that have been experienced by different family members. He must also, on occasion, liaise very carefully with child protection services, domestic violence services, family doctors, teachers and mental health services as well as with the police and refuge workers. A recommendation to the court regarding contact (whether there should or should not be contact, if it should be supervised and by whom, its location and duration) should only come following a careful engagement with all the relevant information and with the views of other professionals involved.

Recommending Supervised Contact

The court-appointed assessor needs to keep certain things in mind when recommending supervised contact. In proposing certain agents or persons in the role of supervisor, care must be taken to see that they are capable and willing to exercise the function that supervision must fulfil in each particular circumstance. A 'supervised visitation checklist' has been developed by Saini and Newman (2010) as a screening tool to assist the decision-making of judges and mental health professionals with regard to the suitability of particular parents and children for utilising particular supervised contact services aimed at 'promoting maximum contact between children and parents' while ensuring child safety (Fidler et al., 2013, p. 260). Where contact centres or agencies are being proposed, the assessor needs to be aware of the specific resources available to these agencies and whether they are offering merely a centre for a parent and children to play in together or whether they will offer some assistance to parents and children to enable them to have a safe and satisfactory experience of being together. Practitioners in this area should also be aware of the risks for children from being further exposed to violence or negative exchanges between parents when they are either entering or leaving the supervision centres.

One final matter is worthy of mention before departing the introduction to this theme. The discourse of 'domestic violence' carries a very high currency now in many of our Western societies, and there is a growing societal awareness of the destructive consequences for individuals, up to and including the loss of life, arising from such violence. For this reason, the discourse can be drawn upon by some separating parents in the course of post-separation conflict as a means of gaining certain advantages within the conflict process. Claims that domestic violence has occurred can be made when, in fact, no violence has occurred at all. These distortions of reality, which can relate either to initial claims of violence or to counter-allegations of violence, are one facet of what makes the work of both the mental health professional and family court judge so challenging. Hence, a careful, critical perspective is required of the mental health professional throughout all aspects of the work.

Skills and Interventions

There are a broad variety of skills and interventions relevant to the practitioner's engagement with the central theme of this chapter, namely parental dispute about child contact in the context of domestic abuse allegations. Some of these skills are to do with information gathering, whereas others are a mixture of assessment, intervention and referral skills. The following six capacities can be thought of as skill areas in which practitioners can monitor their own development over time:

(i) The capacity to inform yourself about the legislation in your country governing domestic violence and abuse, including marital rape, and about the legislative protection open to those experiencing domestic abuse of different kinds.

(ii) The capacity to inform yourself about the range of domestic violence services in the geographical region in which you practice.

(iii) The capacity to make an assessment with adults – whether in the context of therapy, mediation or court-ordered assessment – of the range of domestic abuse behaviours they have experienced in the relationship with their ex-partner.

(iv) The capacity, in the context of post-separation child contact disputes, to assess the pattern of domestic abuse in the past relationship of partners and to assess the relevance of this domestic violence history for the safety of a unique child in the context of any proposed future contact relationship with a unique nonresident parent.

(v) The capacity to construct, where appropriate, a safe post-separation child contact proposal for the consideration of parents, their lawyers and the family court and to provide a rationale for why such a proposal balances advantage and risk in a way that protects a child's best interests.

(vi) The capacity to understand the way trauma resulting from domestic violence might affect an adult or child's presentation in the context of mediation or assessment dialogues and to discuss with them the possibility of referral for appropriate therapeutic assistance.

Personal and Reflective Exercises

The reader may find some of the following exercises more suitable for doing privately rather than in a classroom or group setting. Others can be comfortably done alone in advance of sharing findings in group settings of different kinds.

1. Consider the different intimate relationships you have belonged to since becoming an adult. Write a note about any abusive behaviours you encountered either in yourself or a partner during any of these relationships. How did you and your partner respond to these behaviours?
2. Consider the family or families to which you belonged while growing up. When you look back from the vantage point of the present, do you recall any abusive or violent behaviours being part of these contexts? If you do, can you recall what your response was to these events at the time? Write some notes for yourself about these questions.
3. Consider the range of abuse behaviours that might find a presence in couple life. Which of these behaviours do you think you would find most difficult to hear about in your professional practice? Write a note for yourself in response to this question, and consider why you answered the question in the way you did.
4. Write a note for yourself about the most recent story of domestic abuse you heard in your professional practice? Write a further note for yourself about some aspects of the story you might have heard differently if you belonged to a different gender.

THE INTENSIFICATION OF CONFLICT OVER PARENT–CHILD CONTACT: ALIENATION, JUSTIFIED REJECTION, AND HYBRID CASES

The last chapter examined some of the more manageable conflict scenarios relating to child contact. This chapter moves us towards the more intense end of the conflict spectrum relating to parent–child contact problems following separation and divorce. It is here that we encounter the interruption, to varying degrees, of child contact patterns with nonresident parents as well as the complete cessation of parent–child contact in a small number of cases. Children of different ages may refuse contact with nonresident parents for a host of different reasons, and it is inevitable that a parent whose relationship with a child is threatened through non-contact will invoke the assistance of the family court as a means of restoring his own and his child's entitlements. Although there are a number of nonresident parents who 'walk away' reasonably quickly once they meet what they experience as insurmountable resistance to post-separation child contact, this writer's clinical experience over recent decades suggests that this group is becoming smaller in number. It is probable that increased availability of part or wholly funded legal assistance in many jurisdictions, combined with stronger psychological bonds made by parents with their children during the time the family remains intact, has made it more likely that a 'rejected' parent will appeal to the family court for assistance. Hence, it is at this end of the post-separation conflict spectrum that mental health professionals find themselves increasingly engaged with the family courts. It is in this arena also that they experience a dramatic shift in the way they must realise their conflict containment and management roles as they are joined on the conflict performance stage by a host of others (legal representatives of both parents, judges attached to different levels of the family court system, professional and lay witnesses of different kinds, various 'support' personnel attending court with litigants, siblings and parents of litigants, new partners of litigants) who are differently positioned in relation to the challenges of conflict resolution.

The next chapter considers in detail the different kinds of roles and interventions the mental health professional may be required to perform with families, either at the request of the court or in the 'shadow' of the court. This chapter, however, concerns itself, in its first part, with the developing set of professional reasons and explanations for why post-separation parental contact for some children suffers either significant disruption or a progressive faltering that leads to final cessation. Before setting out on this road, the reader is invited to notice in advance the variety of different theoretical frameworks (psychoanalytic, systemic, attachment, narrative) that have made important contributions to the range of explanations described in the first section of this chapter. The second part of the chapter considers all that is involved for mental health professionals when they are requested to undertake evaluations regarding residence and contact on behalf of the court.

Key Concepts in Understanding Significant Breakdown in Post-separation Parent–child Contact

Three inter-related concepts form the cluster of ideas that represent the best understanding currently available to mental health professionals about why post-separation parent–child contact sometimes runs into significant, if not insurmountable, problems. These concepts are alienation, justified rejection and the concept of a hybrid case. What follows is far from a complete account of the history and development of this network of explanatory concepts but should, nonetheless, provide the mental health and social care professional with a good enough introduction to the meaning of this terminology while clarifying the distinction between the terms themselves. The importance of the practitioner's capacity to distinguish between these concepts and the different realities to which they refer will become more evident in the second section of the chapter, where emphasis is placed on the mental health professional providing an accurate assessment for the family court in cases where an evaluation has been ordered in the context of allegations of either alienation, domestic abuse or both.

Alienation

This writer's first experiences of intense post-separation struggle over parent–child contact occurred in Dublin in the late 1960s and early 1970s. It was a time before the word *alienation* had entered either professional or public vocabularies as a way of describing and/or explaining a process in which a child or children became cut off, either temporarily or permanently, from a separated, nonresident parent. However, both parents and professionals at the time had their own language for describing what they observed. Some referred to certain parental intentions and behaviours as 'using the child as a weapon' in the ongoing 'battle' of a parent with their ex-partner, whereas others spoke of children 'being used as pawns' in post-separation struggles about income and material support. Although this earlier language, compared to later more nuanced descriptions, seems relatively unsophisticated, it retains something of critical importance: it conveys a sense of shared moral concern over what was understood as an inappropriate 'use' of children in the context of intense struggles between their mothers and fathers. These 'uses' were understood as infringements upon what were increasingly seen as the rights or entitlements of children, under most circumstances, to enjoy a continuing relationship with both of their parents, notwithstanding the discontinuity of the couple relationship between those same parents.

The mental health professional assisting at this 'intense' end of the post-separation conflict spectrum will be constantly reminded that the conflicts they attend are not only fuelled by a maelstrom of strong and varied emotions in both parents and children but also by a fiercely contested debate about the rights and entitlements of all involved in the struggle. Both child law and family law outline these rights and entitlements within the different legal jurisdictions to which they refer, but the ordinary daily lived experience of each of the conflict participants sees them attempting to enact and enforce, behaviourally, personally held views of their own entitlements alongside those of their children and their ex-partner adversaries. Mental health professionals also enact and promote, through the medium of their evaluation reports and recommendations, their own preferred perspectives on the themes at the heart of the family conflict before the court. Like the litigant parents, mental health professionals have no built-in immunity from the strength of their own feelings about core conflictual themes and must be constantly vigilant with respect to the difficulty in achieving gender balance both in their narrative descriptions of contested family events and in their processes of judging which underpin recommendations made to the court. Although the challenge of achieving gender balance is present for mental health professionals throughout all levels of intervention in family conflict following separation and divorce, such challenge appears to this writer to increase as the intensity level of family conflict increases. Cross-gender consultation and supervision, as well as participation in mixed-gender peer consultation groups, can all play important parts in raising the level of gender balance achieved by practitioners operating at the most intense end of the conflict spectrum. Readers might also find some of the exercises at the end of the current chapter useful vehicles for progressing a reflection on their own unique challenges in achieving gender balance in their practice.

One of the earliest professional comments within this arena of cut-offs in parent–child contact was provided by Reich (1949) in the context of a study focussed on adult personality types. He noted how some personality types among separated and divorced parents defended themselves from narcissistic injury by fighting for custody of the child and defaming the ex-partner with a view to depriving them of the pleasure of the child. This was a psychoanalytic explanation that sourced the motivation for certain parental post-separation behaviour in the narcissistic ego's need to defend itself from the injury implicit in the event of separation. Within the context of such theory of unconscious motivation, this subgroup of divorcing parents were not thought to be acting with awareness of the psychological basis of their goal-directed behaviour.

An early systemic incursion into this fundamentally psychoanalytic explanation was offered by Wallerstein and Kelly (1980) who described the development of an 'unholy alliance' between an enraged parent and a vulnerable older child or adolescent who acted together in order to wound and punish the other parent. The systemic addition in this explanation is that it draws upon a theory of triangles to suggest how the presence of narcissistic rage in a parent can give rise to a kind of post-separation family formation in which an older child is drawn into a cross-generational coalition ('unholy alliance') with the enraged parent against the other parent. This is a not untypical post-separation family formation in which an older child's relationship with her other parent is sacrificed in the service of containing the rage of her resident parent. Such 'sacrificial' offering often ensures that the relationship of younger siblings with the other parent does not meet the same fate. Nine years later, Wallerstein and Blakeslee (1989), in their study of parents and children a decade after divorce, coined the term 'Medea syndrome' to refer to those parents who seek revenge on their former partners by destroying their child's relationship with the other parent. In the Euripidean Greek tragedy (Euripides, 431 BCE) to which the proposed syndrome refers, the central character, Medea, takes revenge on her husband, Jason, who has betrayed her by leaving her and marrying another woman, by killing their children. By connecting their observation of such parents to the central character in the Euripides tragedy, the authors of this now 30-year-old study remind us of the potential for ultimate destruction that can be unleashed when revenge, following the wounds of betrayal, remains uncontained. In a later section on mental health in this work, we will see how a very small group of separating parents take ultimate revenge on their ex-partners through the murder of their joint children in advance of taking their own lives.

It was Gardner (1985) who provided the mental health field with its first, more extended description of these alienating processes when he coined the term *parental alienation syndrome*. Parental alienation syndrome (PAS) was proposed as a diagnosis for *a child* and, for the most part, was a diagnosis that became relevant in the context of child custody disputes. Gardner felt the diagnosis was warranted by the observation of the following eight *behavioural* factors in the child: (i) a campaign of denigration of the rejected parent; (ii) frivolous reasons offered by the child in support of such denigration; (iii) a lack of ambivalence in the child towards the rejected parent; (iv) the child's claim that her views are completely her own and not simply a replica of the favoured parent's views; (v) support for the favoured parent within the parental conflict; (vi) the absence of guilt in the child over her unfair treatment of the rejected parent; (vii) the presence in the child of stories and scenarios borrowed from the favoured parent; (viii) and the extension of the child's pattern of rejection outwards to include the extended family and others closely associated with the rejected parent. It is noteworthy that Gardner did not see the child as a passive victim in the performance of the syndrome which he saw as arising 'from the combination of a programming (brainwashing) parent's indoctrination and the child's own contribution to the vilification of the target parent' (p. 61). His formulation was clearly limited to certain kinds of parent–child relational histories which did not include contexts where there had been a history of abuse or neglect. For Gardner, the diagnosis was made not as a reflection of the brainwashing parent's efforts to indoctrinate the child into her own negative view of the other parent, but as a result of the degree to which these parental efforts were successfully manifested in the child. The differential success of these parental operations in the life of the child led him to suggest that the diagnosis should be made at one of three different levels – mild, moderate or severe.

The great advantage of Gardner's perspective is that it invites the mental health practitioner to focus closely on observable *behaviours*, past and present, in parents and children. When the practitioner is in the role of informing and advising the family court, as they often are in cases where alienation is present, this behavioural focus fits well with the kind of evidential framework which underpins judicial decision-making. Although courts may be interested in the psychoanalytic frameworks which propose descriptions and explanations of the internal psychic worlds of adults as the motivational basis of their alienating behaviour, the court management of these alienation-based disputes over child contact with nonresident parents normally attends to the performance, or otherwise, of certain behaviours prescribed in court orders. The court will be interested in such matters as whether the 'favoured' parent presented the child for contact with the rejected parent in the time and manner prescribed, and what the behavioural responses of the child were in the context of both handovers and the activities shared with the nonresident parent during contact. These latter matters refer to observable behaviours around which the court can gather and assess its own evidence within the ongoing court management of the case.

Although Gardner's PAS was presented as an individual child diagnosis, it had a strongly *relational* element contained within it. His description of the syndrome also revealed an important emphasis on the history of the *attachment* relationships of the child with both parents. Additionally, there were clear *narrative* features implicit in the final pair of his eight behavioural factors identified in a child warranting the PAS diagnosis. The penultimate behavioural factor referred to the presence within the child of scenarios and descriptions borrowed from the favoured parent. Such 'borrowing' could only refer to a process of narrative transmission from favoured parent to child of negative stories about the rejected parent. Similarly, in the final behavioural factor noted by Gardner – namely the spread of the child's rejection outwards from its focus on the nonresident parent to include extended family, friends and close associates of that same parent – such 'spreading out' could only occur as an instance of narrative development or extension in which the explanations of the negative stories about the rejected parent are expanded to include other characters embedded in the rejected parent's life. For all the richness of Gardner's contribution, however, it seemed to lack the level of complexity required to do sufficient justice to very many of the allegedly 'alienation' cases coming before family courts.

Some 16 years after Gardner had first introduced PAS, Kelly and Johnston (2001) developed a more complex model for understanding the many factors which can together produce the resistance of a child to post-separation contact with a nonresident parent. Theirs was a more systemic model which invited the mental health professional, within the context of her assessment, to consider the way a multiplicity of factors might be interacting with each other in the case of any particular child. The key factors to be considered were as follows: the alienating behaviour of the aligned parent;

the prior parenting of the rejected parent as well as their counter-rejecting behaviour; domestic violence and abuse as well as child abuse and neglect; processes of continuing litigation that develop to include a wide range of others such as extended family, friends, new partners and aligned professionals; sibling relationships; the vulnerability of a particular child who may present as generally anxious and fearful; and developmental factors such as age-appropriate separation anxiety and responses to conflict consistent with the cognitive development of children aged 8 to 15 years. Johnston (1993) had earlier noted that while many parents engaged in high-conflict post-separation struggle use a variety of alienating strategies, not all their children became alienated. Within their model, they see the behaviour of the 'alienating' parent as just one of a variety of factors to be considered, and they place considerable emphasis on the degree to which the child internalises the alienating strategies of the parent to whom she is aligned. Indeed, for them it was this latter factor which should determine whether certain parental behaviours should be considered 'alienating' for the child. Their model took further distance from Gardner (1985) by suggesting that the term *parental alienation* be replaced by the concept of the 'alienated child' on the basis that the latter terminology was more child-focused and less blaming of the preferred parent.

Whereas these authors (Kelly and Johnston, 2001) defined an alienated child as one who 'freely and persistently expresses unreasonable negative feelings and beliefs (such as anger, hatred, rejection, and/or fear) toward a parent that are disproportionate to their actual experience of that parent' (p. 251), Johnston (2010) later proposed moving away from the concept of the alienated child and putting the emphasis back on what an alienating parent is doing. In an interview within the Fidler et al. (2013) study, Johnston comments: 'I prefer to put the word "alienation" into what a parent does; the parent engages in alienating behaviours. A parent who engages in alienating behaviours, which are observable and measurable, is conducting parent alienation upon a child; the child may or may not be able to resist or manage or succumb ... I prefer to keep the term alienation for what a parent does, which I think is emotionally abusive' (p. 17).

A contribution of more recent years to the debate about how parental alienation comes about is provided by Childress (2015). In this instance, the explanatory framework for parental alienation is provided by attachment theory (Bowlby, 1969, 1988). For Childress, the alienating behaviour of an accepted parent can be thought of as a re-enactment of this parent's own traumatic attachment history. Two particular early attachment patterns – the disorganised attachment and a role-reversal (child takes care of parent) type of attachment – give rise in the accepted parent to a narcissistic/borderline personality with a tendency to split the world into all-good and all-bad components. These attachment histories, allied to the splitting processes that flow from them, are what give rise to the accepted parent becoming 'a pathogenic parent'.

Justified Rejection

All of the above commentators (Gardner, 1985; Kelly and Johnston, 2001) on the alienation phenomenon have varying perspectives on how, and to whom or what, the term should be applied, but they all agree that the language of 'alienation' must be kept apart from those situations of child resistance or rejection which are based upon child abuse or neglect, exposure to domestic violence, or significantly problematic parenting. The term *justified rejection* is more fitting in these latter circumstances as it denotes a positively adaptive response in a child to a negative set of circumstance she has had to endure and carries no implication of any undermining behaviour on the part of the more 'favoured' parent. In practice, however, as Johnston (2010) notes, it may be very difficult to distinguish which rejections constitute justified and proportionate reactions on the part of the child from those rejections that would, in all probability, not have occurred were it not for the alienating behaviours of a favoured parent.

Mixed, or Hybrid, Cases

It may be a very challenging research exercise to determine the actual percentages of 'child resistance' cases before the family courts that are based clearly and solely in either the alienating behaviours of a 'favoured' parent or the abusive, neglectful or problematic parenting of a 'rejected' parent. However, a recent study (Friedlander and Walters, 2010) suggests that neither of these types of cases is as common in the practice experience of legal and mental health professionals as what the authors refer to as 'mixed' or 'hybrid' cases. In such cases, the alienating behaviours and strategies of one parent (usually residing with the child) exist alongside a history of some problematic or neglectful parenting in the other parent (usually nonresident).

This relative multiplicity of 'mixed' cases coming before family courts provides a significant challenge for the evaluating professional, as it also does for court management. Within the maelstrom of allegations of past abuse or neglectful parenting and counter-allegations of current and ongoing alienation, they must seek out as much clarity and evidence as possible pertaining to a variety of past and present parental behaviours while gaining access to the child's unique world of experience as a counterpoint to all that their parents allege. It is important both for mental health professional response as well as for family court management that the best possible determination is made with respect to where a particular child's resistance to parental contact fits in on the continuum that stretches from 'alienation' through 'hybrid cases' to 'justified rejection'. Fidler et al. (2013) argue the case for not lowering the threshold too much with respect to the kind of parental behaviours that would allow us to consider some child resistance as instances of 'justified rejection'. When small, historical parenting lapses in a nonresident parent are combined with significant alienating behaviour in a favoured parent, such contact-resistance cases should not fall into the 'hybrid' category and more properly warrant the 'alienation' designation. These determinations are often not easily arrived at either by courts or their assisting mental health professionals, and it can often take some time – for example, more than one judicial hearing and more than one evaluation process – before a determination can be made with some confidence.

NB

The adversarial process also adds to the difficulty in arriving at such determination, as judgements must be made in the context of legal 'cross-fire' which simultaneously attempts, on the one hand, to amplify the extent of past parenting failures and their impact on the child and, on the other, to exaggerate the level and types of alienating behaviours in the favoured parent. Fidler et al. (2013) point out that the key thing that assists both in making such determinations and in choosing appropriate mental health and judicial management strategies 'is the responsiveness to guidance and redirection by the court, lawyers and mental health professionals by both the rejected parent, who may have reacted negatively to being rejected or mistreated by the child, and by the favoured parent, who may have been misguided or mistaken in his conclusion that the child needed protection from the other parent' (p. 38).

Changing Child Residence in the Context of Parental Alienation

One of the most challenging moments in the management of parental disputes where alienation strategies in one parent are central to a child's resistance to contact with a reasonably competent and caring other parent is the decision to change, or not, the residence arrangements for the child from the parent with whom she resides to the nonresident parent. Courts and their assisting mental health professionals will often be as creative as the alienating parents themselves in devising counter-strategies aimed at the maintenance of child contact with the nonresident parent. Such strategies and counter-strategies often take considerable time to play out within the legal arena while the child at the centre of proceedings advances in age, while becoming progressively more alienated from a parent with whom she has less and less contact. It is perhaps unsurprising that mental health professionals and family court judges remain ambivalent about making major changes in children's care and residence arrangements in the context of parental alienation in an arena where best practice guidelines have been slow to emerge.

An Australian study (Templer et al., 2017), aimed at addressing this lacuna with respect to best practice guidelines, made a systematic review of all available English-language literature pertaining to parental alienation. The purpose of their study was to identify available interventions for parental alienation and assess their effectiveness in restoring relationships between affected children and their alienated parents as well as in addressing and resolving psychological symptoms. The investigators also wanted to be able to pinpoint the kind of therapeutic skills that might underpin satisfactory outcomes while identifying broad intervention strategies for restoring relationships and improving overall family functioning. The review finally made a detailed and systematic study of ten key research papers (Dunne and Hedrick, 1994; Friedlander and Walters, 2010; Gardner, 2001; Johnston and Goldman, 2010; Lowenstein, 1998; Rand et al., 2005; Reay, 2015; Sullivan et al., 2010; Toren et al., 2013; Warshak, 2010) on the topic, published between 1990 and 2015. The final criterion for the inclusion of studies in the review was that they address one or more of the following topics: the relationship of children with the targeted parent or alienating parent; attitudes or perceptions of children towards an alienating parent; changes of custody and residence arrangements; and outcomes of therapeutic interventions such as transformation of psychological symptoms.

Within this systematic review, the investigators found a number of different therapeutic interventions being deployed, all of which were 'a specialised form of systemic family therapy' (p. 113). The goals of such therapy were the protection of children from further harm arising from alienation, the improvement of their psychological well-being, the challenging of their distorted thinking and the strengthening of their critical thinking, the improvement of their relationship with the alienated parent and the preparation of the alienating parent for the improvement of the relationship of the child with the other parent, as well as improving the functioning of the parental and other familial relationships. They noted that psychoeducation appeared to be an important ingredient in each of the therapeutic interventions identified in the reviewed studies.

The investigators noted that none of the identified studies recommended waiting for spontaneous resolution of parental alienation or permitting the alienated child to decide her future care and residence arrangements.

A number of the reviewed studies underlined that leaving the child in the primary care of the alienating parent enables the alienation to continue and become more severe. The consequences of continued alienation are further damage to the targeted parent–child relationship (Gardner, 2001) as well as longer-term negative outcomes for the alienated child, such as major depressive disorder, low self-esteem and insecure attachment styles in their adult relational lives (Ben-Ami and Baker, 2012).

Templer et al. (2017) summarise the findings of their systematic literature review study in the following three points. Firstly, parental alienation requires legal and therapeutic management to enhance family functioning. Secondly, awarding primary parental responsibility to the targeted parent and providing specialist family therapy is effective in ameliorating parental alienation. And finally, a specialised form of family therapy, as described above, for parental alienation can improve family functioning and prevent further parental alienation. They emphasise that their findings propose that specialised family therapy should commence as soon as parental alienation is identified. Such therapy needs to be court-ordered, and there must be clearly identified sanctions for parental noncompliance with the goals of the therapy. The range of therapeutic interventions identified in the reviewed literature as contributing to amelioration included workshops, camps, retreats, multidisciplinary family therapy and parallel group therapy for parents and children. They note the importance of the motivation of the alienating parent to participate meaningfully in the therapy being externally driven by such sanctions. Where therapeutic interventions fail to achieve their goal, a change of residence arrangements for the child is warranted. They also underline the findings of certain studies (Dunne and Hedrick, 1994; Gardner, 2001) within their review, which suggest that the removal of the child from their preferred parent does not harm them even when a certain transient distress is experienced by the child.

The Court-ordered Residence and Contact Evaluation

The court-ordered residence and contact evaluation is a *process* with a specified *goal*. The process commences when the court makes an order for such evaluation in the name of a particular mental health assessor or an assessment service. In some jurisdictions, the family courts have their own evaluation services built in to the family justice system which dispenses with the need for parents to pay for such services. In other jurisdictions, the family courts are dependent on a range of differently qualified, privately practising mental health professionals to provide such services. In this latter context, the parents pay the practitioner directly for the evaluation, and the court order will normally specify the proportions of the payment to be met by each parent. In these latter jurisdictions, there may also be a system of legal aid which assist parents, either wholly or in part, with the costs of evaluation.

There has often been a conflicted pre-history to the making of an order for evaluation, with one parent arguing for the need for evaluation and the other parent insisting that it is unnecessary. Although the assessor is not formally made aware of such pre-histories to the matter, it is not unusual for one or both parents to want to 'inform' the assessor of their respective positions in such disputes at the commencement of the process. This information sharing by a parent can and should be thought of as an effort to build an alliance with the assessor against the other parent.

The goal of the evaluation process will be specified in the court order for evaluation, and it is very important that the evaluating mental health professional not commence the assessment process in advance of either receiving a copy of the order or being briefed in writing by a joint letter from both parents' legal representatives. This is because the process needs to be informed from the outset by the specific questions the court needs the assessor to address. Some orders are deliberately general in their focus and require the assessor to provide a perspective for the court on the residence, care and contact arrangements for the dependent children of the separating parents in conflict. Other orders will be quite specific and ask for the assessor's views on such matters as whether there should be overnight contact for an infant in the home of a nonresident parent and, if so, what the frequency and context of such contact should be. Or an order might request an assessor to provide an opinion about the most suitable school placement for a child in circumstances where parents are in dispute about this matter. These specifications of the court order are critical in that they define the scope and extent of the process as the court envisages it in the making of the order. That said, the assessor with a systemic or contextual lens will often discover that an apparently simple and discrete matter requiring the court's adjudication may have a knock-on effect on other matters already decided upon in the same set of orders. For example, in making a recommendation for a child to attend one school rather than an alternative, the assessor may also have to consider how such recommendation impacts the feasibility of contact arrangements already set down in an order.

Once the mental health professional has a copy of the order and understands the scope of the evaluation as envisaged by the court, her engagement with the parents or parties to the dispute, who may be grandparents or others, can commence. The anticipation of the process can fill many parents with a lot of anxiety as they come to terms with the fact that their dispute is entering a phase where a critical level of decision-making about their own and their children's lives is being handed over to the court and it's agents. Providing as much *information* about the process as possible in advance often helps to alleviate such anxiety to some extent. But the matter of information provision is about much more than anxiety containment. It is about acknowledging to some degree *the set of power relations* (Foucault, 1980) that underpin the participation and performance of all involved in the conflict management system. There are few, if any, professional contexts where the power relationship between the evaluation participant and the mental health professional is so unequal as within the evaluation process. The mental health professional has a significant amount of power attaching to her assessment role by virtue of the powers vested in the family courts who appoint her. Already disempowered by the levels of conflict experienced in their own parental relationship, parents become disempowered to a further degree once orders for evaluation are made. Notwithstanding the justifications for such disempowerments arising from the alleged interests of children and vulnerable minors, the whole process of conflict management by the family court through the vehicle of court-ordered evaluation sets up a context in which professional mental health discourses about children and parents are significantly privileged while the voices of parents themselves are, at the very least, temporarily silenced with respect to the immediate future of their children. Such an unbalanced set of power relations creates an ethical demand for the mental health practitioner, which requires that the practitioner work within all stages of the process to re-empower parents to a degree that remains compatible with their children's safety. Working to make the process as collaborative (Anderson, 2012) as possible without denying the imbalance in power relations written into the context is one way that professionals can begin to meet this ethical demand. The provision of good-quality, relevant information to parents in advance of commencing evaluation meetings can be a step in the direction of keeping in mind the power differentials that underpin the process.

Many mental health professionals engaged in this work will have their own information sheet which they send to parents before the process commences. This sheet may contain information about any or all of the following: the qualifications and experience of the assessor; a description of the typical range of interviews and consultations that might be expected in the process; an indication that information might need to be gathered with parental permission from other professionals engaged with the family and its members; the address of the centre or practice at which the assessment will take place and whether some assessment meetings might take place in the homes of the parents; whether there is wheelchair access in the consultation venues; the fee for the evaluation process, and when and how such fee should be paid; the approximate length of time from commencement of the process in the first consultations to its completion, when the assessor's report is lodged with the family court; arrangements for the interviewing of children. Although the provision of such information sheets can be helpful to some degree, they are necessarily very general in their orientation. They represent what an assessor thinks may be helpful information to a broad range of parents. They are no substitute, however, for direct telephone communication with the parents individually, which gives them the opportunity to ask the specific information of the assessor that may be uniquely relevant to them. Such telephone contact can reduce the level of the 'unknowns' about the process as both assessor and parent hear each other's voices for the first time, and the parent has the experience of an assessor who is interested and able to hear and respond to his preliminary concerns. The information sheet is just one of a number of documents referred to in this section of the chapter that will be relevant for the evaluation practitioner both before and during the process of the evaluation. The two tables at the end of the next section of this chapter provide a summary list of these documents, as well as pointing to some of the issues arising in relation to their reception and use.

The assessor needs to be aware if the jurisdiction in which she practises has its own specific *protocol* which governs how the court considers an evaluation process should be conducted. Such protocols, which differ from jurisdiction to jurisdiction, often specify the minimum number and types of consultations which need to be part of an evaluation. For example, a protocol may specify whether children should be interviewed with each parent and/or whether each child should be interviewed alone with each parent. Such protocols often represent the assumptions and current 'prejudices' of a specific group of family lawyers, judges and assessors within a jurisdiction at a moment in time. However, where such protocols exist, it is important for both the written and spoken information of assessors to cohere with such protocols, which may be sent automatically from a court service to litigating parents who are the subjects of evaluation orders.

Whether or not the mental health professional uses a preliminary information sheet with evaluation participants, and regardless of whether there is a protocol for evaluations operational within the jurisdiction, the professional has to be prepared for the litigants' own questions when initial appointments are being set up either by phone or by email. It is important not to be rushed into answering questions by the litigants, who may present as quite demanding in their approach. For example, a litigant who wants immediate advice on how to introduce the topic of the assessment to his three children needs to be told that sensible advice cannot be given about that matter until the professional has gathered both an overview of the whole family situation as well as a detailed account of the progress of each of the three children, who, because of their age differences, may need to be told different things. Likewise, if someone asks on the telephone, in the context of setting up an initial appointment, what the professional's attitude is to overnight contact for children under three years, it is wise not to attempt to answer this question over the phone, but to reassure the parent that the question is both a good one and also a very complex one and that it will receive very careful consideration during the assessment process. Although this may seem a somewhat avoidant response at first glance, it is a safer route than to try to answer the question over the phone with a parent you do not really know at all at this point. Nor is it possible at this early point in your communication to understand where his question is coming from. That said, these preliminary calls can have many functions. One of these functions is to make a beginning engagement with a parent and, as such, it is important to be as informative and helpful as possible without prematurely commencing the assessment process on the telephone.

When the assessment process has begun, one of the most important things the assessor does in the beginning is to *listen very carefully and fully* to the way the parents wants to tell their story of events that led to where they find themselves at that moment, as well as to their perspective on how particular outcomes from the assessment process might improve matters for them, the children and their ex-partner in the future. The listener with a systemic attitude will listen sympathetically to this story and perspective while preparing themselves to listen with equal sympathy to an alternative, and sometimes quite contradictory, story to be told by the other parent. The professional's type of engagement in the assessment process at times resembles that of a qualitative research interview where the interviewer tries to make enough space for the participant to express himself as fully as possible. It is not a therapeutic engagement, yet will often have a therapeutic effect. Recently a father said to me at the end of our first meeting: 'This is the first time in three years of going in and out of court about my daughter that anyone has listened to me fully about what I believe is going on. I am glad the court allowed us to enter this process.'

Even from the earliest stages of the evaluation process, a parent can begin to express a range of very powerful emotions. A mixture of rage, sadness and despair can emerge as individuals seize the opportunity to tell their story at length and in a way that may not have been possible before. They may have written their story out at the request of their lawyer, who will transform this account into an *affidavit*. This type of story construction is not the same as telling their own emotion-filled story in the context of a verbal, face-to-face interaction with the assessor. Although these emotions will not meet a therapeutic response from the assessor, they will meet a *sympathetic* and *containing* response. The assessor may also need to discuss the parent's possible need for a referral for therapeutic support, while reassuring them that such a discussion and possible referral is not going to go against them within the assessment process.

Management of Documentation during the Evaluation Process

Along with receiving a copy of the order for an evaluation in his name, a mental health assessor may also receive a set of legal documents of different kinds which the court has ordered should be provided to them jointly by the legal teams. The volume of this documentation can vary depending on the length of the history of the dispute within the legal process as well as on the disposition of the court with respect to how much background the assessor should receive. Cases that are new to the legal system may well be referred to the assessor with no documentation but a copy of the order itself. Where there is a package of documentation arriving for the assessor's attention, these documents will usually include any or all of the following: a copy of the order for evaluation; a copy of the document setting out what the applicant in the proceedings wants the court to do; a variety of affidavits of each of the parties to the dispute; copies of medical, school, or child protection reports relating to a child or children; copies of legal correspondence between the lawyers acting for both parents; copies of adult mental health reports on either or both parties to the dispute; copies of previous court-ordered evaluation reports; and copies of reports investigating past allegations of child abuse against one or both parents. It is important that the assessor read carefully all the documentation sent to him from the court, but assessors differ with respect to when the documentation should be read. Some assessors like to read all the documentation carefully prior to setting up initial appointments with each of the parents; others like to have the initial adult meetings with each parent/party before they read the documentation. Whatever the timing of the reading of this documentation within the process, the documents must be carefully read in advance of formulating any judgement on the key matters at stake in the process.

In addition to the officially provided documentation, the assessor can expect to be 'offered' a variety of 'other' documentation by one or both litigants when they arrive for their initial appointments. The handling of this material is much more complex. This material can include any or all of the following: email exchanges between the parties to the dispute; old correspondence between the parents; family photograph albums; audio-tapes of the other parent at handovers; video recordings made of the other parent and/or the children. In several jurisdictions, there are clear rules that assessors cannot receive any material that is additional to what the court has already approved. Other jurisdictions may be less clear about these matters and may even lack a set of guidelines altogether with respect to assessor reception of additional material. It is somewhat different when a parent wants the assessor to receive a copy of his own personal notes which were prepared for the purposes of ensuring they did not forget certain details of events as they want to recount them. Even when these notes are received and held, rather than simply used by the parent as an *aide memoir* within the session, the assessor needs to be clear with the parent that she retains the right to discuss any aspect of his notes with the other parent (Tables 7.1 and 7.2).

Table 7.1 Documents Relevant to Court-Ordered Evaluation Prior to Commencement

Document	Issues Arising
Legislative frameworks	Which specific pieces of legislation are relevant to the questions at the heart of the evaluation?
Court order for evaluation	Does the order request *specific* evaluation questions, or is it a more *general* order relating to children's custody, residence and contact arrangements?
Letter of instruction from legal teams	Is the joint letter of instruction sufficiently clear in its request, or should the assessor request further clarification in advance of commencing the evaluation?

Continued

Table 7.1 (Continued)

Document	Issues Arising
Information sheet	How much should be included in an information sheet? Such sheets may include any or all of the following: • The assessors name, qualifications, professional organisation memberships and registration numbers (where relevant). • The address/venue where the evaluation meetings will normally take place. • The number, sequence and focus of meetings normally included in an evaluation process and the persons normally expected to participate in these meetings and in what combination. • A note reminding the participants that the structure just described is only a guide for the evaluation process that may need to be adapted to the unique circumstances of each family context. • Circumstances in which home visits might be part of the evaluation process and the impact this may have on the cost of the process (if relevant). • The length of time of each meeting and arrangements for the cancellation or postponement of meetings. • A range of flexibility with respect to times of the day when evaluation meetings might be held. • The estimated length of time from the commencement meetings to the submission of the evaluation report to the court. • Contact details for the assessor. • Information about transport to the site of the evaluation meetings, contact to and within the building where the evaluation will normally take place and information about parking. • Arrangements for payment of the assessor and methods of payment where this is relevant. • Information concerning the assessor's own note taking during the evaluation meetings and the assessor's permission for participants to make some written notes for themselves, should they wish, during the meetings. • Information that no audio or video recordings of any aspect of the evaluation meetings is permissible.
Evaluation protocols	Evaluation protocols may be formal or informal in nature. Assessors need to be aware of evaluation protocols that have been formally approved for use in the jurisdiction where the evaluation is taking place. Where there are

Table 7.1   (Continued)

Document	Issues Arising
	no formal protocols in operation in a jurisdiction, the assessor may use protocols established by either professional bodies, special professional interest groups or by themselves as individual practitioners. Participants need to be made aware in advance of commencement of the status and content of any evaluation protocol being followed by an assessor.
Affidavits	The court may or may not wish the assessor to have access to the various legal affidavits through which the parties to a dispute (usually the parents, but not always) set out their 'positions' in contested matters and what they are seeking from the court. Assessors need to be sure they have been sent all the affidavits the court has wanted them to have access to.
Reports on the child/children	There may be many different types of professional reports on the child/children (school, medical, psychological, child protection, abuse allegation investigation) at the centre of the evaluation process. Some may be sent to the assessor at the request of the court prior to commencement, but the assessor may need to request others during the process where they feel such reports are pertinent to the answering of specific evaluation questions.
Previous court evaluation reports	The court may or may not want the current assessor to have access to previous evaluation reports, and assessors should never directly receive a copy of previous professional reports from one of the evaluation participants without clarifying with both legal teams that it is the intention of the court that they should receive such reports.
Adult mental health reports	Where the mental health of a parent is an issue of concern at the heart of an evaluation the court may wish that an assessor be furnished with copies of extant reports on the mental health of this parent. The assessor needs to make sure that they have access to those reports, and no others, that the court has decided they should have sight of.
Correspondence between lawyers	Where the court has ordered that copies of such correspondence be sent to the assessor as background to the evaluation process, they can give some insight into the adversarial processes that the parents and lawyers have been engaged in prior to the evaluation. Remember that the assessor is entering and joining a conflict performance and management system that may be up and running for quite some time.

Table 7.2   Documents Relevant during and at Conclusion of Court Ordered Evaluation

Document	Issues Arising
Parent email exchanges	Where such exchanges are not part of the documentation ordered by the court to be sent to the assessor, it is unwise to receive/accept them from one parent. Parents can tell you directly their version of these exchanges, and the assessor can ask the other parent for their version of these exchanges if they think it may assist the evaluative process.
Photograph albums	A nonresident parent may wish to show the assessor what he considers photographic evidence supporting the alleged happiness, fun and ease experienced by his child while on contact visits. Viewing the album relatively briefly with a parent can be affirming of his commitment to the parental role, but it is wise to ensure that the parent leaves the appointment with the album he brought to show the assessor.
Audiotapes & DVDs	These are often offered to the assessor during the process of the evaluation. They are usually offered as evidence of the bad behaviour of the other party/parent in the proceedings. Such recordings are usually made without the knowledge of the person whose bad behaviour they are intended to exhibit. It is unwise to either receive them or allow a parent to play them for you. Even the suspicion in one parent that such recordings may have been played to the assessor can compromise the position of neutrality the assessor must maintain throughout the whole process. The same disposition is recommended towards recordings of what children are reported to have said to one parent at home.
Reports of private investigators	Unless these reports form part of what the court has decided to provide to the assessor by way of background to the evaluation, assessors should not receive these reports from individual parents. The significance of such reports for the evaluation process may be more tied up with the levels of mistrust and/or paranoia in parental systems that their existence proposes rather than with any of their particular 'findings'.
Parents' personal notes	Parents often wish to supplement what they say to the assessor with their own personal typed or handwritten records of their views or experiences. They can feel that there is so much at stake in the evaluation and so little time to explain their position to the assessor. They may worry that they will forget to tell some important pieces from their story. The assessor needs to remind the parent that it is fine to receive some concise notes from both parents in support of what they have had to say, but that the content of their notes may be part of what is discussed with the other parent/party in the conflict.

Table 7.2 (Continued)

Document	Issues Arising
Parental permission records	Where the assessor sees the need to request up-to-date reports on a child or to have sight of reports not already sent to her, the written permission of parents for the seeking of such reports from other professionals must be obtained and kept in the evaluation record.
Children's letters and artwork	Whether children's written 'productions' are in the form of artwork or letters outlining their views and wishes to the assessor, their use should be carefully considered with the child in a manner that fits with the child's age and cognitive capacities.
The evaluation report	In creating a report prepared for the court, the assessor needs to be aware of protocols existing in the jurisdiction with respect to the timing and manner of delivery (post, email, courier).

Deciding on the Boundaries of the Evaluation Process

One of the things the assessor must decide is where to draw the boundaries around the assessment process. Who should the assessor meet as part of the process, and where should they meet these people and with whom? The answers to these questions may not always be clear in the beginning. Therefore, when participants ask the assessor at the outset who they will be seeing, it is important that she signals that the assessment is *a process* and that the outline plan for different meetings may have to be altered in the light of emerging information. It may be relatively easy, for example, to explain why the process needs to engage with a childminder or grandparent who spends several hours each day with a child, but less easy to explain why the assessor might want to meet with an aunt or uncle of the child who may not have been particularly involved with the child up to that point but may be a significant *resource* for the child in the future. However, it may be that one of the principal adult participants in the evaluation process will make strong requests of the assessor to meet with someone who has had a significant involvement with the other key adult participant in the past. The assessor must decide whether the meeting of this request is likely to assist with the evaluation process and questions in relation to the future of the child or children at the centre of the process. In particular, the assessor must guard against engaging with adults who simply want to support one parent's negative perspective on the other participant adult. In these contexts, the assessor needs to remind the participant that although the evaluation process is a type of investigation, it is not a criminal investigation, and if she believes someone has evidence that one of the participants in the process has behaved in a criminal or unlawful manner, it is the police who should receive the communication with rather than the assessor.

Another type of boundary in the assessment process relates to requests by one of the key participants in the process for an extended number of consultations for themselves or their child. Some parents can be extremely anxious around the evaluation process and can worry greatly that they have not yet told the assessor all they need to tell her about their children and the context they understand them to be in. In an earlier part of this chapter, some emphasis was placed upon people in the assessment process emerging with a feeling that they had been heard as fully as possible. The assessor needs to decide whether these requests are legitimate and should be met or whether they are likely to just involve a repetition of material already recounted. Sometimes such requests reflect the fact that an adult has been traumatised by certain events in their relational history and really need a therapeutic referral (Herman, 1998). In such contexts, the assessor needs to remind herself that the evaluation process is just that and must not veer off into a miniature therapeutic process, no matter how distressed a participant may seem to be. In other contexts, the request for further consultations can be a strategy for delaying the completion of the process where such delay is perceived by one parent as being in their interest. Where the request is to have an extended number of consultations with a child, the assessor needs to assess the legitimacy of the request. The argument that a child, following two consultations, is only now feeling sufficiently safe and comfortable with the assessor that she is ready to express herself and her desires more fully may have some merit to it. The assessor will, of course, have the evidence arising from the child consultations as the basis for making such a decision and will not be reliant upon parental report alone. However, the assessor also needs to be aware that such requests can mask further efforts by a parent to 'coach' their child to say certain things within the process.

Observing and Interviewing Children within the Evaluation Process

There is no doubt that meeting with children forms one of the most important and challenging tasks within the overall task of conducting a child custody and contact evaluation. The assessor must take cognisance of what she has already been told by parents and guardians with respect to the age, developmental progress, personality and temperament of a child, or children, in making a decision about how, where and when to see them. In very many assessment processes, children may be seen with both parents separately, with their sibling group, and individually alone. In some situations, a whole family meeting may be a possible and fruitful part of the process. However, there may be many circumstances which make some parts of this sequence of meetings either not feasible or unsuitable. Given the age, developmental stage and numbers of children who are the subjects of the assessment process, the assessor must decide whether some or all of the meetings should be either office-based or in the children's home or homes. Whatever may be decided in collaboration with parents regarding the location of different meetings, parents and children/adolescents need to know in advance how long these meetings are likely to last and how many separate meetings will be held within the one appointment period. The assessor needs to think both of child schedules and child energy when planning the time of meetings.

It is almost always necessary to see a child or adolescent alone on more than one occasion. This is important not simply from a relational perspective but also with a view to supportively involving the young person in an appropriate way in the decisions emerging from the process that impact their lives. When considering care and residence schedules for the future, it can be useful to open up different possibilities with a young person and ask them to give some consideration between sessions to what might work best with respect to their own needs. The assessor might encourage the child/adolescent to think about who she might like to talk the issues over with in advance of meeting with the assessor again. Depending upon the child's age, she will need to be reminded in different ways that the process she is engaged in is in part to do with them having a 'voice', but not always a 'choice', in the critical matters to be decided.

One of the main tasks facing the mental health professional within assessment-based child consultations is the ascertainment of child views and desires concerning matters affecting their future. Assessors will normally try to make it possible for children to share their perceptions of their own relationship with each parent, and to say something of their wishes for the future concerning residence and contact arrangements. There are times when this process seems relatively straightforward, and a child appears to have and feel the freedom to share their perceptions and express their wishes. There are other times this task is anything but straightforward, and assessing the reliability of a child's expressed wishes can be a major challenge. The following two vignettes exemplify two very different reasons underlying this challenge.

Barbara was the nine-year-old only child of two very competent and professionally competitive parents in their early forties. They had decided to separate about one year previously, and were now involved in a court-appointed evaluation process regarding Barbara's future care and residence following the breakdown of mediation. The difference between the parents regarding her future care was that her mother wanted to be her daughter's 'primary carer' while her father insisted that a 50/50 share of her care was in Barbara's best interests. Although aware of her parents' difference about her care, Barbara had been encouraged by both her mother and father to speak freely to the assessor and not to be afraid to say exactly what she wanted for the future. Barbara presented to the assessor as a very pleasant, competent but anxious girl, whose weekend care was already divided exactly equally between her still co-residing parents. When the moment arrived within the child consultation for the assessor to invite her to say something about her wishes or concerns regarding her future residence and contact arrangements, Barbara appeared not to hear a number of the assessor's questions and continued speaking about some of her experiences with school friends as well as about a recent trip she had made to the zoo. When the assessor commented that it seemed difficult for her to say something about these matters, she stopped talking and nodded her head affirmatively as a tear rolled down her face. She later agreed with the assessor when he wondered whether it might be better for her if other people like himself and the judge were to work out good future arrangements for her rather than being burdened with having to know and say what she wanted.

In the above vignette, the child is caught not just in a conflict of loyalties but in a double-bind with each of her parents (Bateson, Jackson, Haley and Weakland, 1956; Bateson et al., 1956). Within the communicational network joining her parents, herself and the assessor, she is told by each of her parents to speak without fear about her wishes for the future while hearing the unspoken command of both parents to align her wishes with theirs. She simply cannot be right with any response she might give to the assessor's questions, and she is caught, as a child, in a relational field from which there is no exit. The assessor is also caught initially between the demands of an evaluation process, legislatively framed, which requires that a child has the opportunity to express her wishes and desires about her future, and an ethical injunction to safeguard the emotional well-being of the child in the process.

A different type of challenge is presented to the assessor in evaluating the reliability of a child's wishes when the child, instead of being unable to say anything because of being caught in a double-bind, seems to be completely clear about what she wants and doesn't want with respect to her future parental care. The following vignette exemplifies a reasonably typical child presentation where severe alienation is present.

Donal was a ten-year-old and the eldest child of Sarah and Tom, who had been separated two years when the court ordered a child contact evaluation because of the ongoing refusal of Donal and his eight-year-old brother, Joseph, to go on the two contact periods per week with their father that had been agreed by their parents at the time of the separation. School and healthcare personnel had independently verified an excellent pre-separation relationship between father and sons. There had been intermittent problems with the contact over the first 18 months of the separation, with the boys refusing to go with father for periods of time without making any specific complaints about their contact time with him. Sarah, a social worker, had told the boys that they were no longer 'little children', and they were free to make up their own minds whether they wanted to spend some time with their father or not. Sarah maintained this position in her own consultations with the assessor. When Donal came for a child consultation alone with the assessor, he told the assessor that he 'hated' his father, that his father only 'pretended' to love him and his brother 'so other people would think he was a great father'. He told the assessor that he didn't want anything to do with his father anymore and that if his dad tried to come to see any of his football matches, he would run off the pitch and run home. When the assessor wondered whether he had enjoyed the contact times when his dad had taken him and his brother on a few occasions to watch their favourite football team in the UK, he immediately responded that he was not his dad and that they were only brought to see those matches because his father wanted to go himself.

Where a child, in the context of very positive pre-separation relationship with a nonresident parent, begins to reject that parent and resist contact with them, a professional must assess the reliability of her expressed wishes within the explanatory framework of parental alienation among other frameworks. Children caught in such dynamics are invited to speak the 'reality' of the favoured parent and will often enter the consultation arena with relative enthusiasm for the idea of having their voice heard. Indeed, as Walters and Friedlander (2016) remark, the call to have the child's voice heard is never more resounding than when made by a favoured parent who will often present himself as champion for the respect of children's wishes. The only problem, of course, is that it is not the child's voice that is being heard. As the dynamics of severe alienation progress over time, the child's relationship with internal and external reality deteriorates. In the process of being conscripted into the alienating parent's campaign of denigrating the other parent, the child gradually denies the existence of any past or present positive feelings for the rejected parent and provides herself with distorted representations of that parent's motivations and emotions. In time she appears to 'forget' the historical reality of enjoyable experiences in the care of the rejected parent. The dynamic promotes in a child a type of black and white thinking where the favoured parent is seen as 'all good' and the rejected parent as 'all bad'.

The psychological and relational make-up of such child presentations are complex in their construction and highly problematic in their consequences. Childress (2013), for example, views these processes, wherein the child gradually shares the delusional world of the favoured parent and comes to view their beliefs as their own, as exemplifying the transgenerational transmission of attachment trauma in the context of parental personality disorder. While the construction processes lying behind such child presentations may differ from family to family, the involvement in such processes are seen to undermine the child's mastery of age-appropriate coping skills such as the capacity for complex thinking and communication that will be needed in the endeavour to resolve problems (Walters and Friedlander, 2016). The emergence of such deficits can, in time, impact the child's ability to maintain positive relationships with peers.

A further matter to be considered in the context of an assessor's relationship with a young person concerns any possible *written communications and/or artwork* the child/adolescent might produce during the evaluation process. The assessor needs to consider whether such letters from the young person should be copied directly into the evaluation report as an appendix, referred to in the report, or simply treated as part of the child's evolving relationship with the assessor. Part of the assessor's respectful communication with the child usually involves a developmentally sensitive conversation about how they would or would not like their 'productions' to be used. It is not uncommon for assessors to receive written communications from children caught in alienation dynamics with the 'instructions' that the letter should be passed on to the judge. Such letters often appear to have a reassuring impact on the child in that they are written proof of her loyalty to the favoured parent and his doctrines.

The emotional and physical safety of children must be a central concern for the mental health professional during the evaluation process. It is up to the assessor to read as best she can whatever risk might be present for children during any part of the process. One of the more usual risk points is when a child is not currently having contact with a nonresident parent, but has agreed to be seen by the assessor with that parent once she does not have to travel with that parent to the meeting and is accompanied to the meeting venue by her resident parent. If the relationship between the parents is acrimonious and volatile, which the assessor should know about from the earlier gathering of the relational history, the assessor needs to protect the child from unnecessary exposure to parental hostility. This can sometimes be done effectively by scheduling different arrival and departure times for each parent. Very often taking care of child safety ensures the emotional and physical safety of parents at the same time.

Collecting Information from Collateral Sources

The family and its individual members may have had multiple involvements with other professionals that may have a bearing upon the questions at the heart of the assessment and/or ongoing court proceedings. It is important that the assessor collect all the relevant information from informed professionals. For example, a child may have particular medical treatment or educational needs that may have a bearing on his post-separation care and residence. Reports may need to be sought from, or consultations had with, a range of other professionals involved with the child. In all of these contexts of information gathering, parental permission will have to be sought (unless the court has made an order overriding such permission), and the assessor must explain carefully to parents the purpose of such consultation or report-seeking and how it is relevant with respect to the specific set of questions to be addressed within the evaluation. Or an adult's mental health challenges may be alleged to be impacting his parenting capacities to some degree, and reports and/or consultations may be required to determine the precise nature of his mental health issues and the treatment he is receiving. As with the direct information gathering from parents, guardians and children, the assessing mental health professional will need to be judicious about what information she seeks from collateral sources. She needs to be clear with herself and with others precisely what information she is seeking and its relevance to the task at hand. Most importantly, she needs to be clear with professionals she consults how the information she receives will be used and whether it will be open to the participants in the process via the court to have access to this information. In some jurisdictions, the courts assist schools and therapists by allowing these professionals to speak confidentially to assessors without fear of being forced to attend court to give open evidence about what they have shared with an assessor. In other jurisdictions, there is no such assistance, and the assessor is obliged to share with the court any information received from any collateral source.

Preparing the Report

The penultimate stage of the evaluation process for the mental health professional is the preparation of the evaluation report. As with all other reports, the professional constructing the report must keep in mind the key purposes for which the report was ordered as well as the context in which it is likely to be received. The evaluation report needs to strike a balance between being clear and succinct in the process of answering the key evaluation questions specified by the court and being sufficiently detailed in its support for the central argument being made. No matter what position the evaluator finally takes on the key matters at stake in the assessment, an argument for a certain line of action should not be made more forcefully than the gathered evidence allows.

Giving Evidence within a Court Hearing

The final step in the evaluation process for the author of the evaluation report is the giving of oral evidence before the court, should this be required. Professional witnesses give their evidence under oath in the same manner as all other witnesses in the hearing of the case. Questions regarding the evaluation, its process and its findings may have to be answered in cross-examination by the legal representatives for both sides in the dispute. It is the job of the professional witness at that moment to answer truthfully and fully the questions she is asked. It is never wrong to ask for clarification regarding a question asked should this be necessary. At times cross-examination can be a reasonably robust process, and the mental health professional needs to guard against consenting to perspectives about the case or about its main participants for which their evaluation provides insufficient support. Additionally, the mental health professional may have to answer questions put to her by the presiding judge in the case. The professional needs to keep in mind that her function in the whole process of giving oral evidence is to provide as much clarity for the court as possible with respect to her perspectives, the data gathered on which these perspectives are based and any other matters on which the court might seek the professional's view.

Achieving Gender Balance in Contexts of Intense Conflict

The last word in this chapter has been reserved for a topic that is relevant to all themes and practitioner skills noted throughout this text: gender balance. The achievement of professional perspectives that are balanced with respect to gender is a challenge across the whole spectrum of post-separation parental conflict and through all the arenas in which this conflict is managed. This challenge can increase in size, however, as conflict becomes more intense and the stakes become higher for parents and their children. The gendered histories of professionals' personal lives may leave them vulnerable to either a greater identification with a father who has been cut off from a child for whatever reason or with a mother who is trying to protect a child from an ex-partner whom she perceives as abusive. Or a professional's strongest identification within a conflict may be with the gender of the child at the centre of dispute. Such identifications are unavoidable to a large degree, and the achievement of gender balance does not depend upon futile efforts to delete them. What gender balance does require is an ongoing reflective engagement by the professional with her own personal and professional histories and a consideration of how facets of these unique histories predispose them to responses of one type or another to the unique components present in the family conflicts with which she becomes involved. The achievement of gender balance by the professional means being able to give equal attention to the different stories told by men and women, giving equal attention to assessing the validity of their accounts and ensuring that the way in which court reports are written and oral evidence made to a court is driven more by the real needs of children and parents and less by the biases arising from the uniquely gendered experiences at the heart of personal and professional lives. These are necessarily high aspirations, and the reader will rightly ask how they might be achieved. In this writer's view, it is the processes of critical reflection engaged in by the professional alone, within their supervisory relationships, or within peer dialogues with trusted colleagues that make the achievement of gender balance more likely. It is hoped that some of the exercises at the end of this and other chapters offer opportunities for readers to further their experience of such critical reflection.

Skills and Interventions

With respect to assisting families where post-separation conflict has reached intense levels and where children are resisting contact with a nonresident parent, the mental health professional needs the capacity to perform a range of both assessment and therapeutic skills, as follows:

(i) The capacity to assess the reasons underpinning a child's refusal of contact with a nonresident parent and to discriminate between those reasons which relate to parental alienation by her resident parent from those reasons which relate to the child's justifiable refusal of contact and/or to make an assessment of the balance of reasons when both types of reason appear to be at work within a child's refusal.

(ii) The capacity to outline clearly in court-ordered evaluation reports the range of evidence gathered, including its source and quality, that underpins professional assessment of the reasons for a child's refusal of contact with a nonresident parent.

(iii) The capacity to consider where the boundaries of an assessment should lie and the capacity to communicate transparently with the key participants in the evaluation process reasons why the boundaries should be drawn in a certain place.

(iv) The capacity to undertake specialist court-ordered family therapy in contexts where parental alienation has been judged to be a central part of children's refusal of contact with their nonresident parent.

(v) The capacity to participate in the multidisciplinary group-based treatment of parents and children subsequent to court orders for such treatment.

(vi) The capacity to liaise effectively with the court about the participation and performance of parents ordered by the court to engage in goal-specific family treatments.

(vii) The capacity to plan with the court and parents for the change of residence of a child where such transition is required. The capacity to appreciate the trauma responses that may lie behind some children's refusal of parental contact after separation and to make appropriate referrals of parents and children to suitably qualified therapists.

Personal and Reflective Exercises

1. Write a few paragraphs for yourself about any personal or familial experiences you have had or are aware of where there was resistance in a child to contact with a parent in the context of post-separation/ divorce family conflict. Write a further paragraph about how you feel these experiences might have a bearing upon the way you perceive the mixture of elements at work when you meet situations in your professional work where there has been a breakdown of parent–child contact in the context of post-separation/divorce family conflict.

2. Retrieve copies of the last three evaluation reports you have completed for the court, and read each of them carefully. After reading each report, write a paragraph for yourself evaluating the quality of the report, noting both its strengths as you perceive them and the places in the report where the quality might have been better. When you have finished this exercise, show the same three reports, minus identifying data, to a trusted colleague working in the same area, and ask him or her to provide you with an evaluative paragraph on each report. When you have received back these evaluative comments, compare the feedback you received from your colleague with the feedback you provided to yourself. Write a final paragraph about your response to any differences noted between the two sets of feedback.

3. Take one of your most recent evaluation reports prepared for the family court in the context of an intense dispute about parent–child contact. Read your report carefully before writing some notes for yourself in response to the following questions about the report:

   (a) If a professional of a different gender had written this report, how do you think the narrative at the heart of the report might have been different? Might there have been differences in the way the content of the report was presented? Might there have been some content included that was not present in your report?

   (b) If a professional of a different gender had written this report, how do you think the recommendations concluding the report might have been different, and in what respects? Might there have been additional recommendations made? Might some recommendations have been omitted?

4. Consider the gender make-up of your current professional supervisory relationship. Is it a same-gender or cross-gender supervisory relationship? Identify an experienced colleague of a different gender from your current supervisor but familiar with your area of practice. Request a one-off consultation about a challenging case with this colleague. Following this consultation, write a few paragraphs for yourself about how your experience of this consultation was both the same as, and different from, how you imagine the consideration of the case might have gone between yourself and your regular supervisor.

ALLEGATIONS OF CHILD ABUSE: SYSTEM EXPANSION, TRANSFORMATION, CONTAINMENT

The last chapter described how post-separation parental conflict intensifies as disputes around contact move into the family court in search of resolution. We saw how the conflict resolution system can expand significantly from a four-person system (parents, child and mediating mental health professional) to a significantly larger system which can include parents, their child or children, lawyers, family court judges and a variety of other lay and professional witnesses. It was noted also how this movement towards litigation as a vehicle of conflict resolution often involved the main disputants increasing their separate dialogues with others in this expanded system while reducing to a minimum level, which may be nothing, their direct dialogue with each other. This context of growing hostility, mistrust and non-communication is often the ground on which allegations of child abuse occur. Such allegations can be of different kinds (neglect, emotional abuse, physical abuse, sexual abuse), and their investigation by child protection and/or police authorities can yield varied outcomes such as that abuse occurred; that it didn't occur, but the allegation was based upon misunderstanding; that abuse did not occur, and the allegation seemed based on malicious intent; or that the question of whether abuse occurred must remain unanswered.

Jurisdictions differ with respect to the number of different outcome categories in which investigation findings are couched. Jurisdictions also differ with respect to the language in which these outcome categories are reported. Some jurisdictions have a simple two-category framework in which an investigation must yield a result stating that an allegation is either 'founded' or 'unfounded', whereas other jurisdictions have a more nuanced system which offers investigators a greater number of categories, including different levels of 'probability', within which to place their findings. Whatever investigation system is in place, the whole territory of investigation of abuse allegations can incorporate many grey zones which invite and permit the participants to construct many competing narratives about, and conflicting interpretations of (Ricoeur, 1974), the allegedly abusive past event and its surrounding context.

Where the allegations are of physical abuse, sexual abuse or severe neglect, there may be, depending upon practice within a particular jurisdiction, two parallel investigation processes with different purposes. The first investigation process will be managed by a child protection system, or a specialist wing of this system, for the purposes of determining whether abuse took place and, if it did, what protection and remediation measures need to be put in place to assist the child and family. The second investigation process will be undertaken by the police and is oriented towards the determination of whether a crime took place and, if it did, whether someone should be brought before the court and charged with an offense under a specific piece of legislation. This chapter is not about child abuse or neglect per se, but about the relational processes that are generated in the context of an allegation of child abuse being made and investigated. It focuses on three main elements governing these relational processes and their implications within this context. Firstly, it focuses on the dramatic *expansion* of the conflict management and resolution system in which parents and child participate. Secondly, it considers some aspects of the predictable *transformation* the post-separation family system experiences in this context. And finally, it considers a range of conflict *containment* strategies open to the court-appointed mental health professional who works with post-separation family systems through the crises of abuse allegation, allegation investigation and investigation outcome. As a prelude to these three major considerations, the chapter commences with a description of the way the key participants develop their narrative understanding (Polkinghorne, 1988) of each other and the situation they find themselves in. Although mental health professionals play many different roles in and around this allegation-investigation-outcome process, including those roles dedicated solely to the investigation, or otherwise, of a specific abuse allegation, the chapter is written chiefly from the perspective of those professionals appointed by the court to assist and advise both court and family in the context of the greatly intensified conflict that usually accompanies the making and investigating of child abuse allegations.

The Child Abuse Allegation as a Multistoried Event

Allegations of child abuse have presented in the context of post-separation family conflict for a very long time. The culture in which these allegations have been received, however, has altered dramatically over the last 50 years. In most parts of the Western world during the last five decades, there has been a developing awareness of different kinds of abuse of children in different contexts and of society's obligation to protect them from such abuse. The ground-breaking North American work of Henry Kempe and his colleagues (Kempe et al., 1985) through the 1960s, 1970s and 1980s on the phenomena of the 'battered child' and 'non-accidental injury' in children began to draw back the veil which concealed a range of different kinds of *physical* abuse of children by their parents and/or caretakers. The 1980s saw a further development in both public and professional sensitivity to the issue of child abuse as victims of child *sexual* abuse began to be listened to and believed (Sgroi, 1982). Simultaneously the mental health professional community began to build its own knowledge base concerning the impact of child abuses of different kinds on the lives of developing children and adults. By the final decade of the twentieth century, most Western societies had in place robust systems of child protection that were underpinned by legal statute and reinforced by strong penalties within the criminal code for those shown to have violated the physical and/or sexual integrity of children. By the start of the current century, these same societies were dominated by discourses about child abuse which strongly emphasised the need to listen carefully to children's accounts of their own experiences and to take their reports very seriously when they attempted to 'disclose' experiences of physical or sexual abuse. Where child sexual abuse was at stake, such discourses often supported a view of those considered to have abused them as perpetrators of one of the most heinous crimes an individual could commit. The strength and power of these discourses are invoked, to different degrees, each time an allegation of child abuse is made.

To make a report of an alleged incident of child abuse in most of our Western societies during the first quarter of the twenty-first century is to press a button that triggers a range of protocol-driven responses in a small number of adjacent professional and institutional fields. Both police and child protection systems become engaged with the family and its members as they interview, often on several occasions, both parents and children in different ways and for different purposes. Although there may be some 'hard' evidence (e.g. X-rays/photographs of bruises or fractures, medical evidence of physical signs and symptoms in genital areas) available, at the heart of some child abuse allegations, the vast majority of investigation data emerge from the telling and retelling by different people of stories about the alleged event. A large number of professionals, through legal obligation, may insert themselves into the space between an allegedly abusive parent and her allegedly abused child, the child's siblings and the child's other parent as the investigations located in both child protection and police systems proceed. Video recordings may be made of some, or all, of these investigative interviews in which individuals of different ages are asked to describe their involvement, direct or indirect, in an alleged past event or events. Such intense investigative processes make for very busy adult and child lives and normally lead to highly increased levels of emotional arousal in all the key participants. Discourses of protection, control and safety dominate the investigation period, and discourses emphasising the maintenance and development of parent–child relationships often appear to take a back seat. Depending upon the resources available within any jurisdiction, such allegations and their investigation may also make for very busy professional lives as the activity and files of mental health, child protection and police personnel grow in response to unfolding allegation-investigation processes.

Part of the evolution of this process may involve either a complete cessation of contact between the allegedly abusive parent and the allegedly abused child and their siblings or a greatly restricted contact context (e.g. reduced contact periods or supervision of contact) while an investigation is in motion. There is so much at stake for the participants that the normal round of life (work patterns for adults, patterns of school attendance and after-school activities for children and adolescents) can be interrupted at every turn of the investigative wheel. For the allegedly abusive parent, what is at stake is the potential of being judged to have abused their child, being charged with a criminal offense and possibly imprisoned for a significant amount of time. Most critically, what is at stake for this parent is the potential loss of contact with her child or children. Even if none of these possibilities become a reality, the process of being investigated involves experiences of shame and humiliation for most accused parents as more and more people within their social, workplace and extended family environments get to know about the presence of allegations even if they are not aware of the details of such allegations. No matter what the many individuals in these environments believe about an allegation, the very presence of an allegation reconstructs the social identity of the parent in a very negative way (Gergen and Davis, 1985). She undergoes a passage from being perceived as a separated parent sharing positively in the raising of her children to being seen as a parent who might have either physically or sexually abused her child and whose parenting role has, to different degrees, been suspended.

For the parent supporting the allegation against her ex-partner, what is at stake is her credibility as a parent whose central motivation is the protection of her child. Her hope and belief is that the investigation outcome will confirm both her credibility and her judgement. Their fear is that the outcome might support the view underpinning an often-made counter-allegation that the making of the allegation is one further move in a parental strategy motivated by malice and aimed at alienating the child from the other parent.

Depending upon his experience of the alleged event and its disclosure in some form and context, the child may have differing responses to being cut off very abruptly from his normal contact with the allegedly abusive parent. He may feel a level of responsibility and guilt for having 'set off' a range of different emergency-type responses in the adults around him, or may feel quietly angry at having to undergo a multiplicity of interview processes that take precedence in his life over such valued activities as football training, dancing classes or, simply, a normal day at school with his friends. His emotional context may change dramatically as he is exposed to the strong responses of his resident parent and extended family members as well as fearing the anger of the parent from whom he has been cut off. This extended family context of the resident parent often presents itself to the child in the form of a heightened sense of protection and care which often comes at the price of being exposed, to some degree, to a range of negative stories about his allegedly abusive other parent.

The above set of contextual changes is the backdrop against which a new set of stories evolves in the minds and dialogues of the key participants. The parent through whom the allegation was made may firmly believe that an abusive act has taken place and may recall 'incidents' in her shared history with her ex-partner which support a view of her as having always been, for example, aggressive, abusive and dismissive of the needs of others. Empowered by a range of negative emotions about her ex-partner, her narrative memory (Kerby, 1991) selects some historical events for inclusion in the new narrative she wishes to make of the other person while 'forgetting' a range of other events that might question the particular kind of identity she wishes to propose (Ricoeur, 2004). These selected historical events, which portray the other parent in a very bad light, are often spoken about repeatedly in front of children and/or extended family members and investigating professionals in the context of dialogues about the current 'allegation' crisis. It is this mixture of narrative remembering and forgetting (Ricoeur, 2004) that promotes an understanding of the alleged event as an event of a particular kind – that is, an act of child abuse with all the implied intentionality on the part of the other parent who has become a 'perpetrator' in the evolving story.

The other side of this story reconstruction process evolves in the parent against whom the allegation is made. The development of her story of her ex-partner now moves from one where the other person may have been seen through a relatively negative lens based upon the way the break-up was experienced to a picture of the other, as we have noted above, as 'an alienating parent' motivated by the 'malicious' intent of destroying the relationship between her and the child (Gardner, 1992). Some 'knowledge' of problematic aspects of the ex-partner's childhood experiences in her family of origin may be 'remembered' as a way of developing a broader, more complex, narrative which attempts to account for how she became the 'evil' person she now appears to be. Just as with her ex-partner, she too casts into oblivion all those historical actions of her ex-partner that might question the likelihood of the vision of the other portrayed in the newly evolving narrative.

System Expansion and Transformation

When an allegation of child abuse occurs within a context of post-separation parental and familial conflict, an unprecedented kind of expansion of the dispute management system occurs. This expansion usually involves the family's simultaneous participation in three other systems, each of which has its own purpose. These three systems are the criminal investigation system (oriented towards the investigation of an alleged crime), the child protection system (oriented towards the assessment of whether child abuse took place and ensuring the child's protection) and the family court system (oriented usually towards the regulation and modification of care/contact arrangements in the light of the allegation and its investigation). The total system comprising all of these activities can, at best, be thought of as a dispute 'management' system rather than a dispute 'resolution' system since the convergence of these activities in time takes the family far away from any visible signs of conflict resolution. It will be seen later, however, how the theme of conflict resolution must always be kept on the horizon by the assisting mental health professional.

At the same time that the family becomes participant in this expanded and complex dispute management system, it becomes transformed with respect to its own internal relational patterns. Typically, a parent alleged to have abused a child no longer participates in the accompanying and collection of a child or children to and from school, and the terms of their altered contact pattern with the child may also debar them from being involved in the child's sporting or extracurricular activities. The 'accused' parent and the alleged child victim will also, in all probability, be cut off from the intimacies that go along with overnight care of the child. The altered care/contact arrangements often mean that the child may be cut off from his regular meetings with grandparents, aunts and uncles on the side of the parent who is the subject of the allegation. These transformations in predictable patterns of familial interaction, bringing about, as they do, ruptures in significant attachment relationships for the child with a range of extended family members (grandparents, aunts, uncles, cousins), have the impact of further intensifying the host of different emotions that normally accompany the performance of post-separation conflict. Such ruptures and cut-offs have the capacity to anger and enrage even the calmest of grandparents, whose previous position of neutrality in relation to the post-separation conflict of one of their adult children rapidly evaporates.

The whole transition brought about by a child abuse allegation in these contexts has been described as a passage from 'intense post-separation intra-familial conflict' to 'inter-familial emotional warfare' (Sheehan, 2013a). The involuntary cessation of contact between a child and one of his parents and set of grandparents can fill individuals with profound levels of anger, sadness, loss, bitterness, rage and revenge. Where two extended families live in the same community or neighbourhood, it is not unknown for such 'inter-familial warfare' to spill over into community-based action and neighbourhood protest (Sheehan, 2013b). All of such extensions of conflict performance indicate how wide the circle can become of those people deeply touched by an allegation and its investigation implications.

This tribal-like emotional warfare intensifies some familial bonds while loosening other attachments. The parent who is supporting the allegation is often drawn closer to her own extended family (parents and siblings), and the alleged child victim may be encouraged to develop even stronger bonds with cousins, aunts and uncles on the same side of the family. Correspondingly, and has been noted above, children often lose contact during this period with one whole side of their extended family and not just with their allegedly abusive parent. Sometimes this loss persists far into the future regardless of the outcome of the abuse investigations. Although many jurisdictions now have facilities for grandparents to make their own independent application for child contact, courts can be reluctant to grant such applications for fear that such contact might be used as a vehicle for gaining unlawful contact hours for the allegedly abusing parent with the child or children in question during the time of the investigation.

Containment Strategies in the Context of Abuse Allegations and Investigations

One of the problems faced by the key participants (usually parents and children) in abuse investigations is the length of time it can take for the relevant agencies and their personnel to complete their investigation tasks and make their reports. A combination of factors, including heavy professional workloads as well as the relative complexity of the task, can lead to investigation periods lasting anywhere from three months to one year. This is usually a period in which emotions run very high, particularly in the key participants. The adult participants usually have no direct contact with each other, and the allegedly abusive parent may have little or no direct contact with the child or children. The common-sense mental health professional intervention logic during these waiting periods has often been to provide as much support as possible for the family members on an individual basis, but not to contemplate any family or joint parental consultations. It is easy to see why such logic might prevail. Very often the parent against whom an allegation of physical or sexual abuse is made may be traumatised by the allegation and enraged by the part she assumes the other parent has played in the making of the allegation (Herman, 1998). The parent supporting the allegation, once the allegation is not fostered with malicious intent, may also be traumatised by the belief that her child has been abused by the other parent. The children in the family may be experiencing the disruption of significantly altered care arrangements during this often prolonged waiting/ investigation period, as well as experiencing a massive conflict of loyalties in the context of the multiple interviews they must endure as part of the investigation processes.

The stakes are so high for all the key participants that it is impossible for family members not to experience the period as one filled with stress and anxiety, in the face of which the offering of therapeutic support to individuals in the family makes a lot of sense while the professional community maintains its twin focus on the protection of children and the unfolding investigation activities. When conflict remains very intense, as it usually does during the investigative phase, parents are often reluctant to accept the offer of individual counselling assistance because of their fear regarding how the receipt of such assistance might be perceived should its existence be 'discovered' by 'the other side' in the conflict. Where parents can be persuaded to avail of such assistance and reassured that their involvement with it will be kept completely confidential with respect to the family court and to all of the investigative agencies in relation to the allegation, counselling can do much to regulate and contain high states of emotional arousal in either parent. The emotional regulation that such counselling facilitates can help by providing some restraint on the growth of poorly grounded narratives of the other parent (often fostered and encouraged by extended family members) as well as supporting a positive parental self-image, which becomes seriously challenged during the allegation-investigation process.

Although counselling for the alleged victims of child abuse is often considered unwise in the context of the many investigative interviews they may have to endure, professionals connected to the family often see the need for the siblings of these alleged child victims to receive some counselling during this period. The resident parent may be really supportive of this idea through seeing in it evidence that the other siblings, although not alleged to have been abused, need assistance to offset the effects of problematic parenting by the allegedly abusing parent. The parent against whom the allegation has been made is often suspicious about how such counselling might be used to advance new allegations against her and will often, in the first instance, withhold her consent for her children's attendance. In such contexts, family courts may ask their assisting mental health professionals for advice regarding the appropriateness, or otherwise, of orders for child counselling to be made, which would dispense with parental consent.

The above paragraphs note some of the dilemmas around the offering and receiving of individual, child or adult, counselling/therapy during the investigative phase, but what can be said of the usefulness of joint parent counselling or family consultations at this stage? Although the logic of intense conflict often drives parents to remain at significant distance from each other while courts, police and child protection all get to work, the mental health professional needs to keep in mind that some of the greatest threats to the longer-term emotional well-being of children in this context may arise from their prolonged disconnection from a loved nonresident parent. In the face of multiple forces inviting disconnections of different kinds, the mental health professional must work to maintain as much connection as possible throughout the family system during this phase.

This principle of maintaining family connectivity at different levels does not apply in the more serious cases of physical and sexual abuse where it is very clear to professionals from an early point in the investigative process that a child has suffered significant abuse and that a parent poses a real threat to child safety. Such situations generally do not come completely out of the blue. They are often preceded by intermittent periods of problematic parenting. On occasion, there may be a voluntary withdrawal from the context by an abusive parent who partially acknowledges her culpability in the circumstances. However, there are many contexts of both physical and sexual abuse allegations where there has been no history of problematic parenting, and where the family relational context has been marked solely by parental dispute over the emotional 'goods' that child contact affords. For example, a parent who feels abandoned by the other parent at the end of a marriage may feel that the departing parent has, through her abandonment, forfeited her entitlement to enjoy the emotional 'goods' that child contact affords.

It is only in the act of engaging the parental dyad or the parents and children together, often with the encouragement of the court, that the mental health professional is able to judge whether the states of emotional arousal in the parents can be sufficiently contained to enable some of the potential benefits for parents and children from joint consultations to accrue. The goals of such consultations may be limited to the following three areas:

1. *Information exchange*. Where child contact has been either temporarily suspended or greatly circumscribed through limited time, restricted location and/or supervision, there is a risk of the 'accused' parent being left out of the loop of much information about the ongoing life of the alleged child victim and/or his siblings. Meetings allow for information exchange not simply between parents and their children but also between children and their nonresident 'accused' parent. Children need the opportunity to share some of their daily achievements, experiences and challenges with the parent they are now seeing less frequently, and parents need the opportunity and encouragement to consult with each other about initiatives that need to be taken about their children. Neither life nor parental responsibility stop simply because an investigation is underway! Depending upon the frequency of parental or family meetings it may be opportune for the mental health professional to suggest a structured but limited email exchange between the parents at agreed intervals and to propose being copied in to such emails should the professional or either parent feel that such regulation might be necessary.

2. *Parental accountability*. The message from the mental health professional must be that the job of being mutually accountable to each other as parents continues despite ongoing investigations. The message must also be that family relationships will continue in some shape or form following the investigation and that the period of intense professional scrutiny and involvement will come to its own resting point. The parent 'supporting' the allegation against the other parent needs to be reminded that his obligation to inform and consult with the other parent remains notwithstanding the existence of an allegation. The 'accused' parent

also needs to be reminded of her ongoing responsibility to parent her children in whatever ways that remain open to her in the light of restrictions placed by both child protection frameworks and the family courts.

Many parents never have the opportunity to hear each other's perspectives either on the alleged abusive event or on the 'disclosures' by the child that form the basis of an allegation and report to child protection authorities. Parental meetings that are well managed by the mental health professional make it possible for each parent to hear the other parent more fully, as they are invited to give their respective descriptions of, on the one hand, the allegedly abusive event, and on the other hand, the details of child 'disclosures' and subsequent parental interaction with health and child protection professionals. It is important that the professional remains tightly in control of such communication exchange, and this is usually achieved by having each parent speak directly to him while the other parent is asked to remain in a listening position. It is not unusual for a considerable amount of new information to be received by each parent in these exchanges.

3. *Planning parent–child communication.* Where direct child–parent contact has been significantly reduced, the mental health professional needs to give consideration to the feasibility of increasing other means of parent–child contact such as telephone, face-time or Skype calls. The professional will, of course, need to give careful consideration to whether such increased indirect parent–child contact is either wanted by the child or children or contributes something to their well-being during the investigation period.

Managing the Outcome of Abuse Investigations

Although the investigation period following a child abuse report or allegation can be filled with tension, anxiety and disruption to regular parent–child contact patterns, the period following the communication of the investigation outcome brings with it a new set of challenges. These challenges vary depending on the outcome. Where the outcome confirms that no abuse took place, the 'accused' parent is challenged to contain her anger relating to the injury both to herself personally and to her relationship with her child that necessarily arises in the interests of child protection during the investigation phase. In particular, she is challenged to contain her appetite for revenge. It is not uncommon for the 'accused' parent to make, or want to make, counter-allegations of abuse against the other parent in this period as normal, or near normal, patterns of child contact are resumed.

Throughout the investigation period and in the aftermath of hearing the investigation findings, the 'accused' parent will have to judge whether the other parent, if she is the individual who brought the 'disclosure' information to the attention of the child protection authorities, did so in good faith or whether her actions were motivated by malice. Furthermore, 'accused' parents have to make this judgement from a position of being relatively traumatised by being in receipt of an allegation against them. The role of the mental health professional in acknowledging the wounds of these parents is immense, and very often individual therapy and support is necessary to help such parents come to terms with the fact that they have suffered an injury for which there is no compensation (Sheehan, 2007). Part of the role of the mental health professional in these circumstances is to assist this parent in her judgement processes regarding the intentionality of the parent who supported the allegation.

The parent who supported the allegation is challenged to accept the findings of an investigation which suggests that no child abuse occurred. Some parents in this position accept such findings and express some relief that, in all probability, their child was not abused. These parents often show willingness to work with the mental health professional to repair the parental relationship. Indeed, such responses are often the strongest indication that their original support of the child abuse report/allegation was made, for the most part, in good faith and with the protection of the child as their primary motive. Another group of parents refuse to accept such findings from the child protection authorities and take the position that they believe what their child said to them and that only they know what the child said directly to them. In other words, by discarding the findings of a professional investigating team, they endorse themselves as the only reliable investigative person in the matter. When the professional encounters this kind of response to such investigation findings, it can be an indication that there may have been a degree of malice in the making of the original report/allegation. Such responses are challenging for the mental health professional to deal with and are often a sign that joint parental meetings are unlikely to be productive. Should a parent displaying these responses attempt to block the restoration of the original contact regime, it is likely that the court will have to deal with the matter. Such responses also give further fuel to the view that the making of the original abuse allegation was one building block in pursuit of alienating the child from the other parent. It is important to recognise, however, that such rigid responses are sometimes a defence against what is experienced as an attack on her parental credibility brought about by the findings of the investigation. It is futile for the mental health professional in these instances to attempt to alter the views of such parents regarding such findings, and the focus of intervention should remain firmly upon the restoration of a level of child contact to the other parent that is in keeping with the child's wishes and interests. Collaboration with a family court judge is a regular part of the mental health professional role in contexts like this, and direct intervention with the parents separately and the child should be solely directed towards order implementation and compliance by both parents and child.

Where investigation findings confirm that abuse took place, such findings often lead to a new set of deliberations by both child protection personnel and the family court regarding the desirability, or otherwise, of continuing parent–child contact with the abusing parent and an assessment of the potential risk to the child from certain kinds of parent–child contact under certain circumstances. The court-appointed mental health professional has an important function of ongoing assessment of the evolving situation and advising the court, following liaison with both parents, children and child protection personnel, about what may be in the best interests of the child and her siblings with respect to contact with the parent judged to have abused a child. The parent against whom findings of child abuse have been made may not accept the findings at all and may request the court to make orders allowing for a review of the investigation data. At this point the family enters a new time period in which its members also await news of whether criminal prosecution will follow.

Skills and Interventions

Allegations of child abuse can arrive at any time in the evolution of the post-separation family life. They may happen as a prelude to, during, or after family court proceedings relating to parent–child contact. Mental health professionals need seven central skills and interventions as they assist families in conflict through the time period spanning the making of an allegation, its investigation and the communication of findings. These skills/interventions can be summarised as follows:

(i) *Containment of the family's heightened emotional field.* An allegation of child abuse against a parent normally throws all the key participants into a state of heightened emotional arousal. Understanding trauma and having a capacity to respond to trauma in different individuals is an essential element in this containment skill.

(ii) *Referrals for therapy and support.* While mindful of the demands of the investigation which is about to proceed, the mental health professional needs to be able to have a conversation with the different family members, adults and children, about their need for therapeutic support during the time of the investigation and the communication of its findings. The mental health professional needs the capacity to navigate issues surrounding parental consent for child therapy as well as the capacity to negotiate boundaries and confidentiality issues for the different therapies in relation to court proceedings. Information should be provided to parents about local self-help organisations offering support to parents who understand themselves to be targets of false allegations of child abuse. In providing such information, mental health professionals should underline for the parents that their action in providing such information is not to be understood as a prejudgement of the investigation's findings.

(iii) *Liaison with other professionals joining the conflict management system.* The mental health professional needs the capacity to liaise with other professionals in an expanded conflict management system as may be necessary. Such liaison communication needs to be performed in an open and transparent way with respect to the family. Care must be taken in these exchanges not to further stimulate an already heightened emotional field.

(iv) *Maintaining and protecting family connection and communication.* The mental health professional must seek out opportunities to keep the different parts of the family connected to each other in the face of the multiple forces that invite distance and disconnection. Joint parental meetings and/or family meetings should focus on exchange of information about children, maintaining a culture of parental mutual accountability and planning interim revisions to parent–child communication.

(v) *Family court liaison and collaboration.* Parents may engage the family court on many occasions during the period of an allegation's investigation and the production and communication of findings. The court-appointed mental health professional has an important role in liaising with the family court as it manages different facets of parent–child contact during this time period.

(vi) *Managing counter-allegations.* In the aftermath of findings which indicate that no child abuse has occurred, the mental health professional has a role in identifying, acknowledging and containing feelings of rage and injustice in the 'accused' parent. The mental health professional will also play a part, alongside child protection personnel, in discriminating between those counter-allegations that are fuelled by revenge from those that warrant independent investigation.

(vii) *Order Implementation in the investigation findings phase.* It is not unusual for the court to make revised orders for child contact at this stage, particularly if no findings of abuse are made. The mental health professional may be required to engage with both parents and children therapeutically, and in a manner accountable to the court, to restore the level of contact that the court feels is in the best interests of children.

Personal and Reflective Exercises

The following three exercises invite the reader to explore their relationship to the theme of the chapter. Like most of the exercises in this book, they can be done in two or more stages. The first approach to each exercise may simply get the reflective 'motor' up and running, and a second approach, made a few days later, may allow for a deeper level of personal experience to emerge.

1. Write an extended note about the range of both your personal and professional experience of the theme of the chapter. Are there some aspects of this theme that you are more connected to in your experience? Are there some aspects of this theme that you have little or no direct experience of in either your personal or professional life? Are there particular memories from either your personal life or professional life that have been evoked in the reading of this chapter?

2. Imagine you are a mother whose five-year-old daughter returned from a contact weekend with her father to tell you, tearfully, that her dad hurt her in the genital area while giving her a bath at the weekend. Write a note about what you think your feelings might be in the face of hearing such a tearful complaint from your daughter. What do you think you would do? Whom might you turn to, apart from your daughter, in responding to such a complaint from your child?

3. Imagine you are a separated father and that you have been contacted by a child protection social worker a couple of days after you have had your five-year-old daughter stay over with you for the weekend. Imagine further that when you meet the social worker at her request, she tells you that your daughter has made a 'disclosure' which suggests that some inappropriate touching of her genital area may have taken place during her bath time while in your care and that she wishes to investigate the matter. Write a note about what your reaction might be in such circumstances. Who might you turn to in the middle of this situation? What might be the range of your different responses to this situation?

THE FAMILY COURT AND KEY MENTAL HEALTH PROFESSIONAL INTERVENTIONS

Most mental health professionals working with family conflict after separation and divorce share an assumption that it is preferable, where possible, for parents to attempt conflict resolution without recourse to the family courts. The rationale underlying this assumption is associated with the host of developments, already mentioned in this book, that seem to foster conflict escalation once entry to the family court has been made. However, there are some separating and divorcing families where, for a variety of reasons, conflict cannot be managed without the assistance of the family court. Where the performance of their conflicts leads to repeated appearances before the family court, these separated parents and their families often draw the description 'high conflict' from the legal and mental health professionals associated with them. In these situations, the mental health professional is regularly required to work with the court to maximise the *containment* aspect of what the court can provide with respect to family conflict in contrast to the more *escalating* effects that court involvement regularly has on these same conflicts. In the collaborative work between court and mental health professional, whether earlier or later in the conflict development cycle, a number of key mental health professional interventions that the court can either suggest or order in the context of its own management of the issues are placed before it. This chapter is about five of these interventions. The first three of these interventions are delivered following an order of the court and on the understanding that the court will be given feedback by the professional regarding the progress of different family members within these interventions towards the goal of the intervention. These three interventions are family therapy, nonconfidential mediation and parent co-ordination. The final two interventions occur when there is either a break in legal proceedings or when legal proceedings have reached a conclusion. These interventions are a multiple family group intervention and interventions relating to the loss of a parent–child relationship. Although these two interventions may happen with the support of the court, neither parent will be accountable to the court for either their participation, or performance, within the interventions. This chapter considers each of these five interventions, gives examples of their use and reflects upon the kind of conflict contexts where such interventions may be useful and the form that collaboration with the family court might take.

Family Therapy

Family therapy (Burnham, 1986; Carr, 2000; Jones, 1993; Lowe, 2004; Minuchin, 1974) has been developed over the last 70 years as a rich array of therapeutic approaches to problem resolution which focuses on the relational context of both child and adult problems. Family therapy has probably been thought about as an intervention more suited to the prevention of problem escalation within 'intact' families than an intervention with families where the processes of separation and divorce are well under way. It is often considered even less when these processes are marked by persistent conflict. In broad terms, family therapy can be thought about as an intervention which brings together some or all family members with a view to assessing the relational context of the problems being experienced by one or more family members, and searching for relational solutions to those same problems. Although much has been written about the effectiveness of family therapy with a wide range of child-focussed (Carr, 2009a) and adult-focussed problems (Carr, 2009b), much less is known about its contribution to problem resolution in the context of the post-separation family crises that regularly present within conflicts coming before the family courts. In this section of the chapter, a small number of post-separation conflict scenarios are considered where a court referral for family therapy has something positive to offer within the context of the court's management of post-separation family impasse. The three contexts named here do not in any way constitute an exhaustive list of the types of post-separation family conflict scenarios where family therapy under the wing of the court may prove a beneficial intervention. Rather, they represent a sample of not untypical post-separation conflict contexts where this writer has found court-ordered family therapy to be of assistance.

Where the court orders or recommends a period of family therapy, it is important that the goal of the intervention is clearly named in a court order if an order is made. Alternatively, the goal of the proposed intervention should be written into the court record if the status of the referral is that of a court recommendation or proposal (Fidler et al., 2013). No matter what the status of the court referral for family therapy, it is important that neither parent nor his or her assisting legal and mental health professionals leave the court with any doubt about the aims of the intervention. The naming of goals does two things. Firstly, it allows the intervention to be evaluated in terms of its progression towards the goal, and secondly, it focuses the minds of parents who are obliged to work collaboratively with the therapist towards the achievement of the goal, rather than just 'sitting out' the process. The goal may be stated simply as the facilitation of contact for a child with her parent in a context where no contact is currently happening. Or, the court may decide to name two goals for the therapy, as when they propose that the goals are 'to facilitate contact for the child with her parent and/or to develop an understanding for the court about why such contact is not being achieved if it is not being achieved'. Such twin goals for family therapy can be set in contexts where the court has already procured an evaluation, and its resulting orders have not been complied with for whatever reasons. Such goals combine a therapeutic input with an element of ongoing assessment in a way that circumvents the need for a further full evaluation process. In all such planned family therapy, the intervention is time-limited and is oriented towards the next occasion on which the court will hear the matter. The court may seek either a written report from the mental health professional about the process or may simply require that the professional give oral evidence about the therapy at the hearing. The following are examples of three different kinds of court-related post-separation family conflicts where a family therapy intervention was found to be useful.

Addressing Children's Sadness and Loss within Post-separation Parental Conflict

Toby and Catherine had been separated nine months, and Toby had made a court application for a contact order in relation to his six-year-old daughter, Rachel, who had failed to join her eight-year-old brother, Matthew, on the twice-per-week contact periods that had been informally agreed between the parents. Catherine had told Toby that she was unwilling to 'force' her daughter to go with her brother when she was showing such tearfulness and upset at the times when the father came to pick up the children. Angry parental scenes at handovers seemed to be the catalyst for even greater levels of distress in Rachel. Toby believed that Catherine was 'not giving permission' for Rachel to go on the scheduled visits with him, and was seeking an order from the court to allow him to pick the children up for contact periods directly from school, thus circumventing the influence he alleged Catherine was having on the process. The court decided to defer its decision on the making of any order, to allow time for a family therapeutic process to occur, with the goal of facilitating the commencement of Rachel's contact with her father. Six family therapy meetings brought to light how distressed both children still were by the losses associated with parental separation and how surprised both parents were about their children's continuing reaction to the separation in the light of how well they felt they had prepared them for the event. The sessions also brought to light how much Rachel missed the small routines she had shared with her father while he was still in the home and how much Matthew missed his mother when he was staying over with his father for a 24-hour period. A mixture of control of parental emotion and interaction at the time of handovers, acknowledging of the children's sense of sadness and loss at the family separation, the planning of one-hour trips to the local shop for Rachel with her father alone, and agreed telephone contact between all four family members (father speaking to mother, Matthew speaking to mother and to Rachel, Rachel speaking to father) while Matthew was overnight with father changed the family's emotional context considerably. By the time the mental health professional made an oral report to the court about the therapy on the date of the subsequent hearing, Rachel was comfortably accompanying Matthew for one of the weekly non-overnight contact periods with their father. The father was sufficiently reassured that the therapy was going in a good direction for both children with respect to contact that he agreed to withdraw his application to the court for a contact order on the understanding that Catherine would agree to continue voluntarily with the family therapy. The court commended both parents for their positive work in family therapy in different ways, encouraged their ongoing voluntary participation in the therapeutic process and reassured them that the court and its services would be there for them if they were needed in the future.

Addressing Family Alliances in Post-separation Family Conflict

As has been observed in a previous chapter, a prolonged in-house phase to the separation process can pose significant challenges for establishing satisfactory levels of parent–child contact in the post-residential phase of the process. When an impending separation is experienced as a very threatening, even though wanted, event by either or both parents, a parental clinging to a child can occur as a means of emotional comfort for both parent and child. Parents often share a bed with one of their children during these time periods, which can be of different lengths. Patterns of parent–child alliance can be set up and solidified during these times, and such alliances do not automatically soften once one parent has transitioned to a nonresident status. As can be seen from the following example, it is not unusual for some children in these circumstances to refuse to participate in very moderate contact schedules ordered by the court following residence and contact evaluation reports.

Michael (12 years) and Nadine (ten years) were the two children at the centre of a court application by their father, Paul (38 years), for enforcement of existing orders for contact. Paul and his wife, Marcia (38 years), had an in-house separation for two years before Paul left the family home as part of an agreement regarding the couple's separation. The family court ordered a residence and contact evaluation during this period, and orders were subsequently made for the children's contact with Paul once the residential separation had occurred. However, during the in-house phase of the separation process, Marcia had slept with Nadine in the couple's bed and bedroom while Paul moved into Nadine's room, with Michael remaining in his own bedroom. Marcia and Nadine had become very close during this period as had Paul and Michael. Father and son had 'gone fishing' a lot together without being accompanied by Nadine as would have happened regularly before the breakdown of the relationship. Similarly, Michael started to decline Marcia's invitations to him to come to the shops with her and Nadine, an activity he would have regularly participated in prior to the estrangement in the parental relationship. After the residential separation, Michael went on all the ordered contact periods, including the overnights, but Nadine refused to go with her father despite coming to the door to see him when he came to collect her and her brother. Following a two-month period of Nadine refusing to participate in the ordered contact periods, and legal exchanges between the lawyers for both parents, Paul took the application for order enforcement, which resulted in the court requesting that the family attend for therapy during an adjournment period of three months. The four family members came together for six family therapy meetings where the objective of the therapy was set by the court as 'facilitating Nadine to fulfil the contact orders already in place'. During the initial meetings, the therapist focussed upon Nadine's experiences over the previous two and a half years and how much of her routine had been disrupted by the particular way her parents' relationship had evolved at home. She had lost out with respect to play dates with her friends, as Marcia had not encouraged her to go to friends' houses as she was unable to reciprocate these gestures because of the situation in the home and was embarrassed that people would find out what was going on. Since her father had left, Nadine had voluntarily let go of her swimming classes, an activity she had really enjoyed, because of her mother's anxiety about not being able to afford basic items for the household. She was also continuing to sleep with her mother, even though her bedroom was now free following her father's departure. The therapist enabled both parents to tune in once more to their daughter's changed life experiences without blaming each other. Michael 'ratted' on his younger sister by telling his parents how much she wanted to go back to her swimming, but knew her mother did not have the money and did not want to upset her mother by asking if she could resume. In the fourth meeting, Paul asked for some time with the therapist alone with Marcia while the children waited in the waiting room. He wanted to talk with Marcia about getting Nadine back into her own bed, and it had transpired that Marcia had already spoken to Nadine about this and they had agreed a date for this to happen one week later. The therapist then raised the issue of a possible return to swimming lessons and wondered whether they might approach a local voluntary organisation for some financial assistance towards the cost of the lessons. Marcia was interested in this suggestion, whereas Paul felt he could not possibly accept such a course of action as he had a full-time job and Marcia worked part-time four mornings per week. Despite having fought hard over a child support order that the court had made, Paul proposed that he would pay two-thirds of the cost of the swimming lessons for Nadine if Marcia would pay one third. Marcia agreed to this proposal so long as she would not have to pay the bus fare to and from the lessons. Paul countered this by proposing that as the lessons were on at 5 p.m., he would bring Nadine to and from the lessons if she would go with him. Marcia felt this was a good solution and asked that she be allowed to talk this idea over with Nadine on her own rather than have it spoken about openly in the family therapy meeting. Paul and the therapist thought this idea made good sense. During the next week, Marcia rang Paul to say that she had successfully persuaded Nadine to go to her swimming lessons with him, and Nadine had told her mother that it didn't matter to her who brought her to the lessons. Paul subsequently booked the lessons and started to bring Nadine to her swimming on a weekly basis. When Marcia privately offered him her share of the money for the swimming lessons, Paul refused to take it and suggested she might want to do something for Michael in case they had 'got his nose out of joint' through what they were doing for Nadine. On the 'swimming afternoon', mother subtly changed the timing of her daily trip to the supermarket to coincide with the swimming lesson and persuaded Michael to come with her again on these trips to help her with the bags. During the shopping, she offered him a 'treat', which he accepted. Within a couple of weeks and a few further therapy meetings, Nadine was back in her own bed and bedroom; Michael had persuaded Nadine to come on the regular weekend visit to the movies with him and his father; and the parents began to take ownership of the contact arrangements by jointly arguing that what had been ordered by the courts did not particularly suit their circumstances in certain respects. In a final meeting before the matter returned to the court, they discussed their amended ideas with the children, who agreed that they made much more sense given the different things they all had to do. When the matter returned to court, the parents, through their legal representatives, reported that their work in family therapy had helped Nadine to partially fulfil the original contact orders and that they were asking the court to modify those orders in line with what they both felt made more current sense for the two children and themselves.

In the above dispute, it is likely that one of the features that enabled family therapy to facilitate some resolution to the issues was the referral by the court for family therapy very early in the conflict development cycle. It is this writer's experience that when such family alliances have crystallised over much longer periods of time, the reconfiguration of family alliance patterns may prove much more challenging.

Addressing Impasses around Parent–child Contact in the Context of Alleged Domestic Violence

In the last chapter, attention was drawn to the power of different discourses that are evoked when sexual abuse is alleged to have occurred. Assertions that domestic violence has occurred as a prelude, of whatever length, to parental separation brings in to play discourses of equal strength. There are many contexts of historical domestic violence where the family courts refuse, with comfort, applications for child contact to a parent who has been clearly and verifiably physically and/or psychologically abusive to an ex-partner and/or their children on foot of court-ordered evaluation reports oriented towards children's wishes and best interests. These contexts form one 'black and white' end of a spectrum which moves through many shades of grey on its way to the other end. Along this spectrum are a variety of familial contexts where historical domestic violence has been alleged and where post-separation contact arrangements begin to falter very soon after an allegedly abusive parent has left the home. In many contexts of post-separation conflict, such allegations of historical domestic violence occur along with denials and counter-allegations of different kinds. Very often there has been no medical evidence of physical abuse, no reports of abuse to the police and no applications for exclusion or safety orders. In many such contexts, parents may agree that there was never aggression directed towards a child. However, a resident parent who understands himself to be a victim of domestic violence may flatly refuse to cooperate with any requests from his ex-partner for child contact. Such refusal is often based on the dual assertion that the child does not wish to go with the other parent and that, in any event, he would not trust his allegedly abusive ex-partner with the safety of their child. Such contexts often present before the courts with two parents requesting the court to foreground two different and competing discourses in the management of their conflict. One discourse bears the title 'domestic violence', and the other opposing discourse is 'parental aliena-tion'. Such contexts often re-present to the court in the form of applications for breach of contact orders made on foot of recommendations arising from prior court-ordered evaluations.

In many of the above 'grey zone' contexts, where such discourses are set in opposition to each other, the court may make a referral and an order for family therapy while leaving orders for small amounts of contact in place. Where the goals of the therapy are set in the form of 'to facilitate the realisation of John's contact time with his father and/or to understand why such contact is not happening if it fails to occur', family therapy under the eye of the court has the possibility of exploring both parental and child experiences and memories of past relationships, as well as giving an opportunity for each person's deeper desires to emerge. Where the therapy fails to facilitate contact, it can at least provide a new platform of information for the court regarding parental behaviour during the therapy from which it can plan its future management of the situation. The following vignette shows how an order for family therapy can be helpful even when it fails to achieve its primary goal of facilitating contact.

Jennifer (40 years) and Stephen (38 years) were separated for two years when the court ordered a period of family therapy following a number of hearings which monitored a stop–start approach to the realisation of Stephen's contact with their four children. Contact for the children with Stephen had been ordered by the court early in the separation process and following a court-ordered evaluation. Jennifer had not agreed with the outcome of the evaluation and made no secret of her opposition to this contact. The evaluation had revealed a very positive and involved relationship between father and all four children before the separation, and the children had expressed a desire to see their father during the evaluation. Despite this early position, the children refused to go for contact periods with father once the order was made. The order for family therapy was made with the twin goals of facilitating the children's contact with father and/or developing an understanding of why such contact was not occurring. The children, two girls of 11 and nine years and two boys of eight and five years, appeared to engage well with father and with the therapist during the two initial family therapy meetings. However, at different points in the meeting when the children were enthusiastically sharing with the father some of their everyday school and sporting experiences, mother interrupted this very positive engagement, saying to father: 'Don't you think you can pull the wool over your children's eyes about what you have done to me. They all know that you have hit me and abused me behind closed doors, and this so-called family therapy is never going to change that.' Following mother's intervention, the children physically and emotionally retreated from the father in the room, with the older girls saying, 'You are bad, and none of us want to see you.' Following a third meeting, in which similar sequences of family interaction occurred, the mother called the therapist to say she was not bringing the children to any more therapy, and she did not see why she had to expose them to the same person who had abused her. In oral evidence to the court at the next hearing, the family

182

therapist reported her observations of these interactional sequences in the family therapy and the fact that the mother had closed the door on the therapy. The court then planned its next intervention based upon the new information available to it.

As noted in an earlier chapter, court-ordered family therapy in contexts where parental alienation is a key element in the breakdown of contact between a child and a nonresident parent will have little chance of succeeding unless it is backed up by clearly defined goals and consistently implemented sanctions for noncompliance with the spirit and aims of the therapy. Where these goals are not predefined by the court and sanctions are either not possible or are not consistently applied, the collaboration between court and therapist will unwittingly foster the longer-term alienation of the child from the nonresident parent while undermining parental respect for the law and its mechanisms.

Nonconfidential Mediation

Mediation has been mentioned several times already in this book. In the context of family and parental conflict following separation and divorce, this intervention occurs in its more 'classical' form, where the parties to a dispute voluntarily enter a process of negotiation with a mediator and where the process remains confidential in the interests of the parties finding their own resolution as an alternative to one being legally imposed. In its classical form, mediation is a dispute resolution process that occurs before parents make an application to the court. Indeed, the justification for commencing legal proceedings is often that the process of mediation has been tried and failed. However, in many jurisdictions the courts can require further mediation efforts by parents even after proceedings have commenced. When this occurs, mediation becomes a within-proceedings event whose processes and content are reportable to the court. Very often classical mediation between separated or divorced parents breaks down because of the unreasonable demands of one or both parents. In nonconfidential mediation, the court charges parents to make further efforts to find an assisted/mediated resolution to some of their disputes but to do so under the eye of the court. The parents are told in advance of the court's requirement that they endeavour to reach as much agreement as they can and that both the content of their agreements and the shape of their dispute processes around matters not yet resolved will be reported by the mediating mental health professional back to the court. For those litigating parents who find themselves repeatedly before the family court with a wide, and often expanding, range of disputed issues, the nonconfidential element of within-proceedings mediation provides another level of containment with respect to the management of their disputes. Such mediation can work well when the time allowed for it by the court is brief and the parties know that the court will make its own orders, based upon the feedback of the mental health professional about both the content and process of mediation, in matters where agreement cannot be reached. Courts may propose that such mediation interventions occur during a break in proceedings on the day of a court hearing itself or may suggest a mediation moratorium of no more than a couple of weeks before the disputed matters are ruled upon by the court if not already agreed by the parents.

Belinda and John, the parents of eight- and ten-year-old boys, found themselves before the court seven years after their residential separation and three years after their divorce. Since the time of the initial separation and the breakdown of their early mediation efforts, the court had, with the assistance of three successive evaluation reports within the first four years of the separation, made orders about daytime contact, overnight care, location of handovers, paternal presence at child medical appointments, as well as about a range of relatively minor matters not anticipated by evaluators as potentially giving rise to dispute. In all, they had been in the family court on 17 different occasions for hearings of different lengths. On this occasion, John had made application to the court to enforce his court-ordered four-hour birthday contact period with the two boys in a context where the birthday of the eldest of the two boys fell on a public holiday Monday where the current orders allowed Belinda's weekend period with the boys to be extended to include the whole of the public holiday Monday. The particular weekend period was coming up three weeks after the application was listed in the court, and Belinda told the court that she was planning to bring the boys away for the full weekend with her parents, whose 50th wedding anniversary occurred on the same day as her son's birthday. She also made the point to the court that she was entitled under the existing orders to have uninterrupted time with her two boys on that particular weekend. The judge acknowledged that there was an anomaly in the Court's orders which this particular conjunction of events had brought to light, and suggested to the parents, whose argumentative style she was familiar with from previous hearings, that they take two weeks to attempt to find a resolution of their own with the assistance of a mental health professional mediator. She reassured them that that she would be seeking a verbal report from the mental health professional about both the content and process of their efforts. This created a new context for the parents, who were becoming used to the court making orders in each new dispute area presented.

When they met with the mediator, Belinda told of the plans she had made for the public holiday Monday and the efforts she had made to book herself, the boys and her parents into a hotel located about 100 kilometres from the town where she and John both resided. She had a table booked for 1 p.m. in the hotel for a lunch to celebrate her parents' anniversary and another table booked in a nearby restaurant for 6.30 p.m. to celebrate her son's birthday. She was adamant that these bookings could not be touched. The mediator explored with John whether he would be willing to avail of his birthday contact in the location of the hotel and at a time that did not disturb Belinda's hotel and restaurant bookings. Belinda then interjected to say she was not going to have John anywhere 'next or near' the hotel on that day as it would be too distressing for her now ageing parents on their 'special day'. John was interested in the mediator's proposal and suggested that he could see the boys from 2 p.m. to 6 p.m. on that day and that he could pick them up from, and drop them back to, the hotel. Belinda protested that John should be able to have his four-hour birthday contact on another day and not be so rigid as to demand it on the birthday in question. In any event, she felt that afternoon contact would interrupt the flow of the day for her parents and restrict everyone's freedom in the afternoon. The mediator proposed to John that he might avail of the court-ordered contact period in the morning of the public holiday, to which he replied that it would take him one and a half hours to get to the hotel location and that he would not be able to commence the contact period until 10 a.m., which would only allow three hours' contact instead of four. The mediator wondered if he would be willing to forgo one of his four birthday contact hours to facilitate a resolution for the boys as well as for themselves. He said he would be prepared to do this. The mediator commended his preparedness to make a sacrifice and told him that the court should know about this flexibility on his part in the middle of this difficult negotiation. Belinda thought it was ridiculous that the court would hear about something as 'puny' as giving up one hour of contact, and said there was still no way she would have John come near the hotel on the day. She spontaneously suggested that she drive the boys to meet their father in the town 30 minutes away from the hotel so that he could meet them there at 9.30 a.m. and keep them until 1p.m., when she would pick them up from the same location. The mediator reminded Belinda of the 1 p.m. lunch booking and that it would be unlikely that she would be back in the hotel before 1.30 p.m. John then interjected to say that if Belinda was prepared to drive the boys to and from the newly proposed contact venue, he was prepared to have the boys just for three hours on that day, which meant that Belinda could pick them up at 12.30 p.m. and get all three of them to the hotel by 1 p.m. The mediator thought this was a good proposal and told the parents that if they went with this resolution, he would be able to report to the court that both parents had exercised some flexibility and made some sacrifices in the manner proposed in the interests of the children. The mediator asked them to take a five-minute break to consider whether they could accept such a deal that the court would later turn into an order. Having considered the matter separately, both parents returned to the mediation room and indicated that they agreed to the proposal. This agreement was then written out by the mediator and signed by the parents. The mediating mental health professional then handed the agreement in to the court on the day of the hearing and was given the opportunity by the court to report on both the content and process aspects of the agreement. Both parents were then commended by the judge for the unique sacrifices and flexibilities they had shown within the negotiations. An order was duly made in the terms of their agreement.

Where nonconfidential mediation achieves some success, it has the advantage of offering parents the means of altering their identities in the eyes of the court. Parents who repeatedly litigate their disputes run the risk of significant admonishment by judges who can grow weary of adjudicating in their disputes, which all carry a similar flavour. This is why the reporting element of the process is so important for some parents, and it is vital that judges and their assisting mental health professionals don't lose the opportunity to be commending and appreciative of parental efforts when these are deserved.

Parenting Coordination

Since the turn of the century, there has been considerable evidence concerning the harmful effects of parental conflict on children from separated and divorced families (Kelly, 2000). Family justice systems are also increasingly aware of the negative impact of adversarial approaches to conflict resolution on post-separation parenting relationships already embroiled in extended dispute. Parenting coordination is a concept and practice that attempts to address these realities in contexts where separated and divorced parents are experiencing protracted conflict and repeated appearances before the family court. As an approach to dispute resolution, it tries to replace the adversarial approach of the courtroom with as much collaboration as possible. Parenting coordination is practised by a parent coordinator who can either be appointed by the court or engaged privately by parents to provide a particular set of services. Higuchi and Lally (2014b) describe the parent coordinator as a legal or mental health professional 'who uses mediation and education techniques to resolve disputes regarding parenting plans but who also has the ability to arbitrate and make decisions when mediation efforts are not successful' (p. 4). The great promise of parenting coordination as an intervention is its capacity to promote parental learning and support mediated resolution of disputes while limiting the amount of time that children are exposed to all the uncertainties that go with their parents' inability to reach agreement over matters which concern them.

Although Kelly (2014) suggests that parenting coordination as an intervention first emerged in northern California in the mid-1980s, it is likely that a variety of less formal approaches to the intervention have existed in different jurisdictions throughout the globe for a much longer time. There is no doubt that increasing levels of marital dissolution, pressures on family justice systems and the high cost for parents of continuing litigation have all contributed to the development and acceptability of the intervention. As an intervention, parenting coordination is relevant for those parents who remain in significant conflict several years after separation or divorce. Research highlighting parenting patterns two to three years post-divorce showed that between 20 per cent (Hetherington, 1999) and 24 per cent (Maccoby and Mnookin, 1992) of parents remained highly conflicted. Such research findings suggest that the intervention may be relevant for as many as one-fifth to one-quarter of all separating parents.

A full review of the extent to which the parenting coordination intervention has been formally established by legal statute in different jurisdictions is beyond the scope of this book. Suffice to say that the intervention has both its formal and less formal faces in different jurisdictions. In some jurisdictions, the role of the parent coordinator is set up by legal statute, which defines and limits the authority of the role as well as specifying the relationship of the role to judicial authority. In these jurisdictions, there is often an Office of Parenting Coordination which both administers the intervention on behalf of the jurisdiction as well as advises judicial authority on the rules required for its successful functioning. In those more formally developed systems, rules can cover such matters as the appointment of parent coordinators, their necessary qualifications, the length of time of their appointment, by whom and how agenda items are set for meetings between parents and their coordinator, the extent of parental obligation to attend meetings convened by the parent coordinator, the extent of mediation efforts required before the arbitration or decision-making function of the parent coordinator kicks in, the manner in which arbitration decisions are to be communicated to parents, the range of issues to which the arbitrating authority of the parent coordinator can apply, whether and to what extent children of different ages can be consulted by the coordinator and the circumstances under which any of the parties in the parenting coordination intervention (either of the parents or the parenting coordinator) can bring disputes back before the court. In general, the intervention is oriented solely to those day-to-day decisions about the care of children which parents are unable to agree upon. It is not used for such larger issues as alteration in children's residential arrangements, significant shifts in care plans or decisions about school placements.

In some jurisdictions, the role of parent coordinator can take on a distinctively case-management function. Fidler et al. (2013) note how the courts in certain Canadian jurisdictions can appoint a parent coordinator in very complex cases where there have been, and may continue to be, a large number of professionals involved (e.g. police, child protection workers, therapists for different family members, school personnel). In these cases, court-ordered evaluations have usually already taken place. The parent coordinator becomes, effectively, a case manager on behalf of the judicial authority and may have the authority to make decisions about the inclusion of additional therapists on the treatment team when parents cannot agree, or about the pacing of parenting plans that have been already given general approval by the court. The advantage of the role in these complex cases is that it leaves therapist figures free of any decision-making role.

In some jurisdictions where the intervention is well developed and underpinned by statute, there may be a Parenting Coordination service available to litigating parents free of charge in cases where the court directs the intervention. In other jurisdictions, parents must pay the parent coordinator directly for the service. In many contexts, parents are free to make their own private contract with a parent coordinator for their services and to be guided in this contract development by the rules laid down by statute in their jurisdiction.

Despite the many disadvantages attaching to less formal systems for deploying the parent coordinating role (e.g. the lack of clarity for parents and parenting coordinators about rules of engagement and limits to the parenting coordinator's arbitration authority), such systems have the capacity to be helpful to some parents and children in some contexts. The following example illustrates the operation of a less formal system in which the role of parent coordinator is not explicitly named.

Natalie and Alan were the parents of eight-year-old Jack and six-year-old Ella. They were separated four years and had been to the family court for 12 separate hearings. They had been in dispute about most things to do with their children since they parted, and three separate evaluation reports had been prepared for the court during this time. The judge at the 12th hearing, having taken hold of the case since the fifth hearing, made orders in relation to the matters at hand while castigating the parents for not making better efforts to mediate resolutions to the normal day-to-day matters that arise with children of their children's ages. He made his frustration known to the litigants, who were now representing themselves as they had both run out of funds to pay for legal assistance. He told the litigants that he did not wish to see them again before him for relatively minor matters and warned that he might deal with matters 'very decisively' should he be faced with such 'intransigence' in the future. He made an additional order that the parents were to consult the most recent evaluator in the case, who was present in court, when they had any differences between them about anything but the most serious matters, and to seek to resolve their issues with this professional's assistance. Should they fail to reach an agreement on any issue, they were to follow the advice of the same professional in the matters under dispute. Furthermore, the order further directed that they were not to make new applications to the court about anything but the most serious matters without having a joint consultation with this mental health professional in the first instance about whatever issues were at stake. The court further ordered that the mental health professional had the freedom to contact the court office directly to have the case relisted for hearing should they have concerns about the children's well-being that they felt the court should be informed about.

Natalie and Alan proceeded to have seven consultations with the mental health professional in the year after the 12th hearing. They had disputes about medical appointments for both children, summer activities for the children, grandparent involvement in the children's birthday parties, the use of particular mobile telephones for telephone contact, and the use of Skype while the children were away on holidays. The mental health professional found that when the emotional climate of the consultations was contained, the parents were able to reach agreement on most issues, and the only issue where advice and direction needed to be given was in relation to the summer activities of the two children when the time for mediation naturally ran out without agreement being reached. The professional insisted that preliminary email exchanges between the parents about any issue should be copied to them. This led to some confidential telephone exchanges with one of the parents, whose emails were felt by the assisting professional to be excessively critical in tone, thereby undermining the likelihood of reaching agreement. This parent agreed to some email coaching in advance of sending mails to his ex-partner. During the second year after the 12th hearing, there were only three consultations with the assisting professional about minor adjustments to court orders for holidays, which the professional noticed were resolved with relative ease. The copying in of the professional to the email exchanges continued even though the email coaching of one parent ceased. The professional noticed an increasing capacity of the parents to resolve minor issues through email alone and without consultation. There were no consultations requested in the third year after the 12th hearing.

Multiple Family Group Intervention

In many Western societies, parents and children going through the normal challenges associated with separation and divorce can avail of group services that offer either education and/or therapeutic support relevant to their transition. Practitioners engaged in this area of practice, however, know how few therapeutic opportunities there are for whole families once parents become caught up in a seemingly endless saga of interpersonal conflict and court appearances that drain them emotionally and financially. So often, parents caught in these conflicts become socially isolated apart from contact with their own extended family members, who seem to professionals to offer them a type of support that does little to contain their developing paranoia about their ex-partners. The creation of space for fresh thinking and speaking becomes a real challenge for mental health professionals working with this particular group of parents and children engaged in significantly high levels of conflict.

Exceptions to this rather bleak picture can be found in therapeutic group projects offered to parents and children caught in high-conflict divorces (Toren et al., 2013; Van Lawick and Visser, 2015). Van Lawick and Visser describe how they developed such a family group project in The Netherlands, which they call 'No Kids in the Middle'. The project runs over an eight-week period where both parents and children meet with other parents and children for a two-hour period each week, with a short break in the middle. The parents can seek to participate in the project without referral or may be referred to the project by the court, mediation services or other voluntary services. They must, however, not be currently engaged in legal proceedings or, at the very least, be on a 'break' from such proceedings. Each project cycle works with six families at a time with two therapists working with the parents and two therapists working with the children in different rooms in the same building. All the parents and children come together in the same large room just before the group work begins, during a break in the middle of the two-hour period, and at the end of the session. The whole thrust of the project is to create a dialogical space for parents and children where they get the support to think and express themselves in new ways while having the possibility to learn from each other. The following six main principles guide the work in the project: the child is always kept in mind; the 'work' happens in groups; legal processes are interrupted; professional-free spaces for family interaction are created; children's creative expressions are shared with the parent group; and the network surrounding the family is reached out to.

Parents and children who are engaged in intense conflict over long periods of time have usually been the subject of equally intense scrutiny and evaluation by professionals over a long period of time. As conflict progresses, the opportunity for anything therapeutic to happen seems to decrease. What is unique about this multiple family group project is that it takes the evaluative pressure off parents and children while creating opportunities for them to interact in an environment where they have the support of other parents and children. The other element of this project that is uniquely creative is the reaching out from the beginning to the networks of others who are involved in supporting the parents and children on an everyday basis. In the literature relating to high-conflict divorce, the members of these networks are too often spoken about simply as 'negative advocates' for the child (Eddy, 2010). Here, the network members are reached out to respectfully, have the goals and challenges of the project explained to them and receive sincere requests from the professionals for their assistance. Although outcome evaluation for this project is ongoing, the project leaders have suggested that those parents who completed the project program report less parental conflict and that conflicts have become more constructive when they occur. Parents also seem, on program completion, to be more accepting of their divorce, more open to forgiveness and more likely to trust each other (Van Lawick and Visser, 2017).

Recording Love and Loss: A Family Intervention Tool in Contexts of High-conflict Divorce

Although the children of many high-conflict divorces experience their parents' disputes over multiple aspects of their care and development, most of them remain in relationship with their nonresident parent and continue to have contact with that parent at different levels of frequency. There are a group of children, however, whose relationship with their other, nonresident parent breaks down fully and finally despite all efforts by the court and it's assisting professionals to keep the parent–child contact alive. Whether such final resistance to parent contact is the result of clear and undiluted alienation of the child from her nonresident parent by her primary carer or the child's own 'decision', made under the weight of exposure to long-standing parental conflict, the result looks the same – a child is finally cut off from her parent, and a parent suffers the loss of both his child and the opportunity to parent his child. The 'end' often comes when that parent runs out of faith in the possibility of the court being able to help him to regain a foothold in his child's life. All interventions, legal and therapeutic, appear to have been attempted, and all have been defeated with respect to their goal. This writer recalls many such incidents, over a number of decades, where the 'rejected' parent begins to come to terms with the collapse of different interventions, realises that the relationship with his child is over for now, and begins to ask questions about the future. 'Will my child come back to me in time? Will he begin to realise in later adolescence what the other parent has done to him and our relationship?' When the uncertainty about all these questions is faced and the parent realises that the future may hold no greater promise than the present, he is left in front of the mental health professional with nothing but an unacknowledged love for his child and a most profound loss that remains unrecognised by those from whom he most needs this recognition.

About 20 years ago, when faced with one such rejected parent, the writer proposed to the parent that he might like to make a DVD recording for his child in which he would tell her of his feelings for her and offer the DVD to the child through the other parent as a way of communicating something from himself without the child having to directly meet him. The parent took up the offer, and the piece of work became the starting point for the gradual refinement of an intervention tool in families where parent–child contact finally ceases. What is described in the paragraphs below is the intervention tool in its developed state (Sheehan, 2016b).

The intervention takes place in five stages but can be aborted at different stages depending upon the responses of the participating parents and child. The first stage of the intervention is discussing the intervention idea with the rejected parent and making it clear that if the child or the other parent does not accept the offer, the DVD can be kept in the file for the child to view when she becomes a young adult if she wishes. The second stage is the making and remaking of the DVD with the parent until they are happy with the production. Many fathers, for example, do not want their children to be burdened by seeing the father's tears and decide to rework the DVD until they are able to express their feelings in a way that feels comfortable to them. The third stage of the intervention is the contacting of the now 'custodial' parent to explain the idea behind the making of the DVD for his child and asking her to think about whether she would like to come to view it and edit out any aspects she feels are inappropriate to communicate to her child. The fourth stage is the viewing and further editing of the DVD with and by the 'custodial' parent if she chooses to become engaged. The final stage of the intervention is the custodial parent making the DVD available to the child to view, or not, as she wishes, receiving feedback from the custodial parent of the child's response to the offer and reviewing the outcome of the intervention with the 'rejected' parent.

Although this family intervention tool has not yet received formal evaluation, Sheehan (2016b) reported that in as little as one-fifth of those families where the intervention was used in its developed form could the intervention be seen to be directly linked to the resumption of contact between an estranged child and a rejected parent. In these families, there were other siblings who had remained in contact with the estranged parent. In approximately half of the families in receipt of the intervention, the resident parent agreed to become involved in editing the DVD recording and subsequently making it available to the child in question. In the other half of the group in receipt of the intervention, the process was aborted at stage three – that is, when the resident parent either refused to become involved in the editing process or failed to respond in any way to the professional's communication about the matter. Where the editing process did take place, the motivation of the resident parent seemed focussed on whether there was anything negative being said on the recording about her rather than on any other aspect of the indirect communication of the other parent with the child. The most consistent finding from the use of the intervention was the reports from 'rejected' parents that the process of making and storing of the recordings for later viewing by the child had helped them considerably in coming to terms with the loss of their child and in regaining a foothold in their own lives.

Skills Required in Key Mental Health Professional Interventions

The small number of examples offered in this chapter as illustrations of some of the key mental health professional interventions in contexts of extended post-separation/divorced family court-related conflict do scant justice to the broad range of situations for which these interventions are relevant. They also do scant justice to the host of uniquely varying circumstances that arise under each category of case that might draw such shorthand descriptions as 'domestic violence' or 'parental alienation'. Indeed, the multifaceted nature of post-separation family conflicts that extend in time and increase in intensity should serve as a warning to practitioners to be wary of settling for singular perspectives within their own understanding of the work. Complex cases require multiple descriptions from multiple perspectives. The practitioner needs to be aware of the strong pull they will feel within these intensely conflicted fields to settle for a singular perspective that holds the promise of clarity. This 'pull' towards singular perspective is the professional analogue of the 'pull' a child often feels when, under the weight of persistent parental conflict, they put all their parental 'eggs' in one basket.

Although there are a host of micro-skills relevant to the performance of the key interventions named in this chapter, many of which skills have already been named in previous chapters, the following are three broad skills that are pertinent to the interventions described in this chapter:

(i) *Court liaison skills.* The first three of the above interventions require very close liaison on the part of the mental health professional with the court. This often means having an ongoing liaison relationship with a particular judge who made orders for an intervention and who may have ongoing judicial responsibility for the case. However, the professional's liaison skill is not just embedded in the relationship with the judge but also in the relationship with both legal teams who are representing the parents in the proceedings. Writing brief reports which give clear and precise updates on the progress of the intervention towards named goals may also be a necessary part of liaison. Standardising communication formats between the mental health professional and the parents' legal teams is a further aspect of liaison skills. For example, it is important that both sets of lawyers receive the same kind of communication from the professional at the same time. Email contact is an excellent facility for ensuring this contemporaneity with respect to communication receipt. The final two interventions described in this chapter may commence with the support of the court but will specifically not happen as a result of a court order. Nor will the court normally seek any feedback regarding the progress of parents or children within these interventions. Despite this, the support of the court for the intervention can have a very positive impact upon the attitude parents adopt in their engagement with the intervention.

(ii) *Maintaining neutrality in the face of complexity.* As conflict escalates within post-separation family relationships, the number of professionals and other persons co-opted in to assist with conflict management and resolution can increase dramatically. This normally means an increase in the complexity of the conflict management system to which the professional belongs. It can be hugely challenging for the professional to maintain her neutrality as she responds to and engages with each part of this complex system. Having a good supervisory relationship can be an essential support for professionals as they try to realise the maintenance of neutrality in these complex contexts.

(iii) *Pointing to the exit door from the family court.* As parents become more deeply embroiled in their post-separation conflicts, they can become dependent upon the courts and their related services for the resolution of both smaller and larger disputes. Whatever intervention the mental health professional is engaged in with parents and their children, whether under the formal eye of the court or simply with the court's support, part of the professional task with parents is to keep their sights on a time in the future when they will have sufficient mutual trust to take back control of matters regarding their children, notwithstanding their differences. The professional can assist with this regaining of trust by noting for parents how the repetitive keeping of small agreements can facilitate a slow, but incremental, redevelopment of mutual trust. An end to legal bills and to having to get time off from work to attend court can also be powerful enticements towards the exit door of the family court.

Personal and Reflective Exercises

1. Think of a family you are currently involved with professionally where post-separation family conflict has already brought parents to the family court on several occasions. What experiences have you had in your personal and/or professional life that might be a resource in your efforts to appreciate and understand the positions of each of the adults and children in this situation? Write some notes for yourself in response to this question.

2. Write a note for yourself about your experiences with any, or all, of the five interventions described in this chapter. Which of these intervention roles would you find most challenging to perform, and why? Write some further notes for yourself about this second question.

PART III

SPECIAL CONTEXTS OF POST-SEPARATION/DIVORCE FAMILY CONFLICT: CHILD RELOCATION AND ABDUCTION, MENTAL HEALTH/ILLNESS AND SUBSTANCE ABUSE

CHILD RELOCATION AND CHILD ABDUCTION: MENTAL HEALTH PROFESSIONAL ROLES AND INTERVENTIONS

Some of the most intense post-separation parental struggles across multiple jurisdictions involve the desire of one parent to move with a child either to another part of the same jurisdiction or to an entirely different jurisdiction (George, 2012). For the last two decades at least, the phenomenon of child relocation has been perceived as presenting international family law practice with an intractable problem (Carmody, 2007). Where parents have little capacity to communicate with each other, for whatever reason, the desire in one parent to relocate with a child may very quickly lead to family court proceedings aimed at seeking either the permission of the court for a child's relocation or the prevention of such relocation. Even where parents have an ability to communicate, the emergence of one parent's desire to relocate with the child can set such fears and anxieties in motion in the other parent that proposals to address the situation in the context of mediation seem like an impossible challenge. This does not mean that mediated resolutions never occur in disputes about relocation. However, in this writer's experience, such resolutions are more likely where the proposed relocation is internal (i.e. within the same jurisdiction) or to a neighbouring jurisdiction, and where parents have had some positive experiences with mediation in the past without necessarily being able to resolve all their post-separation disputes through that medium.

Although mediated resolutions may account for just a small percentage of the total matrix of relocation-related disputes, they bring to light the two key parameters relevant to resolutions of any kind: 'consent' and/or 'permission'. In most jurisdictions where a parent has the written consent of the other parent to take a child to reside outside of the jurisdiction, she will not be found culpable of child abduction if she acts upon that consent and removes the child. If she does not have the written consent of the other parent, whether she has sought such consent or not, she may be charged, in time, with the offence of child abduction should she remove the child from the jurisdiction in which the child normally resides. Where a parent seeks to relocate with a child outside of the jurisdiction where she normally resides, and she fails to get the consent of the other parent, she normally applies to the family court for permission to proceed with relocating the child to her desired destination, thus bypassing the consent of the other parent.

There is a small, but growing, body of empirical research on the phenomenon of relocation. Much of this research endeavour has been conducted in Australia. Some of these studies (Behrens and Smyth, 2010) have examined parents' experiences of family law courts' decisions in relocation applications, whereas other studies (Behrens et al., 2009) have considered the relationship between judicial decisions and parental relationships over time. A study by Parkinson et al. (2011) of mothers' reasons for wanting to relocate described how mothers often expressed more than one reason for their desire to move, with both 'push' and 'pull' factors coming into play. 'Push' factors are those elements in a situation making mothers want to get away from the location they are in, and 'pull' factors are those features in the desired location that are drawing them there. The same study showed how some mothers' desire to move occurred simultaneously with separation, whereas others did not have this desire until a number of years after separation. A New Zealand study by Gollop and Taylor (2012) considered children and young persons' perspectives on relocation following the separation of their parents.

This chapter does not dwell upon those internal or external relocation disputes where mediated resolutions are sometimes possible. Suffice to say that mediation can be an appropriate and relevant mental health professional intervention in these contexts in the first instance. The focus instead is twofold: firstly, the chapter considers the role and function of the mental health professional asked by the court to undertake an evaluation in the context of relocation applications of whatever kind; and, secondly, it considers the different roles and interventions performed by mental health professionals when child abduction has taken place. Some of these roles are also relevant to the assistance of families caught in relocation disputes. Although the law and its exercise provide the key parameters and boundary points through which family court judges make their decisions in specific cases, the chapter is not concerned with the specifics of legislation in different jurisdictions, this being outside the scope of a text such as this. The second half of the chapter, however, gives some consideration to the way an international piece of legislation called *The Hague Child Abduction Convention* (1980) provides protection for abducted children where the states from which they are taken and to which they are brought are signatories to the Convention.

Evaluating Child Relocation Applications for the Family Courts

Reports from jurisdictions in most Western societies suggest that relocation applications as well as child abduction hearings are occupying a gradually increasing share of family court time (Lamont, 2012). This development is unsurprising given the mobility levels in a global workforce, which give rise to an ever-increasing population of international couples in many societies. When some of these couples become parents and later separate, it is not unusual for relocation applications to ensue. The motivation for these applications can often be as simple as the desire to return to family and homeland following the pain and hurt of separation and divorce. Such motivation may also be at the heart of more 'local' relocation applications, where a parent, following separation, just wants to restart her life nearer the residences of her siblings and parents. However, relocation applications may also be motivated by perceived work opportunities within another jurisdiction, by the desire to join a new spouse or partner in his country of residence, or by the need to look after an ageing or ill parent. Not infrequently, however, the desire to relocate with a child is driven by the felt need to get far away from a partner who has been abusive to either the relocating adult or her child, or to both adult and child.

There are many tasks within a relocation evaluation that also form part of any 'ordinary' evaluation undertaken following an order of the court (Stahl, 1994). Children's perspectives and wishes must be ascertained; parental relationships must be assessed; and information from collateral sources must be obtained. This chapter does not repeat here what is common to all court-ordered evaluations, but focuses on aspects of the evaluation process that are more pertinent to relocation applications. Although the task required of the court's evaluation expert in such applications is essentially the same whether the relocation proposed is internal or external to the jurisdiction, the challenges for the evaluation can look very different from family to family and from one proposed relocation to another. It is one thing to undertake a relocation evaluation where a parent is proposing to move a child from London to Birmingham. It is quite a different challenge when the proposed relocation destination is very far away and is part of a very different cultural and linguistic environment to that of the jurisdiction in which the application is made. Hence, one of the first considerations a mental health professional must make when requested to undertake a court-ordered evaluation in a relocation application is whether she has the cultural and linguistic competence to undertake the assessment. If the mental health professional is concerned about this, he may, both wisely and justifiably, either refuse the request to undertake the evaluation or, with the permission of the court, engage the assistance of a cultural consultant and/or interpreter while undertaking the work.

Relocation evaluations also differ from the more general custody and contact evaluations in that their scope is broader and more holistic. Although the more 'routine' evaluation focuses on the specific themes at the heart of parental dispute about a child, relocation evaluations should focus on the totality of elements that contribute to a child's welfare. What is at stake in the relocation evaluation is a consideration of whether the child's welfare, taken in its totality, may be enhanced or diminished by a move with the applicant parent to the requested destination. Although jurisdictions may differ with respect to the law and regulations governing relocation, most systems are predicated upon some version of the 'welfare' principle. Put simply, this means that, although courts may take into consideration a great variety of factors relating to adult lives and responsibilities in coming to their decision, at the end of the day the welfare of the child is of paramount importance in the decision-making process.

It is easy for the evaluation expert to feel somewhat overwhelmed in these contexts given that the stakes are so high for all the participants and their relationships. What the mental health professional needs more than anything in these tasks is a humble disposition allied to a rigorous approach to data collection. Such a disposition will remind the evaluation expert that he is just one part, albeit an important part, of the dispute resolution system. The judge hearing the application bears the burden of final decision-making and judgement. It is critical that the evaluation expert not become attached to the legal outcome of his recommendations and put his energy into the provision of as much accurate and relevant information as possible to the court. This does not mean that the evaluation expert should not give very careful consideration to the final recommendations he makes to the court, but that he should remember that their value to the court may be linked as much to the quality of the information he provides as to the recommendation he finally makes.

The Welfare of the Child

Jurisdictions may or may not have a checklist directing the range of matters a court must pay attention to in dealing with a relocation application. A court-appointed evaluation expert needs to pay attention to such a checklist if it exists in his jurisdiction, as it provides the essential framework within which he must finally assess the relative merits of the application. Section 1(3) of the UK Children Act 1989 provides such a list, and the checklists in other jurisdictions have often taken their lead from this. The section asks the court (and, by implication, assessors) to have regard to the following:

1. The ascertainable wishes and feelings of the child considered in the light of his age and understanding.
2. The child's physical, emotional and educational needs.
3. The likely effect on the child of any change in circumstances.
4. The age, sex, and background of the child and any other of the child's characteristics that might be relevant.
5. Any harm the child has suffered in the past or is at risk of suffering.
6. The capacity of each of the parents and any other relevant person to meet the needs of the child.
7. What the court can do in terms of its powers.

In order to be able to provide an assessment of the child's welfare in the context of a specific application, the expert will need to gather information from the applicant parent regarding her reasons for making the application; where she intends living with the child and how the move to this location will be funded; the care (nurseries, childminders, after-schools), educational (schools), recreational (sports) and medical resources available to the child in the proposed location; the proximity of the applicant and child to family and friends; the employment and work hours of the applicant in the proposed location; the likely impact on the child of a change of culture and language; the curriculum in specific schools being considered for a child; the fee structure in the proposed schools (should private schooling be proposed) and how their curricula fit with the child's educational history; proposals of the applicant parent for the child's contact with the other parent and how such contact and travel will be funded; and the likely impact on the parenting of a parent who has been refused the relocation application.

Enhancing the Quality of Information Provided to the Court

The above information checklist gives an indication of the breadth that can be required within a relocation assessment, and one of the main tasks of the evaluation expert is to orient the court to the key information sets that are most relevant to the welfare of a unique child within a specific application. This may mean challenging or checking the quality of information an applicant parent is providing or asking parents either to furnish more verifiable information themselves or to give the assessor permission to seek further verifiable information directly from third parties. The following vignette illustrates the functioning of such verification processes.

In the context of an application to relocate a school-age child from one European country to another, an applicant mother provided the evaluation expert with information regarding a private school she felt matched the needs of her son. The very full information provided on the school's website suggested to the mother that it had all the facilities and educational expertise provided in the private school her son was currently attending. She had visited the school a year previously and had been assured by the head of the school that there would not be a problem having her child admitted as there were places still available in the class groups at her son's age level. The expert asked the mother if she would mind him calling the head of the school to have his own discussion about the needs of the child, as he had already had direct communication with personnel in the school the boy was currently attending. The mother had no problem consenting to the direct contact and provided the expert with the telephone number for the school. When the expert called the school, the head of the school told him that a decision had very recently been taken by the school board to close the school down over a two-year period and that admissions were formally closed. The school's website was still inviting applications for places in 'a vibrant and innovative educational setting'.

In the above vignette, the applicant parent presented the educational information in good faith, and the expert merely enhanced the quality of the information by updating it. This simple action possibly saved the court from wasting a considerable amount of time hearing argument and counter-argument about the relative merits of a school the child was currently attending and a school that was in a close-down mode. In other contexts, exemplified in the following vignette, the expert may suspect that information being provided in a certain area is either inaccurate or has been deliberately falsified.

An applicant parent of a preschool child provided an expert with a copy of a letter from an employer offering a job contract for a position, with a salary attached and a schedule of work hours. The parent's case for the financial feasibility of the move was based upon the premise that their proposed future salary and work hours would allow her to pay for suitable rental accommodation for herself and her child at the same time as forgoing the need to pay for any additional childcare costs. When the expert challenged the accuracy of the parent's information by suggesting that the salary offered seemed quite high for the job in question and requested permission to speak directly to the head of human resources in the employing organisation, the parent broke down in tears and told the expert that a friend within that department had 'produced' the letter for her to strengthen her case. She then produced a copy of her actual job contract, which carried the appropriate salary and normal working hours for the position. The parent then gave the expert permission to verify the information pertaining to the 'real' job contract.

The evaluation expert needs to remind himself that when the stakes are very high, parents often take liberties with their presentation of the facts in the interests of what they see as the greater good for their child. It does not mean that they are generally dishonest as adults or parents. What it does mean, however, is that the evaluation expert must be constantly vigilant with respect to the possible 'massage' of figures and information pertaining to the case for or against relocation.

Parental Positioning within Relocation Applications

By the time the evaluation expert meets both of the principal parties and their children in a relocation dispute, the family system and its individual members have often tightly positioned themselves in relation to each other around the principal theme of the inquiry. Position theory (Davies and Harre, 1990; Harre and Van Langenhove, 1991; Tirado and Galvez, 2007) suggests that as subjects within a relational, interactive world, we are constantly defining and producing our 'selves' in the ways we speak around a theme in relation to others in that world. In the world of parenthood, for example, we might take up a 'subject position' in relation to our children that invites our partner parent to occupy a reciprocal position. In adopting a particular subject position, we automatically limit the position that the 'other' can occupy within that way of speaking. Within relocation disputes, it is not uncommon for the parent who wants to remove the child, or children, to take up a subject position as the parent who has the only meaningful relationship with the child, who is now, and has always been in the past, the parent who met 99 per cent of the child's needs. The adoption of such a subject position around parenthood automatically invites a reciprocal definition of the other parent as uninvolved, neglectful of parental duties and without meaningful connection to the child. In everyday social life, these 'invitations' and 'offers' are often made and accepted in ways that benefit all of the participants within a particular sphere of exchange. However, we do not have to accept these invitations, and we can contest such offers by taking up alternative positions that invite the other to take up the reciprocal position in relation to the subject position we have adopted. Within relocation disputes, it is not uncommon to find one parent attempting to position herself as 'fully responsible' and the other parent as 'completely neglectful'. The other parent, in response, may position himself as a parent who is 'reasonable and alienated' while identifying the other parent as 'possessive and alienating'.

Within this discursive production process of parental selves, children are also positioned in particular ways and may take a varyingly active part in this process, depending upon their age and stage of development. For example, they may tell an evaluation expert that they want to live in the destination country chosen by their applicant parent because that parent's family or friends residing there are the only people who care about them and that the other parent, her family and friends, never cared about them, never gave them birthday or other presents, and never did anything with them in the past. As the evaluation expert enters the system, he will also feel the weight of being positioned and repositioned by each parent in turn. The invitation from one parent might be to accept the identity of an assessor who can appreciate and respect 'the voice of the child' (which often turns out to be remarkably similar to the voice of the applicant parent!) while the other parent may position the expert as a courageous assessor who is unafraid to uncover and name the parental alienation at the heart of the evolving family dispute about relocation.

The Assessment of Parenting

Whatever different ways of positioning and repositioning self, other and child are at work within the family in conflict over relocation, the assessor must take careful note of these positions. This process points to one very important aspect of the relocation evaluation, which is the careful assessment of parenting in both its quantitative and qualitative aspects. This assessment must carefully trace the history of contact and its changes and the court orders underpinning this history, if there were any. It also means gathering as much relevant information as possible about the historical relationship of parents and children. In a field filled with contested information, the assessor must gather as much 'objective' evidence as possible about this history. Nursery personnel, school principals and after-school managers may provide independent, third-party sources of information about some of the contested matters, although the evaluation expert must take account of the way these professionals may also have been positioned within the dispute through their daily contact with one or other of the parents. Copies of formal records relating to the child's historical participation within these institutions and services may give more grounding to the verbal assertions of parents in relation to contested matters than might be provided by the assessor's verbal conversation with these professionals alone. These can be tedious processes for the assessor, but they certainly add to the quality of the information being provided to the court. A further important social impact of well-organised and documented information made available to the court by the evaluation expert can be that it cuts down on the number of professionals who may be required to give evidence at the hearing of the application. Such consequences can protect institutions from the needless absence of personnel from their services, as well as reducing the legal costs incurred by parents.

Fundamental Questions in Relocation Evaluations

Although this chapter has emphasised the broad nature of the evaluation processes required of mental health professionals within relocation applications, some authors have suggested that, notwithstanding such required breadth, decision-making in relocation applications should be guided by reference to a series of fundamental questions. Both George (2014) and Parkinson and Cashmore (2015), for example, have proposed that these 'fundamentals' can be reduced to three. Firstly, assessors and family courts must ask how close the relationship is between the child and the nonresident parent and how important that relationship is developmentally to the child. Secondly, they must question the viability of the proposed contact arrangements between the child and the left-behind parent in the event of the relocation being permitted. And, finally, if the relationship between the child and the left-behind parent is considered developmentally important for the child and it is considered that a move would diminish this relationship, assessors and the courts should ask what other viable alternatives exist to the parents living a long distance apart and whether relocation with the primary carer might be the least detrimental option for the child's welfare (Austin, 2000, 2008a).

Given the strange set of family dynamics that can be set in motion by a relocation application, it is important that the evaluation expert not rely on direct evidence (i.e. the interviews with the child and the non-applicant parent) alone when it comes to answering the first of these questions concerning the quality and importance, developmentally, of the relationship between the child and the parent who may be left behind. Gathering information from collateral professional sources who have known the parents and children over time is a critical element which supports the arrival at a considered response to the first of these fundamental questions.

Assessing the viability of proposed contact arrangements after relocation between the child and the left-behind parent is, at the best of times, an approximate business. Here, the evaluator must not rely on the information provided by both of the parents in support of their case around the viability or nonviability of such arrangements, but should seek as much independent verification as possible. The concept of 'viability' in this context can refer to such matters as the number of holidays the nonresident parent may have from their employment; the costs of travel and accommodation for the nonresident parent to the child's new country of residence, as well as for the child's return for holidays with the same parent; the reliability of airline, boat and train schedules; the compatibility of school holiday periods in the child's new country with limitations on the nonresident parent's holiday entitlements; whether the child is of an age that he can be permitted to travel unaccompanied or will require paid non-familial accompaniment; and many other matters that may be pertinent within particular application contexts. With respect to all the above matters, the evaluator may have a moderating influence with respect to the contact plan that is finally put before the court. For example, where a relocating parent may propose that a nonresident parent stay in a budget hostel for adults during visitation, but the nonresident parent argues that she requires a junior suite in a five-star hotel to enable her to spend meaningful time with her child, the evaluator may propose that the test of viability, from a financial perspective, might be made with respect to an accommodation that is more costly than the budget hostel, but not as costly as the alternative insisted upon by the nonresident parent.

With respect to the third of the three 'fundamentals' – where the relationship between the child and the nonresident parent is considered important for the child from a developmental perspective and where a move is considered to be inimical to the child's best interests – the evaluation expert must consider such matters as whether the nonresident parent could realistically also move along with the child or whether the circumstances of a 'refused' applicant parent could be made more tolerable by having longer holiday periods with the child each year in the country where she wished to reside. This latter option may enhance the sense of extra-familial support for a disappointed applicant parent. At the end of the day, the answer to this third question often rests upon a number of 'maybes' and 'what ifs' concerning a future that is far from fully predictable, and assessors and the court have to consider whether a child's relocation with a primary carer might be the least detrimental alternative for the child. Although relocation decisions are far from an exact science, they are always based upon unique kinds of risk assessment (Austin, 2008b).

Other Relocation-related Mental Health Professional Interventions

Mental health professionals may provide interventions with family members involved in relocation disputes other than court-ordered expert evaluations. Most of these interventions arise from the very specific nature of the fears and anxieties that arise when relocation has been signalled as a desire in one parent. For the parents who may be left behind, the prospect of their child's relocation can have a traumatic impact (Herman, 1998). Some of these traumatised parents can feel a sense of anticipatory loss in relation to their children. The emotional impact of the relocation application process may leave them unable to focus on their work, to attend appropriately to the other relationships in their life, or to involve themselves meaningfully in the process they have been thrown into. For such parents, personal counselling and psychotherapy may be important in assisting them overcome the immo-bilising impact of receiving news of a relocation application and to cope more adequately with the different demands they face, including the demand of participating effectively in the court-ordered evaluation process (Van Der Kolk, 2014). Other parents threatened with being left behind may respond with increased aggression towards their ex-partners, make complaints to child protection services about the care of the children and enter the evaluation process with a determination to demonstrate that the relocation application is one further example of their ex-partner's poor parenting choices. These parents are unlikely to avail of counselling support or assistance, as their deep fears of abandonment become transformed into energy for 'the battle'.

For the parent who wants to relocate with her child, her time and energy is often taken up with preparing the ground for her relocation assessment and relocation hearing. It is usually a busy time for her, and she can be driven forward by her longing for the promised land of relocation, which seems increasingly near. Regardless of her motivation for departure, her focus on the realisation of her goal leaves little room for dwelling on the possibility of her application being refused. Such parents rarely attend therapists prior to the hearing of their applications unless they are actual, or alleged, victims of domestic violence and where this theme is a major plank in their case for relocation. Where this is not the case, such parents often require con-siderable counselling and therapeutic assistance after a court decision that refuses the relocation. The adjustment required following court decisions can be immense for these parents, and the counselling/therapeutic mental health professional must pay special attention to their mental health needs as they try to cope with the coming apart of their life plans and hopes. Depending upon the ages of their children and the extent to which they have been aware of, and actively engaged in, the relocation evaluation process, 'refused' parents can be vulnerable to drawing their children deeper into the parental struggle by informing them that it was the other parent who prevented them from reaching the goal. Therapists have an important function in these contexts in restraining the disappointed parent from alienating behaviours of different kinds. Mental health professionals should also be aware that relocation evaluations may be the first occasion where a history of intimate partner violence has comes to light.

Children can also require a great deal of therapeutic input in the aftermath of a relocation decision. Play therapy, art therapy and individual counselling may all have a part to play depending upon the age, cognitive capacity and personal disposition of the individual child. Relocated children may feel they need to hide their grief over the loss of their left-behind parents and grandparents, friends, playmates and childminders. Therapeutic input of different kinds can assist these children in finding the emotional energy they need to integrate satisfactorily over time into their new school, recreational and extra-familial settings. Most importantly, it can help the child or adolescent to engage more fully with Skype and telephone contact with his left-behind parent, where such contact has been considered beneficial to the child's interests and ordered by the court.

Child Abduction in the Context of Post-separation/Divorce Family Conflict

There is such a close connection between child relocation and child abduction that they are often considered as two sides of the same coin (Schuz, 2013). Although the wishes and desires of those adults wishing to relocate with a child and others who decide to abduct a child to another jurisdiction are broadly similar, the two situations are governed by different kinds of legislation and have some different consequences for the kind of assistance and intervention families need from mental health professionals. On the one hand, applications for relocation occur within the orbit of domestic law as it operates within a particular jurisdiction. Child abduction, on the other hand, comes under the remit of international law. This section of the chapter begins with a summary description of the key international legal instrument responding to the reality of child abduction. This instrument is *The Hague Convention on the Civil Aspects of International Child Abduction (1980)*.

The additional challenges for mental health professional family assistance arising from child abduction will then be reviewed.

The Hague Convention

This 1980 Convention was the international response to widespread concern about the growing problem of unlawful removal of children from their jurisdictions of habitual residence during the previous half century. As an international legal instrument, it operates in the context of a variety of other domestic and international laws relating to the rights of adults and children. Motivated by the concern to protect children from the harm assumed to be associated with abduction, the Convention provided a legal vehicle for the prompt return of the child to his state of habitual residence. Decisions made under the Convention's mechanisms are not intended as final decisions on the merits of a particular case, but are indicators regarding the jurisdiction in which such decisions should be made. The Convention admitted only a very small number of exceptions to this approach of automatic return. These exceptions related to contexts where it can be shown that a child would be at grave risk of harm should he be returned to the jurisdiction from which he was abducted. The mechanisms of the Convention operate between the states who are signatories to the Convention. The number of states who are signatories to the Convention has grown steadily since its mechanisms were first adopted in 1980 (Schuz, 2013).

Although those who framed the Convention did so with the assumption that the typical abduction scene was a nonresident father removing a child from a mother who was the resident parent of the child, the reality of abduction as it has evolved since the inception of the Convention is that the typical contemporary abductor is a primary caregiving mother removing a child from a jurisdiction where she, the nonresident father and the child habitually reside (Schuz, 2013). The general purpose of the Convention's mechanisms was and remains the protection of children from the harm associated with abduction. Although there is a certain amount of evidence suggesting that abduction does inflict harm on children (Agopian, 1984; Hegar and Grief, 1991), sometimes long-term harm (Grief, 2000, 2009), it has become clear that this is not always the case. A whole group of child abductions concern mother and child victims of domestic violence fleeing from scenes of intense conflict and abuse to places of relative safety for the child and where the parenting of a child can continue in less hostile environments. These are the group of 'hard-core' cases where the exception to automatic return of the child applies. However, the challenges for domestic courts in responding to child abduction where domestic violence is alleged to have occurred are immense, as it is the

211

child's interests alone that are germane to the court's decision to return or not to return the child to his country of habitual residence. The picture becomes even more challenging for the courts with an increasing group of international families who move many times from state to state over relatively short periods of time. Establishing the child's state of habitual residence in these contexts can be very difficult and not always meaningful.

The Convention requires that the voice and wishes of the child be ascertained during its proceedings, and this may be the first involvement of a child with a mental health professional in the context of his parents' struggle. The assessment role of the professional at this point is brief and circumscribed in nature and time, as the court is required to arrive at its determination within a strictly limited time frame. In principle, this assessment is totally oriented to a consideration about whether the child would, in all likelihood, be subject to grave risk of harm should the court decide to return him to the jurisdiction from whence he was taken. If the decision is to return the child, what normally follows is a more extensive evaluation by a child-and-family expert in the context of proceedings in the state to which he is returned. As we shall see later in the chapter, these assessment roles are simply one layer of assistance and intervention required by parents and children in the context of child abduction.

Typical Contemporary Contexts of Child Abduction

Although there are situations where children are abducted by grandparents or others who are not their custodians or guardians, international child abduction is normally 'performed' by one or another of the child's parents in the context of parental dispute. The following list of typical contemporary abduction contexts gives some idea of the variety faced by the assisting mental health professional, as well as of the challenges faced within that assistance. The following contexts all relate to situations where there is a primary carer and a nonresident parent, but it should be noted that abduction can also occur where the care of a child is shared on an equal, or almost equal, basis between the parents:

(i) A mother from an international marriage, being unhappy in her marriage for some years but unable to see a way to separate from her husband on whom she is financially dependent, takes both herself and her children to her country of origin, where her parents and siblings have promised to provide shelter, care and support for her and the children. Residential separation and child abduction happen simultaneously. Child abduction is used in the service of creating the only imaginable residential separation. The mother is psychologically prepared for the move through her telephone contact with parents and siblings. The children are not prepared psychologically for the move but are reasonably familiar with their mother's extended family whom they have seen intermittently during holiday periods in both jurisdictions. The father, realising the marriage is in a poor state but not anticipating an abrupt ending, is traumatised by the simultaneous disappearance of his partner and his children.

(ii) A resident parent/mother and her children flee the jurisdiction in which they reside with the intention of getting away from an abusive father whose patterns of violent behaviour towards mother and children have persisted after residential separation. In these situations, child abduction brings relief and a sense of safety for the mother and children while the father may experience a deep sense of abandonment and accompanying rage.

(iii) A high-earning mother of two children who has primary care, having been embroiled in a bitter, post-separation conflict with the children's father over a two-year period, accepts the offer from her international corporation of a job on the other side of the world which carries twice the salary she currently earns. She travels out of the jurisdiction with her children and believes that her ex-partner, from whom the children are already alienated to some degree, will not have either the personal or financial resources to do anything significant to impede her progress towards a better life for herself and the children. The children are only minimally prepared by their mother for the move to a jurisdiction where they know nobody other than her. The father is devastated, but not totally surprised, by the disappearance of his children, with whom he has had a difficult relationship, primarily because, he believes, of the alienating strategies of their mother.

(iv) The same abducting mother might just as easily be motivated by the desire to be with her new partner in the country where he has employment and residence. The children may already be drawn into the plan for a better future with a new, mother-approved father figure. In this situation, child abduction is accompanied by a maternal strategy directed towards a full eclipse of the children's paternal relationship.

(v) A nonresident father, frustrated by the small amount of contact he has with his child, may take the child out of a jurisdiction to a planned new location. The child is not psychologically 'prepared' for the exit until he is on the plane or has arrived at the desired destination. No contact is made with the primary carer, who only becomes suspicious when the child does not return from a contact visit. The location of the child through Interpol or other agencies may take some considerable time, particularly if the destination is not easily guessed. Friends or contacts of the abductor may hide the parent and child on a temporary basis. Planning of the venture by the abductor is often very poor and the situation often resolves through a voluntary return of the child and the abducting parent. The primary carer mother is traumatised by the disappearance of the child and lives temporarily with the anxiety of not knowing whether her child is alive or dead until either the location of father and child is identified or father and child make contact. The child is often subjected to a degree of brain-washing during and after the abduction process.

(vi) A nonresident father who feels controlled by a primary carer mother in terms of the level of contact they have with their child may decide to extend his one-week holiday abroad with the child and keep him away from the primary carer for several weeks beyond the court-ordered period. The intention of the abductor is not to fully abduct the child in the long-term, but to give the resident parent what he regards as 'a taste of her own medicine'. Contact may or not be made with the resident parent. Motives for the temporary abduction of the child may be mixed. Apart from the desire to make the other parent suffer through depriving her temporarily of her most precious emotional 'good', the nonresident parent may also genuinely long for a closer bond with the child, which he feels would be facilitated by a more prolonged period of time in each other's company. The mother may be shocked and distressed by the non-return of the child in accordance with court-ordered schedules. The child may be subjected to further paternal alienating strategies in addition to those already built in to the abduction itself.

Skills and Interventions

Given the above variety of relocation and child abduction contexts, what are the skills needed by mental health professionals in their various assistance roles with families, parents and children going through these crises? These can be broadly divided into assessment and therapeutic skills.

(i) *Assessment skills.* Unlike the more 'routine' court-ordered evaluations in post-separation parental struggles, where the focus of the assessment is circumscribed by the limited range of themes giving rise to the dispute, relocation evaluations require the mental health professional, in the role of expert assessor, to provide a more holistic and global assessment of the welfare needs of children at the centre of applications. This means not only considering information and data against the welfare checklist that may be operational in a particular jurisdiction but also presenting accurate and verified information to the court upon which the assessor bases his responses to the series of three 'fundamental' questions proposed by George (2014) and Parkinson and Cashmore (2015) as the kernel of relocation assessments. It means having the capacity to make careful assessments of parenting which don't simply rely upon observation of current parent–child interaction but also utilise reliable and independent third-party evidence concerning the history of parent–child relationships. It means assessing for the presence of parental alienating strategies at work in either current or past chapters of parent–child relationships and allowing the information arising from this assessment to inform his perspective on the child's capacity, given his age and maturity, to find a voice of his own within the assessment process. And, most importantly, it means making a safe enough context for the child to express himself as fully as he can about the context and relationships in which he finds himself, without feeling the pressure to make a choice in favour of one parental position or the other. Assessors may also require the skills to avail of cultural and linguistic consultants on occasions.

When the scene of assessment moves to an application under the Hague Convention for the prompt return of the child to the jurisdiction of the left-behind parent, the key assessment skill concerns the capacity to facilitate the voice of the child and his wishes to be heard by the court dealing with the application. Schuz (2013) records that a mental health professional's interview of the child appears to be only one of four ways that the voice and wishes of the child are heard in Hague Convention applications (the others being the judge interviewing the child, the child giving evidence directly to the court or the child having his own separate legal representation). However, when the option chosen by the court is the mental health professional's assessment of the child, the assessor must be the vehicle through which a view on the child's age and maturity level is provided along with a presentation of the child's views, including the nature of any objections he might make to return. This latter matter will often be key to the Court's decision to return the child or not. The mental health professional requires the skill to give clear written and/or verbal evidence to the court regarding these matters.

(ii) *Therapeutic skills.* There are a great variety of therapeutic skills and interventions required by some, but not all, parents and children going through these crises. Adults and children frequently require different kinds of therapeutic assistance. Whether adults or children actually receive the therapeutic assistance they may need depends upon the recognition of this need by either professionals or friends close to the family during the crisis, as well as upon the availability and accessibility of suitable therapeutic resources.

News about the possible relocation or abduction of a child can bring about shock and/or trauma for many parents, who will need strong and consistent therapeutic or counselling support with a professional who understands the psychological dynamics of trauma and the consequent risks to mental health that trauma may engender. In a study of parental child abduction, Grief and Hegar (1991) found that left-behind parents may suffer feelings of loss, rage and impaired sleep. As time moves on, they may suffer from loneliness, fear, loss of appetite and depression. Therapeutic support is certainly required by those parents for whom the matter does not resolve in reasonable time, and symptoms may persist in those whose children have been located and reunited with them because of ongoing fears of re-abduction. These parents often suffer all the symptoms of post-traumatic stress disorder for some years after the 'resolution' of the abduction. In general, the greater impact is suffered by those parents where the abduction crisis remains unresolved for longer periods of time. Therapeutic and counselling intervention often requires close liaison with medical and psychiatric professionals also assisting these parents.

In a small study of abducted children, Agopian (1984) found that the degree of trauma such children experienced was related to their age at the time of abduction, their treatment by the abducting parent, the duration of the abduction, and the counselling and therapy they received after recovery. Mental health professionals referring abducted children for therapy after abduction recovery need to consider the age and general disposition of the child. Although talking therapies may suit some traumatised children and adolescents, it may be that art, music or play therapy will prove a less demanding form of support for others. Where a child is returned to the country of origin of his 'secondary' parent without the accompaniment of his primary carer abductor, the child's therapy will need to take account of the ongoing rupture in the child's primary attachment relationship. Where the abducting primary carer refuses to make any contact with the child, his suffering can be immense, and he may feel fearful of expressing his loss to the parent who has now become his primary parent and carer. It is as though the abductor says to the other parent: 'Now that you have fought so hard to take my child from me, you can have my child completely.' The abductor's private hope is often that, through their strategy of ongoing silence, the secondary parent will feel so overwhelmed by the child's distress that she will plead with him to come and take the child.

A major part of abduction trauma for both parents and children can be the difficulty in building up trust again in other people and relationships.

Although the courts may take whatever steps they feel are required to halt any further alienation by an abducting parent (e.g. by only allowing supervised contact), the therapist assisting in this recovery of the child from trauma will need the kind of predictable and supportive supervision that empowers him to be a predictable therapeutic presence for the child in what often proves to be a long-term and effective therapeutic relationship.

The recovery of trust in the parental relationship is almost always very difficult after a parental child abduction of any kind. In the less severe, more short-term and tokenistic abductions, family therapy and joint parental counselling may have parts to play in rebuilding trust in both parent–child and parent–parent relationships. Such intervention is more likely to yield positive dividends for family members where the abductor makes a sincere apology for the destructive impact her behaviour visited on her child and the other parent.

Personal and Reflective Exercises

Each of the two following exercises can be done privately in the reader's own work journal or undertaken as part of a class group.

1. Imagine you are the female primary carer of two children aged eight and six years and that you have had a conflict-filled, two-year post-separation period with your male ex-partner who is the father of your children. Part of this conflict has been over his unceasing requests to increase his share of the children's care from the court-ordered 25 per cent to the 50 per cent which he believes is in the children's best interests. Imagine further that you have developed a serious relationship with another partner who has persuaded you to come and start a new life with him in another jurisdiction, one hour away by plane, where he has excellent employment. How would you approach this relocation challenge? What conversations and initiatives might you undertake in the pursuit of your goal? Write some notes for yourself about the relocation challenges you perceive in this context and about the conversations and other initiatives you might decide to embark upon.

2. Write a paragraph about your personal responses to each of the six child abduction contexts (i to vi) mentioned above in the section 'Typical Contemporary Contexts of Child Abduction'. Write a further note on those aspects of your own personal or professional experiences that may be playing some part in shaping those responses. If the exercise is done as part of a class, participants could share their written reflections within small groups after each written exercise.

MENTAL HEALTH, MENTAL ILLNESS AND SUBSTANCE ABUSE IN POST-SEPARATION/DIVORCE FAMILY CONFLICT: PROFESSIONAL INTERVENTIONS

This chapter looks at the positive ways that mental health professionals can assist and intervene where concerns about mental health and illness, in both parents and children, are part of the context of post-separation/divorce family conflict. The theme of mental health has been quietly present throughout this text, as it often is throughout the performance of post-separation conflicts of different degrees of intensity. The underlying assumption of the chapter is that practitioners in this area have an important role in safeguarding and promoting the mental health of conflict participants, adults and children while protecting key familial relationships. The context of mental health professional intervention in these circumstances may be voluntary, as when parents jointly request either mediation or family therapy in the process of parting, or court-mandated, as when the professional is requested by the court to undertake an evaluation with respect to where children should reside and the kind of contact they should have with a nonresident parent. Or the court might appoint a mental health professional as a parent co-ordinator for the purposes of implementing its orders and assisting with adjustments required by the contingencies of an illness.

The experience of conflict, as well as direct participation in conflict, can be a stressor that impacts different people in different ways. Practitioners will have met many parents who appear to thrive on their participation in conflict scenarios with an ex-partner. These individuals seem to be energised and activated by the ongoing struggle and appear to almost seek out, if not manufacture, a conflict experience even in times when conflict seems to have disappeared from their lives. When peace reigns and court orders are being appropriately adhered to, such individuals interpret this emergent peace as a sign that their ex-partner must be planning another move in the conflict. This suspicion is enough to drive them into planning and executing counter-strategies of different kinds. The performance of conflict-associated roles appears to give these parents some small sense of agency and competence in lives that have otherwise become progressively contracted and constrained through their involvement in prolonged conflict. In other words, the performance of conflict over time has endowed them with a set of skills which they want to go on using. The continuation of conflict engagement may also be a way of staying in some kind of relationship with an ex-partner and can operate as a psychological defence against the unbearable experience of total loss of the partner that parental peace would signify. Such adults rarely attend counsellors or psychotherapists of their own volition and have usually never been diagnosed by a mental health specialist as having a psychological illness of any kind. They are quick to point out to mental health professionals and their own lawyers the likely presence of a narcissistic, borderline personality disorder in their combatant ex-partner but slow to respond to any invitation to consider the contribution their own mental health status might be making to ongoing struggles. A number of authors (Eddy, 2012; Parkinson and Cashmore, 2015) note that post-separation and post-divorce parental conflicts, particularly those that go to litigation, often involve mothers and fathers with impaired parental capacity arising from personality disorders, mental illness, or drug and alcohol abuse.

Professionals will be equally acquainted with adults for whom the experience of parental conflict over child issues remains deeply stressful no matter how long it persists. The conflict experience can cause these parents to be intermittently sleepless at night, to be unable to focus on their work tasks, to be less perceptive regarding their children's emotional states and to experience mild to moderate degrees of anxiety and depression. These parents are likely to be more open with professionals about their own emotional and psychological states despite articulating a fear that such openness might come against them in the context of parental struggle over their children's care. Yet other parents will conceal information regarding their current mental health status due to precisely the same fears.

What all the above means for the mental health professional is that mental health concerns do not always present openly in the context of assisting families and their members engaged in conflict sequences of different kinds. Sometimes a psychological condition remains buried and unrecognised within the performance of conflict-associated roles. Alternatively, an individual may be aware of his mental health challenges but choose not to reveal them, for strategic reasons, to professionals or to those with whom he is in conflict. Where significant adult mental illness is part of the conflict scene, this is much less easy to hide given the significant behavioural changes and hospitalisations that such illnesses regularly bring about. These illnesses may or may not have had a recognised place in the history of the separating couple's life and may or may not have had a contributory role in the breakdown of the relationship. Or such illnesses may have had their onset either in the process of separating or some years following separation. Each of these different contexts of illness emergence have implications for the way conflict is performed, the range of people who participate in it and how it can be managed.

Where children and adolescents are concerned, their symptoms of psychological stress or distress may often be too easily dismissed by those close to them as a short-term consequence of their parents' conflict. The assumption in this response is that their distress and mood fluctuations will automatically dissipate once parental struggles abate. Adolescent depression, for example, may go unnoticed by parents whose gaze and energy is totally focused on the conflict with the partner from whom they are separating or have recently separated. Or persistent childhood distress may be concealed by one parent or 'outed' by another for different purposes related to the conflict. In such circumstances, the mental health of a child can be compromised by parental conflict over the meaning to be attributed to the child's expressions of distress and whether this distress should be the subject of mental health intervention in its own right. Persistent post-separation parental conflict can create many challenges for both the identification of child and adolescent mental health problems as well as for their treatment.

The chapter commences with a broad consideration of the way mental health concerns in parents, particularly those associated with major mental illnesses, add something of significance to the performance of post-separation family conflict and its management. The chapter continues with an examination of mental health professional interventions with children and adolescents whose mental health is affected to varying degrees in the context of persistent post-separation parental conflict. Attention then turns to the challenges created for conflict management when drug and/or alcohol abuse presents itself in one of the conflict participants. Following this, the chapter attends to the darkest end of the conflict spectrum, where conflict finds a conclusion for some or all of its immediate participants through intimate partner homicide, filicide or familicide. The chapter concludes with a reflection on the mental health of mental health practitioners engaged in different assistance roles with parents and children involved in post-separation/divorce family conflict.

Major Adult Mental Illness and the Performance and Management of Post-separation/Divorce Family Conflict

When a major psychiatric illness strikes a parent engaged in post-separation conflict, he can feel assaulted by fears of different kinds. If he is the parent with whom the children mostly reside, he may fear that his ex-partner will try to capitalize on his vulnerability by suggesting that he is unable to care for the children well enough and that the children's residency arrangements should be altered in favour of herself. He may also fear that his illness might take him to a place where he would be unable to provide the quality of care he knows his children need. His ex-partner may become aware of the problem in its early crisis stage when, for example, she returns the children, following a contact period, to a home from which the resident parent has been recently removed in an ambulance to a hospital emergency department. Or the nonresident parent may arrive to collect children for a contact period only to find no one at home and her ex-partner unable to be contacted by phone to indicate where the children might be picked up. Extended family and friends of the resident parent may 'circle the wagons' in support of the ill parent and play their part, in response to parental fears, in keeping the nonresident parent in the dark about the children's presence in their care. Such dramas around the emergency hospitalization of a resident parent often lead, in the absence of other means of parental communication and negotiation, to emergency court hearings in which applications are made by the nonresident parent for precisely the thing that the resident parent has most feared – namely, the transfer of the residency arrangements for the children to the other, nonresident parent.

Family Courts, Adult Psychiatric Illness and Parental Conflict

The existence of persistent conflict cuts parents off from what they most need in the context of a mental health crisis – namely, the capacity to collaborate as parents and make temporary, flexible adaptations to their children's care schedules for the duration of an illness crisis. Whether the illness manifesting itself in the resident parent is one of depression, bi-polar disorder or a psychosis, the job of managing these emerging crises often falls, at least initially, on the shoulders of the family court and its assisting mental health professional. Although the family courts have a very necessary role to play in the first level response to these crises, they are not good contexts in which to resolve conflicts relating to adjustments in parental care needed when one parent suffers from a major psychiatric disorder. There are two reasons for this. The first is that the stresses and fears associated with family court appearances, notwithstanding the promise they hold for the perceived protection of parental and child interests, regularly create levels of anxiety that do little to assist the stabilization and recovery of parents suffering with the relatively recent onset of a psychiatric illness, and may even set this recovery into reverse. The second is that court systems, unless abundantly resourced, find it difficult to respond in a timely fashion to the challenges faced by an already-conflicted post-separation parental system that has become even more challenged by the unanticipated twists and turns of an illness. For these reasons the appointment by the family court of a parent-coordinator (Higuchi and Lally, 2014a), following the making of an initial set of orders aimed at stabilizing children's residence and contact arrangements with both parents on an interim basis, offers parents a means of managing their challenges over a period of months without the need for repeated court appearances in response to every twist and turn in the ill parent's recovery or deterioration.

Parent Coordination in the Context of Post-separation Illness-related Parental Conflict

Under the guidance of the court, which includes the courts pre-specification of the areas to which the parent coordinator's arbitration authority can apply, parent coordination can be an effective short-term intervention in the management of illness-related crises in post-separation parental conflict. It contains the possibility of gaining as much mediated resolution as possible between parents about child issues even when the parent with the illness either does not want any face-to-face contact with the other parent or is not well enough to meet for face-to-face negotiations. Where the children's resident parent is enduring the illness experience, careful consultations of the parent coordinator with this parent as part of the distance mediation endeavours can limit the sense of disempowerment brought about by his illness and hospitalization. It also has the possibility of reassuring the nonresident parent that there will be an impartial set of professional eyes looking out for the children's interests as the mixture of mediation and arbitration ensues. Should the parent coordinator gain the confidence of both parents over a number of months, the intervention has the added possibility of transitioning into a voluntary arrangement where the mental health professional can be engaged by the parents in either an ongoing mediation role, where family court proceedings are suspended, or a parent coordinator role, where the terms of the role and its duration are agreed in advance by the parents as opposed to being set by the court.

Factors in Assessment

The mental health professional's first role within illness-related crises experienced by parents engaged in post-separation conflict is often that of court-appointed assessor with respect to residence and contact arrangements for children in the context of an unfolding parental illness and its management. The evaluation ordered by the court might be the first evaluation ever undertaken by the family, or family members may be very experienced with respect to such processes. Regardless of whether there has been a history of court-appointed evaluations of the family, the assessor will have to make the best possible assessment of the following factors in the shortest possible time: the children's needs and wishes in the context of both their developmental stage and the situation they find themselves in; the way an emerging illness appears to have impacted parenting capacity in the parent with an illness; this parent's cooperation and responsiveness to agencies offering assistance in the past; the other parent's parenting capacity and her motivation to care for children for longer periods of time; other parenting resources potentially available in the extended families of both parents; the perception of school and after-school personnel regarding children's adjustment since a parent has been hospitalized; the children's understanding of their parent's illness and whether they need any further age-appropriate assistance in this regard.

Many assessments that commence in the crises associated with the emergence of a major mental illness in one of the parents will necessarily occur over time. For example, proposals for longer-term care plans for children of a parent with a significant mental illness must be based upon an adequate assessment of parental capacity across time periods when the parent is well, as well as when he is unwell. This will naturally take several months, and the professional will need to build up a relationship with all the family members during this period. The mental health professional undertaking assessments in these contexts on behalf of the family court should be compliant with whatever protocols regarding risk assessments are in use by the child and adolescent mental health services in their jurisdiction. This professional must liaise closely and effectively with whatever local services are triggered into operation by the very fact of a parent's hospitalization. As with all other crises mentioned in this text, the safety – physical, emotional and sexual – of children is of paramount importance at all times.

Children's Mental Health, Parental Conflict and Mental Health Professional Interventions

Although many children appear to cope very well with the challenges presented by their parents' separation and divorce, mental health practitioners know that there are a whole group of children who don't fare so well and whose mental health and psychological well-being are impacted to varying degrees. Following separation, some children may suffer from mild symptoms of stress and anxiety which appear to have little or no impact on their functioning in educational, recreational or peer contexts, whereas others may suffer from a range of psychosomatic symptoms, mood fluctuations or behavioural disturbances of different kinds. The disturbances in this latter group of children regularly affect their school attendance and performance or draw the disciplinary attention of school or police authorities.

A recent study by Lucas et al. (2013), examining the mental health of a group of eight- to nine-year-old Australian children with both resident and nonresident fathers, found that children from separated families with a nonresident father had a twofold increased risk of mental health difficulties compared to those from intact families. The authors of the study judged that these differences were fully accounted for by parental conflict, the mental health of mothers and fathers, and socioeconomic factors. The differences were explained to a lesser extent by the parenting practices of both parents. Among the factors accounting for this difference, the study confirmed that, consistent with previous research findings demonstrating the adverse effects of family conflict on children's post-separation adjustment (Amato, 2005; Baxter et al., 2011; Hetherington et al., 1998), parental conflict made the greatest contribution. Such findings underline the importance of attending to the central theme in this text – namely, parental conflict after separation and divorce. Mental health practitioners and others working with families in conflict after separation and divorce can be confident that interventions aimed at reducing or containing post-separation parental conflict, or at reducing or eliminating children's exposure to expressions of such conflict, are likely to make a positive contribution to the mental health of children and adolescents. Practitioners can be equally confident that exposure to high levels of parental conflict has negative and long-lasting effects on children's development (Lansford, 2009).

Although it makes sense for practitioner interventions to be addressed towards conflict containment and reduction in the post-separation parental system, it does not make sense to make such conflict the exclusive focus of interventions. Conflict and its performance can have such a hypnotic effect upon observers that it is easy for their attention to be drawn directly towards it and away from other sites of distress in the post-divorce family. Post-divorce parental counselling, as well as parent mediation, certainly carries the potential for conflict management and reduction, which are likely to have positive spin-off effects for children and adolescents. However, the practitioner needs to keep in mind that although these parent-oriented interventions carry hope for all family members, they may take a considerable amount of time before they yield positive results, or they may not succeed in bringing about any improvement at all. In the interim, children and adolescents may be suffering relatively quietly. It always makes sense for the mental health professional to consider what independent, separate assistance children and adolescents might need to help them cope with their experiences of parental conflict. Such assistance might be afforded through their participation in school-based programs for children whose parents live apart or their attendance at play therapy, art therapy or individual counselling, depending upon their developmental stage and unique dispositions. Children and adolescents exhibiting more serious symptoms such as depression, self-harm, school-refusal, substance misuse or eating disorders will need to be referred to their local child and adolescent mental health service or other specialist services.

Other parent-directed interventions that may positively impact child and adolescent mental health in the context of post-separation parental conflict include parent education programs related to post-separation parenting or participation in group-based recreational or educational activities that withdraw parental attention, however temporarily, from the ongoing conflict. Such activities can remind parents that there may be a life to be lived beyond the current struggle. However, parents with significant mental health difficulties may find attending group-based activities too stressful, but may benefit from attending support groups offered by their local mental health services. Where socio-economic factors associated with separation and divorce are a big driver of conflict, the mental health professional should explore whether family members are getting all the financial assistance they are entitled to, and should support parents, individually or collectively, in their approach to local agencies that may have some discretionary power to assist them.

Substance Abuse and Post-separation Conflict Management

Parental abuse of drugs and/or alcohol can provide challenges of different kinds for the management of post-separation conflict. Such conflicts may be different in shape, depending on whether the parent abusing substances is the resident or nonresident parent. Where a nonresident parent has an ongoing and unremitting pattern of substance abuse, there may be little or no conflict between him and the resident parent over child contact. Whether in denial or not about his substance-abusing behaviour, this parent may simply accept whatever limited and/or supervised contact the resident parent imposes. Conflict management challenges arise, however, either when there is a denial of substance abuse by a contact-seeking nonresident parent whose behavioural presentation suggests ongoing abuse or when his pattern of abuse is varying. Practitioners will know that in parents who abuse substances of different kinds, good-quality, nurturing and engaged parenting can be followed quite closely in time with parenting that has become distracted, disengaged and lacking in required levels of vigilance. Substance-abusing parents in varying states of denial may initiate legal proceedings for breach of court orders against the other parent who has withheld a child from parental contact for reasons of safety. It has already been noted that the family court is not a good setting for the ongoing management of contact disputes when major adult mental health conditions are involved. This is also the case with respect to contact disputes where a varying pattern of substance abuse is present in a nonresident parent. In such disputes, the court's appointment of a parent coordinator can facilitate both speedier and safer resolutions than those offered through the court's direct management of contact-related conflicts. In some more serious situations, however, such as those mentioned below, family courts may need to remain centrally involved in dispute management, albeit with the assistance of appointed mental health professionals.

Where the parent abusing substances is the resident parent, the conflict management challenges are often much greater. It is likely, in this instance, that child protection services will play a much larger role on the conflict management team. The court and its assisting mental health professional may face applications from the nonresident parent for longer periods of contact time, and where substance abuse in the resident parent is not contained, there may, in time, be an application by a nonresident parent for a reversal of residence and contact arrangements for exposed children. Mandated testing for levels of substance consumption or ingestion may or may not be part of a court's management strategy in the face of such applications. Where a resident parent acknowledges the problem of substance abuse and is on the road to sobriety or being drug-free, despite slips, the court may decide to leave the matter of contact variations in the hands of a parent coordinator acting in consultation with child protection personnel.

One final matter relating to substance abuse merits particular attention from the mental health professional assisting with contact-related post-separation conflict. This concerns a group of separated families where the presence of substance abuse in a parent occurs in conjunction with psychological illness and aggressive/violent behaviour towards an ex-partner. Several studies (Brown et al., 1999; Easton, 2012; Easton et al., 2008; Kessler et al., 1996; Rhodes et al., 2009) have pointed to links connecting substance-abusing adults, mental health problems and aggressive and/or violent behaviour towards an intimate partner or ex-partner. Easton (2012), for example, in a study of male substance-abusing domestic violence offenders in receipt of group behavioural therapies, found that those men with co-occurring mental health problems had more pretreatment impairments, more substance abuse within treatment, more problems with aggressive behaviour throughout treatment and more impairments in anger control after treatment than those men without co-occurring mental health symptoms. Brown et al. (1999), in a study of a cohort of men in domestic violence treatment, found that in those men with the dual problem of domestic violence and substance abuse, the dangerousness and frequency of abusive behaviours increased as their substance abuse increased. These dual-problem men also reported more hostility, apprehension, frustration and suspiciousness and more previous arrests than the violence-only males in the study.

Such studies alert mental health practitioners to the need for careful risk assessment in post-separation contact disputes where two or three of these factors co-occur. Female victims of domestic violence may do informal 'deals' with their violent partners about levels of post-separation child contact as a way of securing their exit from shared accommodation, in the mistaken belief that residential separation will bring an end to violence and harassment. Not only do many such deals fail to deliver this cessation for victims, but, as some studies (e.g. Humphreys and Thiara, 2003) indicate, they merely open the door for abusive ex-partners to continue a campaign of aggression, harassment and threats through the medium of child contact. Such contexts, which often result in 'no-contact' orders for at least a period of time, require the closest possible liaison between the court's assisting mental health professional, the court itself, law enforcement agents, child protection, domestic violence treatment and mental health services if victims and their children are to be protected from ongoing abuse.

Intimate Partner Homicide, Filicide and Familicide

On several occasions in this text, the place of domestic violence has been noted as a key factor in post-separation parental conflict. Despite the significant (for men) and moderate (for women) decreases in intimate partner homicide since 1975 (Stockl et al., 2013) in the United States and other relatively wealthy parts of the globe, due perhaps to the increase of both public awareness of domestic violence and of improved state responses to domestic abuse of all kinds, the context of post-separation conflict still encounters adult and child victims who pay the ultimate price of their lives through being killed by a parent/ex-partner. These events, though rare in their occurrence, keep a horrendous horizon in view for all those working with parents and children where the anger and rage that often accompanies the performance of post-separation conflict has the capacity to spill over into interpersonal physical violence. In writing and reading about the theme of post-separation family conflict, it is our duty to remember these child and adult victims whose individual names and profiles the media keep before us until the time of the next tragedy. Although it seems almost certain that the mental health of the perpetrators of these crimes plays an important part in such tragedies, it has been difficult for researchers to clearly establish this role, given that most perpetrators of filicide, for example, also take their own lives, and researchers must rely on secondary sources of information to make inferences regarding their psychological states and motivation.

In a small qualitative Western Australian study of seven cases of familicide, where post-separation conflict over residency and contact were identified as being a concern between the conflict participants, Johnson (2006) found that the couples involved had experienced long-standing unhappiness and discord; the wives had been the principal instigators of the separation; and their male partners appeared to have had great difficulty in accepting the separation. Each of the seven female survivors of these familicides reported experiencing their couple relationship as marked by the dominance and control of their male partners, whom they experienced as possessive both in relation to themselves and their children. The study also found that although the surviving women spoke in interview of their history of domestic violence, neither the police nor the family court had adequate information about this prior to the tragic events. Three of the seven couples had not used the family courts at all, and those that had did not fully disclose either to their lawyer or the court the extent of the violence that was occurring in the relationship. In only one case was there clearly a current dispute before the court at the time of the murder-suicide event. The study found that even when physical violence had not been part of the couple history prior to separation, violence was triggered in the male partner by the event of separation. In six of the seven familicides studied, threats had been made by the male perpetrator to harm either himself or others prior to the offence.

The study also reported that it was difficult to gain any evidence concerning the existence of a mental disorder in the male perpetrators given that there were no psychiatric, psychological or assessment reports available on the men. However, most of their surviving female partners thought, retrospectively, they had seen signs of depression or disturbed behaviour in their ex-partners in the weeks or months prior to the catastrophic event. Information regarding these matters, it appeared, only came out retrospectively. Studies such as the above provide a small but important insight into how lightly, if at all, the families involved may engage, prior to the event, with services that might assist them. Mental health professionals are more likely to come into the scene *after* a tragedy has occurred. Indeed, Johnson (2006) reported that the traumatic impact of the familicides in her study went far beyond the female survivors in the immediate family and gained a foothold in the lives of extended family members and family friends. In that particular study, the effects ranged from severe illness resulting in death, to chronic mood disturbance and depression, to increased use of alcohol and drugs. A range of post-traumatic symptoms was also recorded. This wider circle of impact of trauma and trauma effects is even more noticeable in larger studies of familicide, where the term is confined to those events where a whole family is wiped out through the murder and suicide actions of one of its members (Websdale, 2010). Although the psychotherapeutic treatment and support of traumatised survivors may remain the central site of mental health assistance in these post-separation tragedies, the role of the same professionals in strengthening preventative measures must also be considered. Such measures might include fostering better co-ordination between family court, child protection and mental health services or facilitating the operation of a triage service (like that operated in many emergency departments of general hospitals) at the point of litigants' first entry into a family court system for whatever reason. In many jurisdictions, it is still too easy for extremely vulnerable adults, who are usually parents of highly vulnerable children, to slip in and out of the court system without any warning signals being triggered. The hope is that further research can assist in identifying early warning signs in families and individuals vulnerable to the occurrence of this kind of tragic behaviour and, in the process, allow for the refinement of preventive strategies.

The Mental Health of the Mental Health Professional

Intermittent comment has been made throughout this text about the different kinds of price adults pay for their ongoing immersion in interpersonal conflict. Conflict engagement takes its toll in different ways on the mental health and functioning of its participants. Mental health professionals assisting those in conflict through the many intervention roles described in the forgoing pages also, and inevitably, pay some personal price for their persistent immersion and necessary depth of engagement in conflict scenes where the stakes can be very high. Indeed, just as with those directly engaged in post-separation conflict, it may take the observations of others close to them to alert mental health professionals to signs of vulnerability in their own mental health. Depending upon personal history and the presence or absence of personal support, the impact of constant engagement with scenes of intense interpersonal conflict, which may or may not involve physical violence, can range from mild symptoms of stress to misuse of alcohol and other substances, to a full-blown burnout with all the emotional/psychological sequelae that flow from this state (Hanks and Vetere, 2016).

One of the key supports mental health professionals engaged in this work require is a good supervisory relationship with a senior colleague familiar with the area of practice. This supervision should not only focus upon the challenges of particular pieces of practice and the skill development needed to meet an ever-changing set of assessment and therapeutic demands, but should also be a real support for the professional in examining the two-way impact between professional practice experiences and personal life and relationships (Jensen, 2016). A good-enough supervisory relationship in this practice arena should also have a periodic mental health check built in. Included in this check for the mental health professional must be an exploration of how the supervisory relationship itself is experienced by the practitioner and whether any adjustments in supervisory pattern need to take place. It is likely that the supervisory process will be greatly enhanced through supervisors themselves having periodic supervision-of-supervision consultations where they are also supported to examine their supervision practice experiences and the bidirectional impact at work between their own professional experiences and their personal life.

The mental health needs of practitioners in this area also find great support through peer supervision and consultation groups. It is likely that such groups will vary in the degree of trust they engender in their participant members, and some groups may be able to fulfil some supervisory needs, but not others. Hence, it is not an unusual pattern for professionals to have more than one supervisory structure in place to support their different supervisory and support requirements.

Personal and Reflective Exercises

1. Write some notes for yourself about any personal or familial experiences you have had with psychological illnesses or addictions of any kind. What impact do you think these experiences might have upon your professional practice when assisting families engaged in post-separation conflict where such themes are part of the context?
2. What psychological illnesses and conditions do you feel you are sufficiently informed about? Write a note for yourself about why you feel this way. What psychological illnesses and conditions do you feel you need to be better informed about? Write a note about how you feel you could inform yourself more about these illnesses and conditions.
3. Write a few paragraphs for yourself concerning the relationship you believe exists between your own mental health and the professional practices you are engaged in. How do aspects of your personal lifestyle impact upon your professional practice with family members engaged in post-separation family conflict, and vice versa?
4. Write a letter of no more than ten lines to your professional practice supervisor, saying you would like her assistance within a future supervisory session to look at your mental health needs in the context of the unique mix of professional practice and personal life experiences that currently make up your life.

BIBLIOGRAPHY

Agopian, M.W. (1984) 'The impact on children of abduction by parents'. *Child Welfare*, 63(6): 511–19.

Ahrons, C. (2007) 'Family ties after divorce: Long-term implications for children'. *Family Process*, 46(1): 53–65.

Ainsworth, M. (1967) *Infancy in Uganda: Infant Care and the Growth of Love*. Baltimore, MD: John Hopkins University Press.

Ainsworth, M., Blehar, M., Walters, E., and Wall, S. (1978) *Patterns of Attachment: A Psychological Study of the Strange Situation*. Hillsdale, NJ: Erlbaum.

Akhtar, M. (2017) *What Is Post-Traumatic Growth?* London: Watkins.

Amato, P.R. (2005) 'The impact of family formation change on the cognitive, social and emotional well-being of the next generation'. *Future of Children*, 15(2): 75–96.

Anderson, H. (2012) 'Collaborative relationships and dialogic conversations: Ideas for a relationally responsive practise'. *Family Process*, 51(1): 8–24.

Arbuthnot, J., and Gordon, D. (1996) 'Does mandatory divorce education work? A six-month outcome evaluation'. *Family and Conciliation Courts Review*, 34: 60–81.

Arendt, H. (1958) *The Human Condition*. Chicago, IL: University of Chicago Press.

Aristotle. (1895) *Poetics*. Introduction, text, translation and commentary by S.H. Butcher. *Aristotle's Theory of Poetry*. London: McMillan.

Atkins, D.C., Baucom, D.H., and Jacobson, N.S. (2001) 'Understanding infidelity: Correlates in a national random sample'. *Journal of Family Psychology*, 15: 735–49.

Augustine, R. (1991) 'Marriage: The safe haven for rapists'. *Journal of Family Law*, 29: 559–90.

Austin, W. (2000) 'Relocation law and the threshold of harm: Integrating legal and behavioural perspectives'. *Family Law Quarterly*, 34: 63–82.

Austin, W. (2008a) 'Relocation, research and forensic evaluation: Part 1: Effects of residential mobility on children of divorce'. *Family Court Review*, 46: 137–50.

Austin, W. (2008b) 'Relocation, research and forensic evaluation: Part 2: Research in support of the relocation risk assessment model'. *Family Court Review*, 46: 347–65.

Bacon, B.L., and McKenzie, B. (2004) 'Parent education after separation/divorce: Impact of the level of parental conflict on outcomes'. *Family Court Review*, 42: 85–98.

Bank, S., and Kahn, M. (1982) *The Sibling Bond*. New York: Basic Books.

Barky, A.E. (2015) *Conflict Resolution for the Helping Professions: Negotiation, Mediation, Advocacy, Facilitation, and Restorative Justice*, 3rd edn. New York: Oxford University Press.

Barocas, B., Emery, D., and Mills, L.G. (2016) 'Changing the domestic violence narrative: Aligning definitions and standards'. *Journal of Family Violence*, 31(8): 941–47.

Bateson, G. (1972) *Steps to an Ecology of Mind*. New York: Ballantine.

Bateson, G. (1979) *Mind and Nature: A Necessary Unity*. New York: Bantam Books.

Bateson, G., Jackson, D.D., Haley, J., and Weakland, J. (1956) 'Toward a theory of schizophrenia'. *Behavioural Science*, 1(4): 251–64.

Bauman, Z. (2003) *Liquid Love*. Cambridge: Polity Press.

Baxter, J., Weston, R., and Qu, L. (2011) 'Family structure, co-parental relationship quality, post-separation paternal involvement and children's emotional well-being'. *Journal of Family Studies*, 17(2): 86–109.

Behrens, J., and Smyth, B. (2010) 'Australian family law court decisions about relocation: Parents' experiences and some implications for law and policy'. *Federal Law Review*, 38: 1–20.

Behrens, J., Smyth, B., and Kaspiew, R. (2009) 'Australian family law court decisions on relocation: Dynamics in parents' relationships across time'. *Australian Journal of Family Law*, 23: 222–46.

Belesky, J., and Cassidy, J. (1994) 'Attachment theory and practice'. In M. Rutter and D. Hay (eds), *Development Through Life: A Handbook for Clinicians* (pp. 373–402). Oxford: Blackwell Science.

Ben-Ami, N., and Baker, A.J.L. 'The long-term correlates of childhood exposure to parental alienation on adult self-sufficiency and well-being'. *The American Journal of Family Therapy*, 40: 169–83.

Birnbaum, G.E., Orr, I., Mikulincer, M., and Florian, V. (1997) 'When marriage breaks up: Does attachment style contribute to coping and mental health?'. *Journal of Social and Personal Relationships*, 14: 643–54.

Bornstein, M.H. (2013) 'Parenting and child mental health: A cross-cultural perspective'. *World Psychiatry*, 12(3): 258–65.

Bourdieu, P. (2004) *Science of Science and Reflexivity*. Trans. R. Nice. Chicago, IL: University of Chicago Press.

Bowlby, J. (1969) *Attachment and Loss:* Vol. 1: *Attachment*. London: Hogarth Press.

Bowlby, J. (1973) *Attachment and Loss:* Vol. 2: *Separation: Anger and Anxiety*. London: Hogarth Press.

Bowlby, J. (1980) *Attachment and Loss:* Vol. 3: *Loss: Sadness and Depression*. London: Hogarth Press.

Bowlby, J. (1988) *A Secure Base: Clinical Applications of Attachment Theory*. London: Hogarth Press.

Brown, E.M. (1991a) *Patterns of Infidelity and Their Treatment*. New York: Brunner/ Mazel.

Brown, E.M. (1991b) 'Children and affairs: Issues and interventions'. In E.M. Brown (ed.), *Patterns of Infidelity and Their Treatment* (pp. 245–304). New York: Brunner/Mazel.

Brown, T.G., Werk, A., Caplan, T., and Seraganian, P. (1999) 'Violent substance abusers in domestic violence treatment'. *Violence and Victims*, 14(2): 179–90.

Burnham, J.B. (1986) *Family Therapy: First steps towards a Systemic Approach*. London: Routledge.

Burnham, J. (1993) 'Systemic supervision: The evolution of reflexivity in the context of the supervisory relationship'. *Human Systems*, 3/4: 349–81.

Campbell, J.C. (1995) *Assessing Dangerousness: Violence by Sexual Offenders, Batterers and Child Abusers*. Thousand Oaks, CA: Sage.

Campbell, D., and Draper, R. (eds). (1985) *Applications of Systemic Therapy: The Milan Approach*. London: Grune and Stratton.

Campbell, J.C., Sharps, P., and Glass, N. (2001) 'Risk assessment for intimate partner homicide'. In G.F. Pinard and L. Pagani (eds), *Clinical Assessment of Dangerousness: Empirical Contributions* (pp. 136–57). New York: Cambridge University Press.

Cano, A., and O'Leary, K.D. (2000) 'Infidelity and separations precipitate major depressive episodes and symptoms of non-specific depression and anxiety'. *Journal of Consulting and Clinical Psychology*, 68: 774–81.

Carmody, T. (2007) 'Child relocation: An intractable international family law problem'. *Family Court Review*, 45: 214–46.

Carpenter, G.L., and Stacks, A.M. (2009) 'Developmental effects of exposure to intimate partner violence in early childhood: A review of the literature'. *Children and Youth Services Review*, 31: 831–39.

Carr, A. (2000) *Family Therapy: Concepts, Process and Practice*. Chichester: Wiley.

Carr, A. (2009a) 'The effectiveness of family therapy and systemic interventions for child-focused problems'. *Journal of Family Therapy*, 31(1): 3–45.

Carr, A. (2009b) 'The effectiveness of family therapy and systemic interventions for adult-focused problems'. *Journal of Family Therapy*, 31(1): 46–74.

Carter, E., and McGoldrick, M. (1980) *The Family Life Cycle: A Framework for Family Therapy*. New York: Gardner Press.

Childress, C.A. (2013) *Reconceptualizing Parental Alienation: Parental Personality Disorder and the Trans-generational Transmission of Attachment Trauma*. Retrieved from http://drcachildress.org/asp/admin/getFile.asp?RID=69&TID=6&FN=pdf

Childress, C.A. (2015) *An Attachment-Based Model of Parental Alienation: Foundations*. Claremont, CA: Oaksong Press.

Cicirelli, V.G. (1995) *Sibling Relationships Across the Lifespan*. New York: Plenum Press.

Clinton-Sherrod, A.M., and Walters, J.H. (2011) 'Marital rape and sexual violation by intimate partners'. In T. Bryant-Davis (ed.), *Surviving Sexual Violence* (pp. 48–58). Lanham, MD: Rowman and Littlefield.

Cloke, K. (2001) *Mediating Dangerously: The Frontiers of Conflict Resolution*. San Francisco, CA: Jossey-Bass.

Coles, P. (ed.). (2006) *Sibling Relationships*. London: Karnac Books.

Cook, A., Spinazzola, J., Ford, J., Lanktree, C., Blaustein, M., Cloitre, M., and Kolk, B. (2005) 'Complex trauma in children and adolescents'. *Psychiatric Annals*, 25(5): 390–98.

Cooper, D. (1994) 'Productive, relational and everywhere? Conceptualizing power and resistance within Foucauldian feminism'. *Sociology*, 28: 435–54.

Crittenden, P. (2008) *Raising Parents: Attachment, Parenting and Child Safety.* Cullompton: Willan Press.

Crittenden, P.M. (1995) 'Attachment and psychopathology'. In S. Goldberg, R. Muir and J. Kerr (eds), *Attachment Theory: Social, Developmental and Clinical Perspectives* (pp. 367–406). Hillsdale, NJ: Analytic Press.

Crittenden, P.M., and Claussen, A.H. (eds). (2000) *The Organization of Attachment Relationships: Maturation, Culture and Context.* New York: Cambridge University Press.

Dallos, R. (2006) *Attachment Narrative Therapy.* New York: Open University Press.

Dallos, R., and Vetere, A. (2009) *Systemic Therapy and Attachment Narratives.* London: Routledge.

Davies, B., and Harre, R. (1990) 'Positioning: The discursive production of selves'. *Journal for the Theory of Social Behaviour*, 20: 43–63.

Denzin, N.K. (1987) 'Caring for children'. *Society*, 24(3): 32–36.

Derrida, J. (1981) *Positions.* Chicago, IL: University of Chicago Press.

de Shazer, S., and Berg, I.K. (1992) 'Doing therapy: A post-structural re-vision'. *Journal of Marital & Family Therapy*, 18: 71–81.

Deutsch, M. (1973) *The Resolution of Conflict.* New Haven, CT: Yale University Press.

Deutsch, M., Coleman, P., and Marcus, E. (eds). (2006) *Handbook of Conflict Resolution: Theory and Practice*, 2nd edn. San Francisco, CA: Jossey-Bass.

Dickerson, V.C. (2014) 'The advance of poststructuralism and its influence on family therapy'. *Family Process*, 53(3): 401–14.

Dunne, J., and Hedrick, M. (1994) 'The parental alienation syndrome: An analysis of sixteen selected cases'. *Journal of Divorce and Remarriage*, 21: 21–38.

Duvall, E. (1977) *Marriage and Family Development.* Philadelphia, PA: Lippincott.

Easton, C.J. (2012) 'Co-occurring mental health problems among substance dependent offenders of intimate partner violence'. *Advances in Dual Diagnosis*, 5(2): 86–93.

Easton, C.J., Lee, B., Wupperman, P., and Zonana, H. (2008) 'Substance abuse and domestic violence interventions: The need for theoretical based research'. *The American Journal on Addictions*, 17(4): 341–42.

Eddy, B. (2009) *New Ways for Families in Separation and Divorce: Professional Guidebook for Judicial Officers, Lawyers and Therapists.* Scottsdale, AZ: High Conflict Institute, LLC.

Eddy, B. (2010) *Don't Alienate the Kids! Raising Resilient Children While Avoiding High-Conflict Divorce.* Scottsdale, AZ: High Conflict Institute, LLC.

Eddy, B. (2012) *The Future of Family Court.* San Diego, CA: HCI Press.

Elizabeth, V., Gavey, N., and Tolmie, J. (2012) 'The gendered dynamics of power in disputes over the postseparation care of children'. *Violence Against Women*, 18(4): 459–81.

Ellis, D., and Stuckless, N. (2006) 'Domestic violence, DOVE, and divorce mediation'. *Family Court Review*, 44(4): 658–67.

Euripides (1993) *Medea*. Trans. A. Elliot. London: Oberon Books.

Fackrell, T.A., Hawkins, A.J., and Kay, N. (2011) 'How effective are court-affiliated divorcing parents education programs? A meta-analytic study'. *Family Court Review*, 49: 107–19.

Fidler, B.J., Bala, N., and Saini, M.A. (2013) *Children Who Resist Postseparation Contact: A Differential Approach for Legal and Mental Health Professionals*. New York: Oxford University Press.

Flaskas, C., McCarthy, I., and Sheehan, J. (eds). (2007) *Hope and Despair in Narrative and Family Therapy*. London: Routledge.

Folberg, J.A., Milne, L., and Salem, P. (eds). (2004) *Divorce and Family Mediation: Models, Techniques and Applications*. New York: Guilford.

Folger, J.P., and Jones, T.S. (eds). (1994) *New Directions in Mediation: Communication Research and Perspectives*. Thousand Oaks, CA: Sage.

Foucault, M. (1980) *Power/Knowledge: Selected Interviews and Other Writings*. New York: Pantheon Books.

Freedman, J., and Combs, G. (1996) *Narrative Therapy: The Social Construction of Preferred Realities*. New York: Norton.

Freud, S. (1957) 'Mourning and melancholia'. In *The Standard Edition of the Complete Psychological Works of Sigmund Freud* (pp. 245–68). Translated and edited by James Strachey, London: Hogarth Press.

Friedlander, S., and Walters, M.G. (2010) 'When a child rejects a parent: Tailoring the interventions to fit the problem'. *Family Court Review*, 48: 97–110.

Gardner, R.A. (1985) 'Recent trends in divorce and custody litigation'. *Academy Forum*, 29(2): 3–7.

Gardner, R.A. (1992) *The Parental Alienation Syndrome: A Guide for Mental Health and Legal Professionals*. Cresskill, NJ: Creative Therapeutics, Inc.

Gardner, R.A. (2001) 'Should courts order PAS children to visit/reside with the alienated parent? A follow up study'. *American Journal of Forensic Psychology*, 19: 61–106.

Garrido, E.F., Culhane, S.E., Petrenko, C.L.M., and Taussig, H.N. (2011) 'Psychosocial consequences of Intimate Partner Violence (IPV) exposure in maltreated adolescents: Assessing more than IPV occurrence'. *Journal of Family Violence*, 26(7): 511–18.

George, R. (2012) 'The international relocation debate'. *Journal of Social Welfare and Family Law*, 34: 141–52.

George, R. (2014) *Relocation Disputes: Law and Practice in England and New Zealand*. Oxford: Hart.

Gergen, K.J. (1991a) 'The saturated family'. *The Family Therapy Networker*, 15(5): 27–35.

Gergen, K.J. (1991b) *The Saturated Self*. New York: Basic Books.

Gergen, K., and Davis, K. (eds). (1985) *The Social Construction of the Person*. New York: Springer.

Goldberg, P.D., Peterson, B.D., Rosen, K.H., and Sara, M.L. (2008) 'Cybersex: The impact of a contemporary problem on the practices of marriage and family therapists'. *Journal of Marital & Family Therapy*, 34(4): 469–80.

Gollop, M., and Taylor, N. (2012) 'New Zealand children and young people's perspectives on relocation following parental separation'. In M. Freeman (ed.), *Law and Childhood Studies* (pp. 219–42). Oxford: Oxford University Press.

Grief, G.L. (2000) 'A parental report on the long-term consequences for children of abduction by the other parent'. *Child Psychiatry and Human Development*, 31: 59–66.

Grief, G.L. (2009) 'The long-term aftermath of child abduction: Two case studies and implications for family therapy'. *The American Journal of Family Therapy*, 37: 273–75.

Hague Convention on the Civil Aspects of International Child Abduction (1980). 25 October, Hague, Netherlands.

Haley, J. (1976) *Problem-Solving Therapy: New Strategies for Effective Family Therapy*. San Francisco, CA: Jossey-Bass.

Hanks, H., and Vetere, A. (2016) 'Working at the extremes: The impact on us of doing the work'. In A. Vetere and P. Stratton (eds), *Interacting Selves: Systemic Solutions for Personal and Professional Development in Counselling and Psychotherapy* (pp. 65–84). London: Routledge.

Hans, J.D., Haselschwerdt, M.L., Hardesty, J.L., and Frey, L.M. (2014) 'The effects of domestic violence allegations on custody evaluators' recommendations'. *Journal of Family Psychology*, 28(6): 957–66.

Hare-Mustin, R.T. (1987) 'The problem of gender in family therapy'. *Family Process*, 26(1): 15–17.

Harre, R., and Van Langenhove, L. (1991) 'Varieties of positioning'. *Journal for the Theory of Social Behaviour*, 21: 393–408.

Hawes, S.E. (1998) 'Positioning a dialogic reflexivity in the practice of feminist supervision'. In B.M. Bayer and J. Shotter (eds), *Reconstructing the Psychological Subject: Bodies, Practices and Technologies* (pp. 94–110). London: Sage.

Hazan, C., and Shaver, P. (1987) 'Romantic love conceptualised as an attachment process'. *Journal of Personality and Social Psychology*, 52: 511–24.

Hegar, R.L., and Grief, G.L. (1991) 'Abduction of children by parents: A survey of the problem'. *Social Work*, 36: 421–27.

Herman, J.L. (1998) *Trauma and Recovery: From Domestic Abuse to Political Terror*. London: Pandora.

Hetherington, E.M. (ed.). (1999) *Coping with Divorce, Single Parenting, and Remarriage*. Mahwah, NJ: Erlbaum.

Hetherington, E.M., and Kelly, J. (2002) *For Better or Worse*. New York: Norton.

Hetherington, E.M., Bridges, M., and Insabella, G. (1998) 'What matters? What does not? Five perspectives on the association between marital transitions and children's adjustment'. *American Psychologist*, 53(2): 167–84.

Higuchi, S.A., and Lally, S.J. (eds). (2014a) *Parenting Coordination in Postseparation Disputes: A Comprehensive Guide for Practitioners*. Washington, DC: American Psychological Association.

Higuchi, S.A., and Lally, S.J. (2014b) 'Introduction'. In S.A. Higuchi and S.J. Lally (eds), *Parenting Coordination in Postseparation Disputes: A Comprehensive Guide for Practitioners* (pp. 3–10). Washington, DC: American Psychological Association.

Hildebrand, J. (1998) *Bridging the Gap: A Training Module in Personal and Professional Development*. London: Karnac.

Hilton, N.Z., Harris, G.T., Rice, M.E., Lang, C., Cormier, C.A., and Lines, K.J. (2004) 'A brief actuarial assessment for the prediction of wife assault recidivism: The Ontario Domestic Assault Risk Assessment'. *Psychological Assessment*, 16: 300–12.

Hoffman, L. (1981) *Foundations of Family Therapy*. New York: Basic Books.

Hoffman, L. (1992) 'A reflexive stance for family therapy'. In S. McNamee and K.J. Gergen (eds), *Therapy as Social Construction* (pp. 7–24). London: Sage.

Howard-Bostic, C.D. (2013) 'Is mutual violent combat (MVC) a gender neutral conceptualization of intimate partner violence'. *International Journal of Arts and Sciences*, 6(2): 361–75.

Howe, D. (2011) *Attachment Across the Lifecourse: A Brief Introduction*. London: Palgrave.

Huang, L.C., Vikse, J., Lu, S., and Silai, Y. (2015) 'Children's exposure to intimate partner violence and early delinquency'. *Journal of Family Violence*, 30: 953–65.

Humphreys, C., and Thiara, R. (2003) 'Mental health and domestic violence: 'I call it symptoms of abuse'. *British Journal of Social Work*, 33(2): 209–26.

Irving, H.H., and Benjamin, M. (2002) *Therapeutic Family Mediation: Helping Families Resolve Conflict*. Thousand Oaks, CA: Sage.

Jaffe, P.G., Crooks, C.V., and Bala, N. (2009) 'A framework for addressing allegations of domestic violence in child custody disputes'. *Journal of Child Custody*, 6(3–4): 169–88.

Jensen, P. (2008) *The Narratives Which Connect: A Qualitative Research Approach to the Narratives Which Connect Therapists' Personal and Private Lives to Their Family Therapy Practices*. Doctorate of Systemic Psychotherapy awarded by the University of East London in conjunction with the Tavistock Clinic, UK.

Jensen, P. (2012) 'Family therapy, personal life and therapeutic practice: The map of relational resonance as a language for analyzing therapeutic processes'. *Human Systems*, 23: 119–38.

Jensen, P. (2016) 'Mind the map: Circular processes between the therapist, the client and the therapist's personal life'. In A. Vetere and P. Stratton (eds), *Interacting Selves: Systemic Solutions for Personal and Professional Development in Counselling and Psychotherapy* (pp. 33–49). London: Routledge.

Johnson, C.H. (2006) 'Familicide and family law: A study of filicide-suicide following separation'. *Family Court Review*, 44(3): 448–63.

Johnston (2010) 'Research interview'. May 10th, cited in B.J, Fidler, N. Bala and M.A. Saini (2013) *Children Who Resist Postseparation Contact: A Differential Approach for Legal and Mental Health Professionals* (p. 25). New York: Oxford University Press.

Johnston, J.R. (1993) 'Children of divorce who refuse visitation'. In C. Depner and J.H. Bray (eds), *Non-Residential Parenting: New Vistas in Family Living* (pp. 109–35). Newbury Park, CA: Sage.

Johnston, J.R., and Goldman, J.R. (2010) 'Outcomes of family counselling interventions with children who resist visitation'. *Family Court Review*, 48: 112–15.

Jones, E. (1993) *Family Systems Therapy: Developments in the Milan-Systemic Therapies*. Chichester: Wiley.

Jones, T. (2015) *Heart of Conflict*. Thousand Oaks, CA: Sage.

Keating, A., Sharry, J., Murphy, M., Rooney, B., and Carr, A. (2016) 'An evaluation of the Parents Plus-Parenting When Separated programme'. *Clinical Child Psychology and Psychiatry*, 21: 240–54.

Kelly, J.B. (2000) 'Children's adjustment in conflicted marriage and divorce: A decade review of research'. *Journal of the American Academy of Child and Adolescent Psychiatry*, 39: 963–73.

Kelly, J.B. (2007) 'Children's living arrangements following separation and divorce: insights from empirical and clinical research'. *Family Process*, 46(1): 35–52.

Kelly, J.B. (2014) 'Origin and development of parenting coordination'. In S.A. Higuchi and S.J. Lally (eds), *Parenting Coordination in Postseparation Disputes: A Comprehensive Guide for Practitioners* (pp. 13–34). Washington, DC: American Psychological Association.

Kelly, J.R., and Johnston, J.R. (2001) 'The alienated child: A reformulation of parental alienation syndrome'. *Family Court Review. Special Issue: Alienated Children in Divorce*, 39(3): 249–66.

Kempe, C.H., Silverman, F.N., Steele, B.F., Droegemueller, W., and Silver, H.K. (1985) 'The battered child syndrome'. *Child Abuse and Neglect*, 9(2): 143–54.

Kerby, A.P. (1991) *Narrative and the Self*. Bloomington, IN: Indiana University Press.

Kessler, R.C., Kessler, C.B., Nelson, K.A., McGonagle, M.J., Edlund, R.G., and Frank, P.J. (1996) 'The epidemiology of co-occurring addictive and mental disorders: Implications for prevention and service utilization'. *American Journal of Orthopsychiatry*, 66(1): 17–31.

Koutselini, M., and Valanidou, F. (2014) 'Children living with violence against their mothers: The side effects on their behaviour, self-image and school performance'. *Pedagogy, Culture and Society*, 22(2): 213–31.

Kropp, P.R., Hart, S.D., Webster, C.W. and Eaves, D. (1994) *Manual for the Spousal Assault Risk Assessment Guide*. Vancouver, BC: British Columbia Institute on Family Violence.

Kropp, P.R., Hart, S.D., Webster, C.D., and Eaves, D. (2000) 'The Spousal Assault Risk Assessment (SARA) Guide: Reliability and validity in adult male offenders'. *Law and Human Behaviour*, 24: 101–18.

Lamont, R. (2012) 'Free movement of persons, child abduction and relocation within the European Union'. *Journal of Social Welfare and Family Law*, 34: 231–44.

Lansford, J.E. (2009) 'Parental divorce and children's adjustment'. *Perspectives on Psychological Science*, 4(2): 140–52.

Lowe, R. (2004) *Family Therapy: A Constructive Framework*. London: Sage.

Lowenstein, L.F. (1998) 'Parent alienation syndrome: A two-step approach toward a solution'. *Contemporary Family Therapy: An International Journal*, 20: 505–20.

Lucas, N., Nicholson, J.M. and Erbas, B. (2013) 'Child mental health after parental separation: The impact of resident/non-resident parenting, parental mental health, conflict and socioeconomics'. *Journal of Family Studies*, 19(1): 53–69.

Lusterman, D.D. (1998) *Infidelity: A Survival Guide*. Oakland, CA: New Harbinger.

Lusterman, D.D. (2005) 'Helping children and adults cope with parental infidelity'. *Journal of Clinical Psychology*, 61(11): 1439–51.

Maccoby, E.E., and Mnookin, R.H. (1992) *Dividing the Child: Social and Legal Dilemmas of Custody*. Cambridge, MA: Harvard University Press.

Maheu, M., and Subotnik, R. (2001) *Infidelity on the Internet: Virtual Relationships and Real Betrayal*. Naperville, IL: Sourcebooks.

Mayer, B. (2015) *The Conflict Paradox: Seven Dilemmas at the Core of Disputes*. San Francisco, CA: Jossey-Bass.

McGoldrick, M. and Gerson, R. (1985) *Genograms in Family Assessment*. New York: Norton.

McHoul, A., and Grace, W. (1995) *A Foucault Primer: Discourse, Power and the Subject*. London: UCL Press.

McIntosh, J.E., and Long, C.M. (2006) *Children Beyond Dispute: A Prospective Study of Outcomes from Child Focused and Child-inclusive Post-secondary Family Dispute Resolution*. Canberra: Australian Government Attorney General's Department.

McIntosh, J.E. Wells, Y.D., Smyth, B.M., and Long, C.M. (2008) 'Child-focused and child-inclusive divorce mediation: Comparative outcomes from a prospective study of post separation adjustment'. *Family Court Review*, 46(1): 105–24.

Minuchin, S. (1974) *Families and Family Therapy*. Cambridge, MA: Harvard University Press.

Minuchin, S. (1984) *Family Kaleidoscope*. Cambridge, MA: Harvard University Press.

Moylan, C.A., Herrenkohl, T.I., Sousa, C., Tajima, T.A., Herrenkohl, R.C., and Russo, M.J. (2010) 'The effects of child abuse and exposure to domestic violence on adolescent internalizing and externalizing behaviour problems'. *Journal of Family Violence*, 25(1): 53–63.

Murphy, J., and Rubinson, R. (2015) *Family Mediation: Theory and Practice*, 2nd edn. Los Angeles, CA: LexisNexis.

Napier, A., and Whitaker, C. (1978) *The Family Crucible*. New York: Harper and Row.

Ney, T. (2015) 'Constructing conflict: A discursive analysis of family law conflict'. *Conflict Resolution Quarterly*, 33(3): 177–201.

Ney, T., Blank, G.K., and Blank, A. (2007) 'Affidavits in conflict culture: A discursive analysis'. *Conflict Resolution Quarterly*, 24(3): 305–26.

O'Brien, K.L., Cohen, L., Pooley, J.A., and Taylor, M.F. (2013) 'Lifting the domestic violence cloak of silence: Resilient Australian women's reflected memories of their childhood experiences of witnessing domestic violence'. *Journal of Family Violence*, 28(1): 95–108.

Overlien, C. (2010) 'Children exposed to domestic violence: Conclusion from the literature and challenges ahead'. *Journal of Social Work*, 10: 80–97.

Parkinson, P., and Cashmore, J. (2015) 'When mothers stay: Adjusting to loss after relocation disputes'. *Family Law Quarterly*, 47: 65–96.

Parkinson, P., and Cashmore, J. (2015) 'Reforming relocation law: An evidence-based approach'. *Family Court Review*, 53(1): 23–39.

Parkinson, P., Cashmore, J., and Single, J. (2011) 'Mothers wishing to relocate with children: Actual and perceived reasons'. *Canadian Journal of Family Law*, 27: 11–51.

Parry, A., and Doan, R.E. (1994) *Story Re-Visions: Narrative Therapy in the Postmodern World*. New York: Guilford.

Peluso, P.R. (2007) 'Infidelity: Introduction and overview'. In P.R. Peluso (ed.), *Infidelity: A Practitioner's Guide to Working with Couples in Crisis* (pp. 1–7). New York: Routledge.

Polkinghorne, D.E. (1988) *Narrative Knowing and the Human Sciences*. New York: State University of New York Press.

Rand, D., Rand, R., and Kopetski, L. (2005) 'The spectrum of parental alienation syndrome part 3: The Kopetski follow-up study'. *American Journal of Forensic Psychology*, 23: 15–43.

Reay, K.M. (2015) 'Family reflections: A promising therapeutic program designed to treat severely alienated children and their family system'. *American Journal of Family Therapy*, 43: 197–207.

Reich, W. (1949) *Character Analysis*, 3rd edn. Trans. T.P. Wolfe. New York: Orgone Institute Press.

Rhodes, K.V., Houry, D., Cerulli, C., Straus, H., Kaslow, N.J., and McNutt, L. (2009) 'Intimate partner violence and comorbid mental health conditions among urban male patients'. *Annals of Family Medicine*, 7(1): 47–55.

Ricoeur, P. (1974) *The Conflict of Interpretations*. Trans. D. Ihde. Evanston, IL: North Western University Press.

Ricoeur, P. (1984) *Time and Narrative*, Vol. 1. Trans. K. McLaughlin and D. Pellauer. Chicago, IL: Chicago University Press.

Ricoeur, P. (1991) 'Narrative identity'. In D. Wood (ed.), *On Paul Ricoeur: Narrative and Interpretation* (pp. 188–99). London: Routledge.

Ricoeur, P. (1992) *Oneself As Another*. Trans. K. Blamey. Chicago: University of Chicago Press.

Ricoeur, P. (2004) *Memory, History, Forgetting*. Trans. K. Blamey and D. Pellauer. Chicago, IL: University of Chicago Press.

Roberts, J. (1994) *Tales and Transformations: Stories in Families and Family Therapy*. New York: Norton.

Rothschild, B. (2017) *The Body Remembers*, Vol. 2. New York: Norton.

Saini, M., and Newman, J. (2010) *Supervised Visitation Checklist (SVC)*. Unpublished manuscript.

Schapp, W. (1976) *In Geschichten Verstrickt*. Wiesbaden: B. Heymann.

Schluter, M., and Lee, D. (1993) *The R Factor*. London: Hodder and Stoughton.

Schon, D. (1991) *The Reflective Practitioner: How Professionals Think In Action*. London: Ashgate.

Schore, A.N. (2014) *The Science of The Art of Psychotherapy*. New York: Norton.

Schuz, R. (2013) *The Hague Child Abduction Convention: A Critical Analysis*. Oxford and Portland, OR: Hart.

Sgroi, S. (1982) *Handbook of Clinical Intervention in Child Sexual Abuse*. New York: The Free Press.

Sheehan, J. (1995) Psychotherapy as Narrative: A Critical Application of Paul Ricoeur's Philosophy of Narrative to Psychotherapy. Unpublished Ph.D dissertation, University College Dublin.

Sheehan, J. (2004) 'Positioning narrative in psychotherapy'. *Eisteacht*, 3(3): 6–11.

Sheehan, J. (2007) 'Forgiveness and the unforgiveable: The resurrection of hope in family therapy'. In C. Flaskas, I. McCarthy and J. Sheehan (eds), *Hope and Despair in Narrative and Family: Adversity, Forgiveness and Reconciliation* (pp. 161–72). London: Routledge.

Sheehan, J. (2013a) 'Child and adolescent development in the context of lesbian and gay parenting: What to make of the evidence?'. Presentation to the Irish Constitutional Convention on Same-Sex Marriage, Dublin, 13 April.

Sheehan, J. (2013b) 'Allegations of child abuse in post-divorce family process: Conflict management and harm reduction'. Presentation, 8th European Family Therapy Association Congress, Istanbul, 26 October.

Sheehan, J. (2016a) 'Children in the mediation process'. Presentation to the Mediators Institute of Ireland, Dublin, April 2016.

Sheehan, J. (2016b) 'Recording love and loss: A family intervention tool in high conflict divorce'. Presentation at the European Family Therapy Association Conference, Athens, 18 September.

Shorter, E. (1975) *The Making of the Modern Family*. New York: Basic Books.

Snyder, D.K., Baucom, D.H., and Gordon, K.C. (2007) *Getting Past the Affair: A Program to Help You Cope, Heal and Move On – Together or Apart*. New York: Guilford Press.

Sori, C.F. (2007) 'An affair to remember': Infidelity and its impact on children'. In P.R. Peluso (ed.), *Infidelity: A Practitioner's Guide to Working with Couples in Crisis* (pp. 247–76). New York: Routledge.

Sousa, C., Herrenkohl, T.I., Moylan, C.A., Tajima, E.A., Klika, J.B., Herrenkohl, R.C., and Russo, M.J. (2011) 'Longitudinal study on the effects of child abuse and children's exposure to domestic violence, parent-child attachments, and antisocial behaviour in adolescence'. *Journal of Interpersonal Violence*, 26(1): 111–36.

Spring, J.A. (1996) *After the Affair: Healing the Pain and Rebuilding the Trust When a Partner Has Been Unfaithful*. New York: Harper Collins.

Stahl, M. (1994) *Conducting Child Custody Evaluations: A Comprehensive Guide*. London: Sage.

Sternberg, K.J., Caradaran, L.P., Abbott, C.B., Lamb, M.E., and Guterman, E. (2006) 'Type of violence, age and gender differences in the effects of family violence on children's behaviour problems: A mega-analysis'. *Developmental Review*, 26: 89–112.

Stockl, H., Devries, K., Rotstein, A., Abrahams, N., Campbell, J., Watts, C., and Moreno, C.G. (2013) 'The global prevalence of intimate partner homicide: A systematic review'. *The Lancet*, 382(9895): 859–65.

Subotnik, R. (2007) 'Cyber-Infidelity'. In P.R. Peluso (ed.), *Infidelity: A Practitioner's Guide to Working with Couples in Crisis* (pp. 169–90). London: Routledge.

Sullivan, M.J., Ward, P., and Deutsch, R.M. (2010) 'Overcoming barriers family camp: A program for high-conflict divorced families where a child is resisting contact with a parent'. *Family Court Review*, 48: 116–35.

Templer, K., Mathewson, M., Haines, J., and Cox, G. (2017) 'Recommendations for best practice in response to parental alienation: Findings from a systematic review'. *Journal of Family Therapy*, 39: 103–22.

Thoennes, N., and Pearson, J. (1999) 'Parent education programs in the domestic relations courts: A multi-site assessment'. *Family and Conciliation Courts Review*, 37: 195–218.

Tirado, F., and Galvez, A. (2007) 'Positioning theory and discourse analysis: Some tools for social interaction analysis'. *Forum: Qualitative Social Research*, 8(2): 1–28.

Toren, B., Bregman, B.L., Zohar-Reich, E., Ben-Amitay, G., Wolmer, L., and Laor, N. (2013) 'Sixteen session group treatment for children and adolescents with parental alienation and their parents'. *American Journal of Family Therapy*, 41: 187–97.

Van Der Kolk, B. (2014) *The Body Keeps The Score: Mind, Brain and Body in the Transformation of Trauma*. London: Penguin.

Van Lawick, J., and Visser, M. (2015) 'No kids in the middle: Dialogical and creative work with parents and children in the context of high conflict divorces'. *Australian and New Zealand Journal of Family Therapy*, 36(1): 33–50.

Van Lawick, J., and Visser, M. (2017) 'High conflict divorce and no kids in the middle-where clinical practice and research go together and influence each other'. Presentation, International Systemic Research Conference, Heidelberg, 11 March.

Varga, A., and Budinayte, G. (2015) 'New marriage trends: The contemporary marriage. *Human Systems*, 26(2): 205–19.

Von Bertalanffy, L. (1968) *General System Theory*. New York: Braziller.

Wallerstein, J.S., and Blakeslee, S. (1989) *Second chances: Men, women and children a decade after divorce*. New York: Ticknore and Fields.

Wallerstein, J.S., and Kelly, J.B. (1980) *Surviving the breakup: How children and parents cope with divorce*. New York: Basic Books.

Walters, M.G., and Friedlander, S. (2016) 'When a child rejects a parent: Working with the intractable resist/refuse dynamic'. *Family Court Review*, 54(3): 424–45.

Warshak, R. A. (2010) Family Bridges: Using insights from social science to reconnect parents and alienated children. *Family Court Review*, 48: 48–80.

Websdale, N. (2010) *Familicidal Hearts: The Emotional Style of 211 Killers*. New York: Oxford University Press.

White, M. (2007) *Maps of Narrative Practice*. New York: Norton.

White, M., and Epston, D. (1990) *Narrative Means to Therapeutic Ends*. New York: Norton.

Wilmot, W.W., and Hocker, J.L. (2014) *Interpersonal Conflict*, 9th edn. Boston, MA: McGraw-Hill.

Windslade, J., and Cotter, A. (1997) 'Moving from problem solving to narrative approaches in mediation'. In G. Monk, J. Windslade, K. Crocket, and D. Epston (eds), *Narrative Therapy in Practice: The Archaeology of Hope* (pp. 252–74). San Francisco, CA: Jossey Bass.

INDEX

CPSIA information can be obtained
at www.ICGtesting.com
Printed in the USA
LVHW08s1702011018
592009LV00043B/1706/P